From
Mother Divine
to the Corner Swami

From
Mother Divine
to the Corner Swami

RELIGIOUS CULTS IN PHILADELPHIA

THOM NICKELS

AMERICA
THROUGH TIME®
ADDING COLOR TO AMERICAN HISTORY

Dedicated to Carolyn Nickels-Campitelli

Cover images courtesy of Lori and Tommy Garcia.

America Through Time is an imprint of Fonthill Media LLC
www.through-time.com
office@through-time.com

Published by Arcadia Publishing by arrangement with Fonthill Media LLC
For all general information, please contact Arcadia Publishing:
Telephone: 843-853-2070
Fax: 843-853-0044
E-mail: sales@arcadiapublishing.com
For customer service and orders:
Toll-Free 1-888-313-2665

www.arcadiapublishing.com

First published 2020

Copyright © Thom Nickels 2020

ISBN 978-1-63499-263-3

Typeset in 10pt on 13pt Sabon
Printed and bound in England

Contents

Prologue   7

1   Father and Mother Divine   15
2   The Cultic Lure of Philadelphia Psychics   47
3   When the Secular Meets the Religious: Earth Day and   61
      the Rise of the Secular Guru
4   Cults That Have Become Mainstream   76
5   Philadelphia's Pop-Up Messiahs   90
6   The Empire Cult of Scientology   113
7   Hare Krishna to All and To All a Good Night   122
8   Tea for Two: The Cult of Theosophy   133
9   Processing Satan   152
10 Philadelphia's Radical Faeries   167
11 The Cultic, Scenic Amish   174

Bibliography   191

Prologue

The question of what constitutes a religious cult may differ from person to person. Generally, most people would agree that organizations like Jim Jones' Peoples Temple, where on November 18, 1978, 909 people voluntarily drank cyanide poisoning and went to their death, was unquestionably one of the more dangerous cults of our time.

Yet there is also a sliding scale of religious cults, as I explain in the chapters in this book.

The Mormons, or the Church of Jesus Christ of Latter Day Saints, began as an unpopular cult with illegal practices such as polygamy, a radical and almost unheard of departure from the American religious mainstream. Through time and social adaptation, the tenets of the Church of Jesus Christ of Latter Day Saints changed, and as a result that religion's cult status diminished in the eyes of the public. The abandonment of polygamy helped the Church to be seen as less of a cult.

I grew up in an Irish-German Roman Catholic household, the eldest of six children. As a child, I was schooled in the tenets of pre-Vatican II Catholicism when Sunday Mass was in Latin, when the fasts before communion were arduous, when nuns wore traditional habits and passed as nuns. The Baltimore catechism taught that the Roman Catholic Church was the true Church of Christ and that all the other branches of Christianity split off from Rome to form their own "man-made" churches. The key words here were "man-made," implying a defective mechanism and something less than divine. In the vestibules of the average Catholic Church in those days, one could find pamphlet racks filled with pocket-sized books on the multitudes of existing Christian denominations. The range of topics was breathtaking: Are Anglican Religious Orders Valid? Are Jehovah's Witnesses Christian? What About the Schismatic Eastern Orthodox churches? Needless to say, it was consoling for a young Catholic person like myself to read how vastly inferior (and far from the Truth) many of these "man-made" denominations were.

This was the upbringing that formed the lens from which I viewed the various religions in my hometown of Frazer, Pennsylvania. Not far from my house there were Episcopal churches with tall steeples and nineteenth-century graveyards; a plain Mennonite church on the top of a hill where on Sundays one could see processions of white bonnet-capped ladies. Presbyterian churches also predominated: the one that I am thinking of was an old stone structure set back among a clump of trees and a spectacular garden.

This was the Presbyterian Church where I was brought as a teen by a Protestant friend who fooled me into thinking that we were going to a Halloween party. The surprise for me would be that we were not going to a party at all but rather to a round table inquisition, albeit friendly, where twelve members of the Presbyterian youth group piled me with thorny questions about Catholicism. Put on the defensive, I stuttered and stammered out answers as best I could, and in the end I left the "Q&A" with the feeling that I did not do so well. Debating twelve people at once is hardly an easy task. Later, somewhat embarrassed, the friend who had tricked me into thinking I was going to a party offered an apology.

Catholics in the 1960s in Chester County, Pennsylvania, were treated as religious oddities. In many ways, Catholics were viewed as centuries-old superstitious cultists who worshipped statues and the pope. There was, however, a heavy "pope veneration" among Catholics in those days. When I was a grammar school student, I can remember sitting with my family in front of the television watching a special from Rome that featured Pope Pius XII being carried into Saint Peter's Basilica on the *sedia gestatoria* flanked by two large Egyptian feathered fans, also known as flabella. The remarkable scene by today's standards was pure Cecil B. DeMille. Watching the ceremony, everyone in our family who could kneel on the floor did so when the pope extended his right hand in an Apostolic Blessing.

As Catholics, we knew we did not worship the pope but telling that to the local Presbyterians, the Baptists, or the Mennonites was an impossible task that recalls the passage from Matthew 7:6: "Do not give what is holy to the dogs; nor cast your pearls before swine, lest they trample them under their feet, and turn and tear you in pieces."

When John F. Kennedy ran for president, most of Chester County heralded its Richard Nixon Republican colors. Nixon for President bumper stickers could be found on most of the cars on the highways, while John F. Kennedy stickers were a rarity. Our family station wagon was heavily adorned with JFK stickers. This was my doing, influenced as I was by the nuns at school who made it known to us on a daily basis that if elected, Kennedy would become the first Catholic president of the United States of America. This fact was a problem for many strict, stalwart Protestants of a certain mindset who saw a Kennedy presidency as an excuse to build an underground tunnel from Washington, D.C., to Rome so that the pope and the new Catholic president could conspire and come up with a plan on how to turn everyone in the United States Catholic.

This was no mild fear mongering but a horrific vision many people took seriously. Protestant neighbors of mine, boys my own age, debated me on the length and breadth of this tunnel; how soon it would be built and how life in the United States would crumble as the pope and his legions made their way, huge Egyptian feather fans in tow, through the tunnel in order to conquer Washington and force all the states to submit to the pope. I was at a loss when it came to countering these tunnel arguments, but their commonality showed me just how queerly Catholics were perceived.

The public high school I attended after eight years of Catholic grammar school mandated student homeroom readings of the King James Bible. This presented a problem for Catholics because the King James Bible was not the Douay Rheims Catholic Bible, so Catholic students were urged not to participate in the King James readings. This caused an even greater separation anxiety and divide because now Catholics were perceived as anti-scripture, as "being against the Bible," which seemed to confirm the mistaken belief that in the Roman world "the pope was the one and only Bible for Catholics." Catholics then were looked at by many Protestants the way that the Amish in their broad rim hats and horse and buggies are looked at by many people today.

Today, the perception that Catholics are anti-Bible has been wiped clean given that the differences between Protestant and Catholic were radically minimized after the Second Vatican Council in 1963.

When I told a Russian Orthodox priest friend that I was writing a book on religious cults in Philadelphia, he asked me if I was going to include the Quakers or the Society of Friends. The question gave me pause. Philadelphia and the state of Pennsylvania were both founded by a Quaker, William Penn, and Philadelphia itself was once commonly referred to as the Quaker City. The Quakers, of course, began as a conventional Christian religion but over time there was a gradual metamorphosis into peace and social justice issues while the tenets of traditional Christianity were cast aside. Today, even atheists and agnostics can now comfortably call themselves Quakers.

Gurus of all sorts populated Philadelphia in the '60s and '70s. Holy men and women from India, self-appointed avatars like Ira Einhorn who, while having no religion, behaved in the manner of a charismatic evangelist in order to attract followers from the city's psychedelic and countercultural communities to join with him in preparing to raise the planetary consciousness and to help lay the groundwork for a new Utopian society. It has been said that when personal belief in a deity fades from consciousness, the whole of life becomes a search for meaning—any kind of meaning, even ones that invent messianic systems to save the Earth or transform it into a working Utopian dream. Instant-mix messianic systems can taunt the borders of sanity, inviting disaster (Jonestown), or they can have a deleterious effect on the originator of the messianic dream itself.

One such "messianic" case can be found in the life of West Philadelphia activist Kathy Change, who set herself on fire on the University of Pennsylvania campus.

In 1996, *The New York Times* reporter Ian Fisher wrote:

Tall, striking and complicated, Kathleen Chang grew up in the Bronx feeling "stared at, giggled at" for being of Chinese descent. She was disowned by her brilliant and demanding family, whose patriarch was one of China's leading intellectuals before he went on to prominence at Harvard University.

She endured a disastrous marriage to a respected Chinese-American author and lived either on inheritances or on men's money. For a time in New York she worked as a prostitute.

In 1978, she had a vision that she could redeem her many perceived failures with an act of utmost ambition: saving the world.

But after nearly two decades of pamphlets and protests and stripping naked in public, if that was what it took, there came the realization that no one was listening and nothing had changed.

"It was not occurring and that terrified her," said Ray Cairnes, 48, her boyfriend for most of the last 13 years. "She was running out of costumes that she could make and outrageous stuff she could do in order to make people pay attention to her."

Around Penn, her death set off a debate about whether students had become too cynical for ignoring Ms. Chang, a child of the 60's whose vision was, at worst, unattainable in this world. But there was also anger that an act she had presented as an idealistic final statement had inflicted so much pain on the people, mostly students, who had watched helplessly on Oct. 22 as she burned to death before a steel sculpture of a peace sign.

The popularity of consulting psychics or mediums can be considered a form of cultish activity. In this book, the section entitled "The Cult of the Psychic" presents an overview of some of Philadelphia's well-known seers.

Years ago I came into contact with a number of fortune-telling families. Sometimes I would go into their little tarot card reading shops and see what the future had in store for me.

My first fortune-teller experience occurred as a student in Baltimore. Strolling down East Baltimore Street one evening, I spotted a gypsy shop and decided to have my palm read for $2. The ablaze-with-neon curtained-off room was no larger than a broom closet. The gypsy woman held my palm and told me that I needed instant karmic cleansing. She suggested that I take three coins and throw them into the Baltimore harbor—only I had to do this with my back to the water and throw the coins over my shoulder like coins are thrown into Rome's Trevi Fountain. I walked down to the dark and gloomy harbor and did as the fortune teller advised.

The very day after the instant karmic cleansing, my landlord told me that he was selling his house and that I needed to find another place to live.

One year later, in Boston, I was walking downtown when I passed another fortune-teller shop. An old woman in a headscarf winked at me and asked if I wanted a life reading for $3. It was a tremendously hot day and the only thing I wanted to do was get out of the sun, so I went inside the little curtained-off room, sat down, and watched as she shuffled some cards. Behind another curtained-off area I could hear children. In fact, I no sooner heard a child's voice than I saw a little round face with large brown eyes peeking up at me from underneath another hanging curtain.

The Boston fortune teller said I had many obstacles in life; that many people were jealous of me; and that there was a curse on my family going back to the fourteenth century. The fourteenth century is a long time ago, so I asked her why I should be responsible for the antics of a diabolical ancestor. The woman offered a solution: for an extra $5, she would burn a special candle in her secret temple. That candle would be lit in my honor and melt the wax walls of the family curse.

She went ahead and lit the candle and then held her hand out for the money. This was followed by her husband's appearance from behind another curtained-off area; after this, a number of doe-eyed children flooded the room. What was happening? After questioning the family, I discovered that they needed eggs. They had not had breakfast and they wanted scrambled eggs. They were hungry.

"I'll get you eggs," I said to the woman. I knew that eggs were cheaper than $5, so I volunteered to walk to a nearby grocery store and buy them a dozen. They thought my offer was a con and did not expect me to return, but I got them the eggs, and we parted on a civil note. I have no idea what happened to the wax walls surrounding the family curse.

I stayed away from fortune tellers for a long time after that, although one time in downtown Philadelphia I went undercover as a reporter and had my fortune read at a number of shops. In almost every case, I was told that people were jealous of me and that there was a family curse that I had to "melt."

"I thought that wall was melted a long time ago," I said to one old woman in a headscarf.

"The walls come back, just like bedbugs," the woman said. "They melt and then they return."

A young woman seer in downtown Philadelphia told me that my father had had an affair with a young woman neighbor in Frazer when I was a teenager (not true). Another seer, this one an old woman in the Italian Market frightened me when she put her hands over mine in a healing embrace, then told me to keep very still as a shock of electricity shot from her hands into mine. Was this witchcraft? How did she do it? She also told me to mark May 16 on my calendar. Mindful of the date, I was doing laundry in the laundry room of the apartment house where I was living and on that date I met a guy who would later become my best friend.

During a trip to Florence, Italy, I would go out at night and hang around the Piazza Duomo near the great cathedral, Santa Maria del Fiore. Piazza Duomo was a melting pot of Moroccan and North African visitors and immigrants, some selling trinkets like wooden toy trains and leather goods, others sitting on the cathedral steps smoking their peculiar brand of tobacco. Piazza Duomo was a busy place. Lovers openly displayed their affection for one another on the cathedral steps; these displays went a lot farther than the conventional French kiss. People lingered in doorways, said hello to strangers, and drank wine in the moonlight. There were no surprise visits by police officers who ordered people to "vacate the premises."

At a card table at the Piazza Duomo, an old Italian woman was busy reading tarot cards. She was doing her readings in Italian, and the line of people wanting readings was very long. She was obviously well known for her accuracy. I had to opt out of a reading because I did not speak Italian.

Watching the woman read client after client, I had intense thoughts of Philadelphia writer Charles Godfrey Leland, a spiritual descendent of the infamous occultist Aleister Crowley. Leland began to write books about Italian witches when he first visited Florence. In one book, Leland talks about meeting a famous local reader named Maddalena. It occurred to me that perhaps Leland had met the queen of Italian witches in Piazza Duomo.

Leland's time with the Italian witches changed his life.

Born in 1824 to merchant Charles Leland and Charlotte Godfrey, both direct descendants of the first settlers of New England, his boyhood was a mixture of privileged wealth and an obsession with the mystical. He loved folk magic and walking in the woods, where he claimed that he heard words in the songs of birds and even in the sound of running water. At eighteen years of age, he wrote his first book, *Hermes Trismegistus: His Divine Pymander*. The book was later published and became an inspiration for a variety of hermetic writings.

Leland graduated from the College of New Jersey, now Princeton University, in 1845. After graduation, he studied in Munich, Germany, then traveled in Europe. In his book *Memoirs*, he writes about the physical impression he made as a young man:

> At this time I was a trifle over six feet two in height, and had then and for some time after so fair a red and white complexion, that the young ladies in Philadelphia four years later teased me by spreading the report that I used rouge and white paint! I was not as yet "filled out," but held myself straightly, and was fairly proportioned.

After his post-graduate European travels, he returned to Philadelphia to begin a career in journalism where he wrote for, and edited, a number of newspapers and magazines, including *The Philadelphia Evening Bulletin*, *The Philadelphia Press*, and *Vanity Fair*. During the Civil War, he enlisted in the Union Army, but his experiences on the battlefield were limited.

He moved to England in 1870 where his mystic inclinations and fluency in several languages helped him to immerse himself in what used to be known as

"Gypsy society," studying their culture to such an extent that in time he came to be accepted as one of their own. In Florence, his friendship with Maddalena led to his discovery of a number of witch cults with roots going back to ancient times.

From the time he was a toddler, Leland had been well-schooled in the world of spirits. In *Memoirs*, he writes about the haunted feeling many felt in Philadelphia's Washington Square:

> …Washington Square, opposite our house, had been in the olden time a Potter's Field, where all the victims of the yellow fever pestilence had been interred. Now it had become a beautiful little park, but there were legends of a myriad of white confused forms seen flitting over it in the night, for it was a mysterious haunted place to many still, and I can remember my mother gently reproving one of our pretty neighbours for repeating such tales…

Leland wrote books like *The English Gypsies and Their Language* (1873), *The Gypsies* (1882), *Gypsy Sorcery and Fortune Telling* (1891), and *Legends of Florence* (1895–6). In *Memoirs*, he even writes about witches in Philadelphia:

> As for the black witch, as there were still four Negro sorcerers in Philadelphia in 1883 (I have their addresses), it may be imagined to what an extent Voodoo still prevailed among our Ebo-ny men and brothers. Of one of there my mother had a sad experience. We had a black cook named Ann Lloyd, of whom, to express it mildly, one must say that she was "no good." My mother dismissed her, but several who succeeded her left abruptly. Then it was found that Ann, who professed, had put a spell of death on all who should take her place. My mother learned this, and when the last black cook gave warning she received a good admonition as to a Christian being a slave to the evil one. I believe that this ended the enchantment…

Before his death in Florence on March 20, 1903, Philadelphia's own "Aleister Crowley" wrote of his impressions of the city after a long time away in Europe:

> Its inhabitants were all well-bathed, well-clad, well-behaved; all with exactly the same ideas and the same ideals…. And they were so fond of flowers that I once ascertained by careful inquiry that in most respectable families there was annually much more money expended for bouquets than for books.

Unlike Piazza Duomo, there are plenty of flowers in Philadelphia's Rittenhouse Square.

1

Father and Mother Divine

On March 14, 2017, *The New York Times* ran the following headline: "Mother Divine, Who Took Over Her Husband's Cult, Dies at 91." Mother Divine actually died on March 4, 2017, but it took *The Times* a while to print an obituary.

Mother Divine was a mysterious figure. Little is known about her early life. She was born Edna Rose Ritchings on April 4, 1925, in Vancouver, where her father, Charles, ran the Strathcona Floral Company, a nursery and flower shop. Her mother was the former Mabel Farr.

At fifteen years old, she became fascinated by Father Divine and his religion, which preached a gospel of self-help, abstinence, economic independence, and social equality. By providing cheap meals and social services during the Depression, Father Divine attracted a large following in Harlem, where he maintained his headquarters, and through his many missions, known as heavens, elsewhere in the United States.

The revelation came to her, she wrote in *Ebony* magazine in 1950, "that Father Divine is God Almighty personified in a beautiful, holy body."

I met Mother Divine in June 2010 when I visited her estate at Woodmont in Gladwyne, Pennsylvania. At that time, I teamed up with Philadelphia artist Noel Miles who wanted to set up his easel and paint the Woodmont mansion for a possible book project. Mother was gracious during that visit. We were not only invited to dinner—Mother's followers called it a "holy communion" service—but were also told that we could have a special interview with Mother after the meal.

The Gladwyne mansion is a multi-room French Gothic masterpiece designed by Quaker architect William Price (1861–1916) for Philadelphia industrialist Alan J. Wood, Jr., in 1892. Wood, Jr., was an engineer and U.S. Congressman as well as the head of the Alan Wood Company, which specialized in iron making. Woodmont was modeled after the Biltmore or George Vanderbilt estate in Ashville, North Carolina. In 1929, Richard Wood, the son of Alan, sold Woodmont to J. Hector McNeal, a corporate lawyer. At this point, the interior of Woodmont began to be transformed. McNeal redecorated the dining room with imported wood paneling from a Catholic chapel in Avignon, France. The importation of medieval fragments for installation in great American homes was then very popular. McNeal also decorated the dining room with statues of many Catholic saints. The statues were installed on a rim or shelf near the ceiling and circled a large part of the room.

The year 1952 brought more changes to Woodmont when, after McNeal's death, the 70-acre estate was sold by his daughter to the Peace Mission Movement. It was then that the grand house was officially named Woodmont— The Mount of the House of the Lord.

The sale to Father Divine for a relatively humble $75,000 coincided with the passing of the Gilded Age and the selling off of many of Philadelphia's old mansions.

The Peace Mission Movement began as a force for peace and goodwill between different racial groups. The movement, as Mother Divine noted in her book *The Peace Mission Movement* (1982, Palace Mission, Inc.) was to make people "industrious, independent, tax-paying citizens instead of consumers of tax dollars on the welfare rolls." By 1952, the Peace Mission Movement was already well-established in Philadelphia. Mother Divine listed several established mission churches and homes as Peace Mission residences beginning with the Circle Mission Church, Home, and Training School of Pennsylvania at 764–772 South Broad Street; the Unity Mission Church, Home and Training School at 907 N. Forty-First Street, and the Nazareth Mission Church and Home at 1600–1614 West Oxford Streets in North Philadelphia.

"These were the churches at which religious services were held and which housed the members of the congregation on a donation-for-services-rendered basis, and offered low-cost meals to the public, as well as the services of a barber shop and dress shop," Mother Divine wrote. The Peace Mission Movement also offered hotel accommodations at rates comparable to the YMCA to people who were willing to abide by the moral code of the movement.

Father Divine's International Modest Code included prohibitions against smoking, drinking, obscenity, vulgarity, profanity, undue mixing of the sexes, and the receiving of gifts, presents, tips, or bribes. These hotels included the 300-room Divine Lorraine Hotel at Broad Street and Fairmount Avenue and the Divine Tracy Hotel near the University of Pennsylvania at Thirty-Sixth and Chestnut Streets.

One of the groups within the movement were the Rosebuds. Mother Divine writes that the Rosebuds "are the feminine youth group who pattern their lives after the Virginity of Mary and the Holiness of Jesus." They are the movement's official choir.

"They volitionally sing of their sacred love for GOD, their Husband and Maker, as well as of their love for America, Democracy and Brotherhood," Mother Divine wrote. "Their uniform consists of a red jacket with a white 'V' for Virtue and Victory, a blue skirt and white blouse."

Peace Mission men were known as Crusaders. Crusaders modeled their lives on the virginity of Mary and the holiness of Jesus Christ. Their uniform consisted of a light blue jacket with black trim and black trousers. The Crusaders acted as waiters during the banquet Holy Communion service. Mother Divine described the Lily-buds as "those sisters who were redeemed from the mortal, carnal life, and made virtuous as the Rosebuds." The three groups had their own creed and goals.

Since the passing of Father Divine in 1965, the Peace Mission Movement had been under the direction of Father Divine's second wife, Edna Rose Ritchings, a white Canadian woman he met in 1946:

"In 1946, FATHER DIVINE chose one from among HIS followers to be HIS Bride," Mother Divine wrote. "She, in Her Spotless Virginity, was a Sample and Example for all others to emulate." "The Virgin Mary recognized Her LORD and bowed before HIM in HER day. MOTHER DIVINE is the same Virgin Mary, reincarnated, recognizing and bowing before Her LORD in this day and time. She appeared first in the Person of Peninnah, who married FATHER DIVINE on June 6, 1882. Peninnah, the first Mother Divine, recognized FATHER DIVINE to be the living CHRIST Through Their Marriage." Mother Divine then goes on to explain how Peninnah desired to die "and be reborn in a more youthful body in which She could be of greater service."

Adam Morris, in his book *American Messiahs, False Prophets of a Damned Nation*, writes:

Peninniah never made it to the City of Brotherly Love. After the establishment of the Ulster County [New York] colonies, Sister Penny, aka Peninniah, spent most of her time upstate, far from the bustle of Manhattan. Her health had begun to fail as early as 1936: during that year and the next, heart trouble and kidney failure forced her hospitalization on two occasions; her second stay lasted for a period of months. Although her status was meant to be a secret, reporters discovered Mother Divine's whereabouts after her absence became conspicuous. Father Divine did not visit his wife in the hospital. Initially, he might have avoided her sickbed because doing so would have drawn attention to her illness, as his movements were closely watched by New York reporters. But the most likely explanation is also the most perverse: if Father Divine truly believed that impurity of thought was the cause of illness and death, then Mother Divine was a backslider who was just as corrupted as numerous others whose deaths he had blamed on their own mental failings. Her last known appearance was at a 1942 Holy Communion banquet in New York, during which she felt well enough to sing. But as of 1943, Peninniah Divine had completely disappeared.

The myth states that "the spirit of the Virgin Mary, reincarnated in the first Mother Divine, was again reincarnated in a young girl who was not under Father Divine's immediate jurisdiction, but three thousand miles away on the west coast of Canada." This then led the young Edna Rose Ritchings to travel all the way to Philadelphia so she could declare to Father Divine: "I want to marry you because I know you are God."

In a sermon about this meeting, Father Divine explained that he had always been in touch with his future bride because his "spirit went across the border and taught this virtuous, untouched, incorruptible and undefiled bride from infancy…" The marriage, it was explained, was purely spiritual. Neither lust, passion, or physical propagation played a part in the marriage but rather it was comparable to the marriage of Christ to His Church.

Father Divine's greatest contributions were probably in the area of Civil Rights. As early as 1951, he advocated for reparations for the descendants of slaves and for integrated neighborhoods. Decades before the Civil Rights Act, before the NAACP, Stokley Carmichael, Angela Davis, and the Black Panthers, Father Divine preached peaceful non-violent social change. Unfortunately, Father Divine's "preaching" work on behalf of Civil Rights is a mostly understated fact.

My first view of Mother Divine was when she was descending the grand staircase in the Woodmont mansion. She was dressed in what resembled a nineteenth-century ball gown while being escorted by a Rosebud dressed in red who also wore a small red beret tilted to the side in the style of Che Guevara. The Rosebud was a thin black woman and Mother was white—she had snow white hair and skin that seemed much paler than the color of Dove soap. She carried herself with confident elegance, her head erect and her eyes focused on some invisible point on the horizon. Her walk down the staircase was so slow it called to mind the walking styles of European aristocracy, namely Queen Elizabeth II of England.

Emblems of royalty were very evident in the mansion, not only in the grandiose architecture and design of the place but also in the studied attentiveness and seriousness of Mother's other sentries, who also wore cocked berets. The Rosebuds were stationed throughout the house like Vatican Swiss Guards. The atmosphere definitely evoked the formality of a royal court because it was obvious that the Rosebuds would not tolerate any foolish action, like presupposing it was okay to sit on the furniture, which of course we did not do.

In situations like this, the human tendency is to be formal, even though I longed to see just one of the Rosebuds smile or show some warmth. Feel-good camaraderie is not in the Woodmont style book, however. The Rosebuds, when they did smile, did it in a fixed way as if they were ready to retract it at a moment's notice. I knew this to be the case when I asked one of them, a Miss something-or-other, if I could take a photograph. My request was met with a stern "No, you may not take photographs," as if I should have known better. I replied with a somewhat stunned "Oh… okay," the "Oh" in my reply signaling my dismay at such a silly rule. What could possibly be wrong with taking a snapshot? Everything, as it turns out.

Often the "secondary" people around any high-ranking leader have an inflated sense of self-importance and behave in a manner that may "out-formalize" the personal style of the big boss, the very person one would expect to flaunt attitude. Mother Divine had an easy and light spirit and it was easy to see a mischievous glint in her eyes. She was quick to smile and laugh, yet it was my impression that she was surrounded by stiff wooden Cigar Store Indian types who were quick to find fault and scold.

Dinner began when Mother rang a large hand bell. A female cook in a white uniform produced the platters from a small kitchen directly behind Mother. Numerous platters of salad items, including a wide assortment of vegetables, condiments, and sauces, set the pace for more complicated platters offering meats and fish, rice, potatoes, breads, and more vegetables and meats until at last diners could devote their attention to the business at hand, eating, rather than the elaborate ritual of passing platters.

When platters were passed from one diner to another, they never touched the table. Diners were not allowed to hold two platters at the same time, so the synchronization of the plates had the movements of a dance. While this was going on, diners listened to old audio tapes of Father Divine sermons. The mostly elderly crowd, men in suits and women in Peace Mission uniforms, combined eating with the singing of hymns. A few elderly white women, European by birth, clapped their hands in a singsong fashion in between mouthfuls, reminding me of the antics of patients in a mental institution.

After dinner, Mother invited my artist friend and me into her private office where she showed us old photographs of Father Divine. This had also been Father Divine's old office and it was modeled, she said, on the John F. Kennedy Oval Office in the White House. It was such a time capsule that I expected to see little JFK, Jr., crawl out from under Father Divine's old desk at any moment.

A rosebud stood beside her as the four of us chatted. I found myself occasionally looking out of Mother's office window at the tomb of Father, believed by followers to be God incarnate. The conversation was not profound but filled with cursory pleasantries. There were even several photo ops in which Mother snuggled up against Noel Miles and me. Photographs were no longer an issue because the rosebud who greeted us in the foyer was not the one standing by Mother's side.

By the time we left Woodmont, we had the feeling that the Rosebuds around Mother were much like a covert army. It was much like the feeling you get when you visit a couple who are in a bad marriage but who put on a happy face when company comes. You can somehow feel the tension and repressed emotion coming from the couple, but there is no way you can prove that it exists. Mother, after all, was sitting on a vast fortune and a huge empire. She was elderly and had to be helped around the mansion on her daily walks around the estate.

While in a cab leaving the estate, we passed Mother as she began her daily walk, escorted by several dour-looking Rosebuds. During our chat with Mother, she appeared strong, but seeing her outdoors there seemed to be a profound change. She not only looked weak and vulnerable but also seemed to be almost totally under the care and direction of the women propping her up.

The word "care" in this sense can also be a code word for power and control. We have all heard stories of what happens to some elderly mothers when their care is relinquished to their children, and how one child can claim power of attorney and have the mother committed to a nursing home while her assets are funneled into other family bank accounts.

Noel Miles and I were certain that Mother liked us and so we were very surprised when we were turned down by a secretarial rosebud when we called later to schedule a follow-up interview. The rosebud told us that we were not permitted to visit. No reason was given but it was obvious that we were no longer welcome at Woodmont.

Since that time, we have both felt that Mother was really a prisoner behind pearly gates and that she was not acting as a free agent.

This is why I think it is a good thing that *The New York Times* called the Peace Mission a cult.

THE HUNT FOR A LITTLE BROWN BOY

The story of the little brown boy cannot be understood without first understanding the relationship between Jim Jones (of Jonestown, the jungles of Guyana, infamy) and Mother and Father Divine.

If the walls of Woodmont could talk they would tell how Jim Jones, who preached a strange blend of the gospel and Marxism, came to visit Mother Divine with a large number of his followers.

Adam Morris writes that in the summer of 1956, Jim Jones left his native Indianapolis with his wife, Marceline, to visit Mother and Father Divine at Woodmont:

> At this point in his career, Jones theoretically disapproved of any religious group
> that indulged in excessive veneration of a living leader: it didn't seem very socialist.

His doubts were further raised in Philadelphia. Upon arrival to a Peace Mission hotel, a concierge informed Jones that he and Marceline would not be allowed to occupy the same room. The couple decided to lodge elsewhere, and were so put off by this oddity that they nearly concluded their reconnaissance mission then and there. However, after spending time with the other congregations he intended to visit while in Pennsylvania, Jones decided to give the Peace Mission another chance. This broad-mindedness notwithstanding, Jones admitted to feeling "revulsion" as he entered the Circle Mission Church on Broad and Catharine. But the kindness of the angels slowly wore down his defenses. Although initially "nauseated" by their meek veneration of Father Divine, Jones wrote that he "could not help but help but see a peace and love that prevailed generally throughout the throng of the enthusiastic worshippers. Every face was aglow with smiles and radiant friendliness." After returning to Indianapolis, Jones took out ads in one of the city's black newspapers to advertise "*2 free fellowship meals*" *in addition to the miracles he worked several times weekly.*

In the late spring of 1971, having achieved new heights in Peoples Temple business expansion and much success as a traveling evangelist, Jones, who had visited Woodmont before when Father Divine was alive, contacted Mother Divine and asked to visit her at Woodmont. She was agreeable; in her new role as head of the Peace Mission, Mother Divine often received visitors.

Jones chose about 200 of his most dedicated followers to accompany him on the trip, and prepped them rigorously before their departure. He explained that Father Divine had failed and that he died before completing his life's work. Jones had long ago come to understand that it was now his calling to lead the Peace Mission down the same "socialist" path followed by Peoples Temple. Economic and social equality were the goals of both movements.

Peoples Temple buses took almost three days to make the cross-country trip. According to Jeff Guinn in *The Road to Jonestown, Jim Jones and Peoples Temple*, stops along the way were made only for gas and bathroom breaks. Guinn writes that when they arrived in Philadelphia, Temple members were housed in Peace Mission apartments although Jones himself stayed at Woodmont. Later, Jones and the members were taken on a tour of the property and treated to an elaborate banquet where the dessert was ice cream shaped like flower petals. Mother Divine invited Jones to make a few remarks; he praised the ministry and memory of Father Divine. By all accounts, it was a pleasant evening.

Guinn goes on to say that the Temple visitors stayed a second day, during which Jones spent time talking with Mother Divine. Jones, however, was dissatisfied. That night, there was another gathering for dinner, a barbeque with all the trappings, and Jones stood up to speak again. This time his tone was critical. He criticized the Peace Mission and its luxurious trappings, and told the assembly that Father Divine had "conferred his mantle" on Jim Jones. "His spirit has come to rest in my body," he said, and he urged the Peace Mission to follow him.

Mother Divine took offense and ordered Jones and his people to leave the Woodmont estate. The group did leave, but they also managed to take about a dozen elderly Peace Mission members with them; however, all of the former Woodmont residents died shortly after arriving in their new Peoples Temple California home.

Guinn writes:

> The drive back to Mendocino County was tense. When they arrived, Jones gathered the followers who'd made the trip and explained that what had happened at Woodmont was not his fault. Mother Divine had been enthusiastic about merging their ministries under Jones' leadership, so much so that, after maneuvering so they were alone, she tore open her blouse and insisted that they have sex. Jones refused—"She flaunted her sagging breasts in my face but I wasn't tempted." This was why she had ordered him and his followers to leave Woodmont. Everyone was urged to help the defecting Peace mission members, who were mostly old women, to assimilate to the Temple. Jones asked for contact information provided by others back at the Peace Mission apartments, and for a while nothing more was said about Mother Divine and the Peace Mission ministry.

Long after Jones's return to California, however, he continued to send Peace Mission members at Woodmont letters with the headline: "This May Be Your Last Chance For Life."

When Father Divine was alive, both he and Mother Divine knew that Jim Jones had his eye on Woodmont. According to Lori Garcia, wife of Tommy Garcia, the adopted son of Mother and Father Divine, Jones wanted to take over the Peace Mission movement when Father Divine passed away. In a series of telephone interviews, Lori Garcia told me that her husband, Tommy, was present at least two times when Jones and his group visited Woodmont. The first was at a banquet, but the second time the group visited, Mother Divine took Tommy aside and said, "It is not safe for you to be here," and had a bodyguard take him to another Peace Mission building. At the other meetings between Jones and Mother and Father Divine, Jones often spoke in churches in Center City Philadelphia. At one rally in 1977, after his eviction from Woodmont, Jones spoke to a large group of followers on North Broad Street. At that time, several followers spoke about cancer and bone-related miracle cures they had received from Jones. There were hymns and then Jones himself, his charismatic voice rousing the crowd into a frenzy of "Amens," would address the people.

In recordings archived by the Jonestown Institute, at that 1977 rally, Jones said:

Jones: (Moderates) It is written, the love of money is the root of all evil. Love of money is the root of all evil—(Pause) (unintelligible comments off mike, back to mike) That's marvelous. Said that they got the Ku Klux Klan here in Philadelphia now too, and they're wanting equal time because of *Roots*. (Short laugh) That's— That's the thing. That's all they can see out of Roots, out of our precious people that suffered and bled and died, and then they made us think we made it. They said Roots. I knew—I knew we started—(Stumbles over words) now hold in here tonight. Last night we saw cancers passed, uh, but when you get to preaching the truth, everybody gets nervous. But you—you're going to get the truth tonight, if it kills you, because it's already crucified me.

While there was no solid Ku Klux Klan presence in Philadelphia in the 1970s, there were scattered attempts at organizing KKK marches and parades in the Philadelphia suburbs and in the neighboring town of West Chester, formerly called Turk's Head. These marches were usually small and occurred without incident, but in the city of Philadelphia itself, the KKK's presence was more rumor and innuendo than actual fact. The mention of the made-for-TV movie *Roots*, however, is an accurate portrayal of the mood of the city in 1977, when race-related issues and concerns were becoming hot topics in the press and among residents. Jones' captivating preaching style had the rollicking cadence of an old time Baptist preacher mixed with the verbal acuity of a Spoken Arts poet. The power and energy in his voice had a sort of messianic fire that held listeners spellbound.

On that day in 1977, Jones continued:

We're going to be in the first time ever healing services conducted in the greatest cathedral in New York. 110 Amsterdam. You hear what I'm saying? What's the name of that cathedral? St.—St. John's Divine. You've heard of that great cathedral? I'm a friend of the bishop of the Episcopalian church [Rt. Rev. Paul Moore, Jr., Bishop of New York]. I've reached out to people in various levels. So how many will tell your loved ones up in New York? You need to give them the truth, 'cause we're gonna have shakin' of truth over there. 'Cause God is shaking up everything that can be shaken, so that (voice grows loud) that which cannot be shaken will remain! Praise his name. (voice moderates) How many will tell your loved ones? Some of you oughta come on over with us. We're gonna be in New York for two nights. Tomorrow night, and the next night. I'm gonna be speaking to the Council of Churches, and then tomorrow night at seven-thirty at one-one-ten, is it? 110 Amsterdam, St. John the Divine, the great big cathedral, worldwide-known, one that's supposed to be the world's largest temple. So be there, be there, and tell your loved ones. Put your hand on your neighbor and tell them of three miracles. That's what we call agreement—two, three, greeting together. Tell 'em of three miracles that you've seen God do here, in the land of the living. The sister tonight got healed, that was crippled in her back, because she said, "I perceive you're more than a pastor." You've heard what I told, I'm not gonna repeat it. You are the living. What do you see tonight? Because as you think, so is it. As you think, so is it. Put out your hand, by the faith and by the power of the hundredfold (singing becomes louder; Jones's voice grows to ministerial fervor) I am, so art thou! What thou seeth in me I see in you!

It is doubtful that any of Jones's Philadelphia listeners in 1977 were aware that as a young kid growing up in Indiana, he would kill cats and small animals and then force the kids in the neighborhood to attend the funeral services he would arrange for the dead pets. It is also doubtful that Jones's Philadelphia followers were aware that Peoples Temple was a gay-affirming church, unlike the bulk of black churches in Philadelphia at the time. Jones liked to say, "I have to be all things to all people," and that included his sexual relations with followers, both male and female.

Guinn writes that "Jones was clearly bisexual, though he chose not to openly admit it. For a long time he discouraged gay relationships among his followers.... Most of his followers had no idea that Jim Jones had numerous sex partners among Temple members."

The mid-1970s was a traumatic time for gay rights organizations in Philadelphia. The Reverend Melvin Floyd, a former Philadelphia police officer who had established Neighborhood Crusades, Inc., with offices on West Queen Lane in Germantown, dedicated his life to ministering to gangs and troubled youth, most notably in the black community. He also fought against street crime, absentee fathers, and drug dealing. He was famous in the city for his one-of-a-kind van, which was outfitted with a stuffed dummy's torso sitting atop a coffin on the van's roof. The corpse-dummy was supposed to represent the danger and stupidity of taking drugs.

Floyd was a controversial but powerful figure in the black community in the 1970s, but he was often referred to as a bigot and a homophobe by gay activists. In the 1976, one year before Jim Jones gave his 1977 talk on North Broad Street, Floyd was awarded the prestigious Philadelphia Bar Association Award, The Edward Bok Philadelphia Award for his neighborhood activism. The award explains the ambiguity many Philadelphia leaders at the time felt about gay rights.

Much of Floyd's activism included his opposition to the first Philadelphia gay rights bills that were being proposed in City Council. The bills called for a ban against the discrimination of homosexuals in housing and employment. Rev. Floyd testified at an early City Council meeting and said, "The one thing about everything else that can destroy that kind of manhood is to come up with a generation or generations of homosexual black males."

Floyd was not alone in his opposition to what was often referred to as "the legitimatization of homosexuality into law." A multiplicity of churches and religious organizations set up tables near Philadelphia City Hall and promoted the signing of petitions to stop gay rights from being enshrined into law. City Council Bill 1275 was one such bill that never made it out of committee, and the suppression of the bill caused an eruption of angry protestors in City Council chambers, mainly lesbians who belonged to an activist group called DYKETATICS. The city was fairly well polarized on the gay rights issue with some church groups telling passersby through bullhorns that the sin of homosexuality caused homosexuals to have rotten teeth.

This prejudice, of course, was in direct opposition to the philosophy of Peoples Temple.

In "A Queer Look at Jonestown," Irene Monroe wrote about the Peoples Temple for the L.A. Progressive:

As an "open and affirming" church that welcomed LGBTQs in the era of the Florida sunshine homophobe poster-girl Anita Bryant and her "Save the Children" campaign, the Peoples Temple was a safe and sacred sanctuary. The Peoples Temple marched in Gay Pride and embraced a social gospel of radical inclusion. Jones had a sizeable LGBTQ following that kept growing as did his African American audience. The LGBTQ community followed Jones and expanded in numbers at each church he had from Indiana, Ukiah, San Francisco to Guyana. LGBTQ parishioners were involved in every aspect of church life, governance, and activities.

My interviews with Lori Garcia continued over a period of several months. One topic that most interested me was how her husband, Tommy Garcia, a boy born in Los Angeles, wound up in Woodmont as the adopted son of Mother and Father Divine. This long, complicated story will probably be told at greater length when Tommy Garcia publishes his own book about that period. Still, Garcia was forthcoming when speaking about how an anonymous little boy from Los Angeles wound up in Gladwyne, Pennsylvania.

"The final visit between Jim Jones and Mother and Father Divine," Lori Garcia said, "was the firecracker that set things in motion." It was at that time that Father Divine told Mother Divine, "I need a brown little boy who can be groomed, who has not been tainted by the movement, who is intelligent, and that I can groom to be your assistant." The obsessive lurking around of Jim Jones had put something unpleasant in the air, a tone that more or less seemed to say: "Look, Father Divine, you are a sick old man, and once you're gone I'm going to come here and take over the Peace Mission movement." An adopted son who could be trained to be Father Divine's successor as well as an aid to Mother Divine was an investment in perpetuity. It was at that point that a universal call went out to everyone in the movement at every location around the world to keep an eye out for such a boy. "Everyone wanted to be the one who delivered the child to Father Divine," Lori Garcia said.

In Los Angeles, meanwhile, a woman named Georgia Julia Costa, the thirteenth of fourteen children born to Greek-Albanian parents in New Hampshire, met the very handsome and athletic Tomas Garcia, a semi-professional soccer player who played for the Mainland Mexico team and who came to the United States on a work visa in 1949. The two met in Los Angeles in 1952, and little Tommy Garcia was born in 1954.

"Georgia fell in love with Tomas," Lori Garcia said. "Tomas was very handsome and very well built. Both were very young. Georgia, a photographer, was 22. They spent a lot of nights dancing at the Hollywood Palladium. After Tommy was born, his sister Susan was born in August of 1958."

Life for the little brown boy from the time of his birth to March 1962 was a combination of harmony and falling victim to his father's demons. Tommy was constantly complaining of severe headaches to his mother as the relationship between Georgia and Tomas began to go downhill. The headaches continued. Tommy was even sent home from school because of the headaches and his mother, at her wits end, took him to Children's Hospital in Los Angeles to find out what the problem was. The source of the headaches could not be traced to a medical condition but rather to trauma, such as a blow to the head. This was in fact what was happening, although Tommy refrained from telling his mother beforehand that his father had kicked him in the head.

At the same time that this was happening, Georgia found herself in the Self Realization Fellowship's Lake Shrine gardens, camera in hand and looking for the perfect photo. As a photographer, she was always looking for places that were perfect for taking photos. Whatever that vista might be—Disneyland, Santa Monica Beach, Pacific Ocean Park, or Lake Shrine—they were always locations in the public domain. But here she was in this Paramahansa Yogananda-inspired garden where, according to Lori, she had her first interaction with a woman from the Peace Mission movement.

"I believe that when a person meets someone, makes a new friend, sometimes it is easier to speak with that new friend about what's going on in your life than telling an old friend," Lori Garcia offered. That is what Georgia Garcia did. Georgia showed the woman, whose name was Louise, a photograph of her son, Tommy, and immediately Louise must have thought of the call for a brown little boy that had been made by Mother and Father Divine back in Gladwyne, Pennsylvania.

What transpired between Georgia and Louise from that moment on was something that Lori Garcia could not tell me, although it can be assumed that a deal was made regarding the photo, meaning that Louise sent the photo to Mother and Father Divine. This set the wheels of progress in motion. Years later, Tommy Garcia would reveal to his wife Lori how he spotted the photo of himself at the Woodmont estate. He explained to her that Father Divine had two special secretaries entrusted with a sort of high-security clearance, Miss Saint

Mary Bloom, his black right-hand assistant, and Miss Dorothy Darling, his white right-hand assistant. Miss Saint Mary Bloom was also the treasurer of the movement's Palace Mission and president and treasurer of the Circle Mission. Miss Saint Mary Bloom had a private office on the second floor of Woodmont with a sofa that Lori Garcia recalls being "over six feet long and a large safe that contained important papers and lots of cash." One day when Tommy was sent to the Bloom office, he spotted the picture of himself in the safe.

"Somehow that picture was sent to Woodmont. I don't know if it was sent to the attention of Mother Divine or Father Divine, I don't know that answer," Lori Garcia told me, "but I do know that upon receipt of that photo Father Divine said, 'Bring me that child!'"

LIKING WHAT THEY SAW

Mother and Father Divine obviously liked what they saw and further negotiations ensued. Eventually it was agreed that Georgia would drive to Philadelphia from Los Angeles with Louise, Tommy, and Susan. The little brown boy, after all, was needed to thwart the advances of Jim Jones. With Louise in the passenger seat and Tommy and Susan in the back seat, the group headed east.

But leaving Los Angeles was not easy. Tomas Garcia had to be left out of things, and so he was told what basically amounted to a lie: Georgia had told Tomas that she wanted to take the children across the country to New Hampshire to introduce the kids to her large family. No one in Georgia's family had ever come to California with the exception of one sister, and certainly Georgia had never returned to New Hampshire since she married Tomas. It was summer break, and the excuse worked. Tomas suspected nothing when the one car caravan pulled up in front of Saint Thomas parochial school in Los Angeles to pick up Tommy, and then to the Jefferson Street Peace Mission building to pick up Louise. The crew spent five nights on the road. In June 1962, Georgia and Louise delivered Tommy and Susan to the Peace Mission's Divine Lorraine Hotel on North Broad Street.

Georgia told Tommy to take his sister up the steps and then go right to the cafeteria while she parked the car. Tommy and Susan were then met by Peace Mission sentries who separated them in different sections of the hotel. It was an emotional situation for the eight-year-old boy and his even younger sister. Tommy was then chauffeured to Woodmont to begin a life under Mother and Father Divine's care, while his sister was sent away to live in one of the movement's lesser houses on Broad Street, a communal extension for girls, although only five girls lived there at the time.

Immediately after Tommy's personal introduction to Mother and Father Divine, he was taken to the King of Prussia Mall where he was outfitted in a new wardrobe. But his new life as the prince of Woodmont would not last long because almost immediately after his arrival, he was molested by a male Peace Mission member who was the head of security.

Tommy's mother, Georgia, who was promised the position of Mission photographer, was sent to live in another property. In 1962, there were hundreds, even thousands of buildings owned by the Peace Mission—in Philadelphia, New Jersey, New York City, Harlem, and even upstate New York. These buildings were places where people—workers—were needed. In exchange for room and board, Peace Mission members participated in worker duties. Lori Garcia says she is certain that Georgia fell right into step because she remained with the movement for the rest of her life under her new name of Miss Harmony Faith Love. "In most cases new names were given by Father Divine but in some cases people chose their own names and Father gave his okay. Georgia worked at the Key Flower Dining Room at the Divine Tracy Hotel and died in 2001. She never left Philadelphia," Lori Garcia said.

Located at 20 South 36th Street in Philadelphia's University City neighborhood, the Divine Tracy Hotel was often eclipsed by the far grander edifice on North Broad Street, the Divine Lorraine Hotel. Both hotels offered impeccable living quarters and a much touted "wholesome atmosphere," where smoking, drinking, obscenity, profanity, vulgarity, undue mixing of sexes, receiving of gifts, presents, tips, or bribes were prohibited. Men and women were housed on different floors.

Father Divine would die three years after Tommy Garcia arrived at Woodmont. "I am certain that Father Divine expected to have far more time with Tommy than he had," Lori Garcia recalls. "But certainly the three years he had with Tommy were intense and very special." The two shared many confidences, including the revelatory fact that Father Divine was not really God, as his followers believed. Lori Garcia, who says that she believes in God although she is not sure what house of worship she belongs in, said: "Tommy not only knew that Father Divine was not God, but in one of their first meetings Father Divine said to Tommy, 'I am not God.'"

In the beginning of his ministry, Father Divine had some very forward-thinking ideas on race and civil rights and his fight for racial justice made him a pioneer and a sort of prophet in the eyes of the black people who were still suffering from discrimination in all areas of life, including being barred from living accommodations, rest rooms and to use water fountains of their choice (unless marked "Colored"). Restaurants were also problematic because many did not serve blacks unless one had an ingenious imagination and was able to break through the skin color barrier by claiming that they were Indian or from the Hawaiian Islands. Father Divine's worldwide Peace Mission network created a safety net for many blacks. "I think they called him God because to them no one but God could have created for them on earth what was happening and then I think it got out of hand and it took on a life of its own. There was an avalanche of activity and then the opportunists got involved and then some of them did questionable things," Lori Garcia said.

God or no God, the plan to find a little brown boy was well thought out and well executed. "When Tommy was delivered to Father Divine, it was up to Father Divine to decide whether Tommy stays or goes. One of the first things Father Divine asked Tommy was would he agree to stay there with him," Lori Garcia recalls. "Tommy looked around Father Divine's office where there were 13 or 14 secretaries with their steno pads writing down every word that is uttered. Tommy notices that some people are smiling, some are frowning and some have no expression whatsoever. The first thing this eight and a half year old child says is, 'What about my sister and my mom?'"

This sentiment demonstrated to Father Divine that this was not your average selfish kid. At this point, Father Divine stated that they would be well taken care of but would not live at Woodmont. Tommy agreed and spent the next three years in uninterrupted consultations with Father Divine. At banquets, he was seated between Father and Mother Divine. Essentially, once the boy began living at Woodmont it was a three-month crash course, arriving in Gladwyne in June and then starting school in September. In addition to his Woodmont training, the chosen son was taken around to all the Peace Mission locations where he was introduced as Master Tommy.

"Once school began, since Father Divine told him that he wasn't God, he was taught how to be compassionate and a caring person and to take care of your fellow men and women and especially to take care of the elderly." As for the so called "God Secret," Father Divine instructed the boy to tell no one that he was not God. "Tommy has kept that secret. From the time he was eight years old this secret has been kept because Father asked Tommy to keep it," Lori Garcia adds.

Sometime after Tommy's arrival in Woodmont, Mother Divine took him aside and told him that she feared for her life. How was this possible? When Father Divine married Mother Divine, some Peace Mission members did not believe in her (so-called) divinity. According to Tommy, Mother Divine was not as well received as everybody would have wanted her to be. Even their marriage was done in secret—there was no grand ceremony or celebration. When it came time for Father Divine to present her to the Peace Mission, he had to present her as the reincarnation of Peninniah, his first wife. Mother was only aged twenty-one and Father was in his forties at the time of their marriage, an age span that would engender eye rolls in any strata of society. But here at Woodmont, where the followers were very simple people, people who did not think anything of standing for eight hours a day polishing silverware, the reaction was mixed. Some followers accepted the new Mother Divine while others said they did not believe in her deity and were going to fight her tooth and nail.

The real power struggle at Woodmont began after Father Divine's death.

Lori Garcia told me how Tommy was required to stand by Mother's side during the funeral ceremonies, during which no one was permitted to show any expressions of sorrow. If anyone cried, Mother Divine had them removed. "It was a very different side of her that you have probably never seen," She explained:

> One of the very first things she did after the funeral, the memorials and meeting people who came to Woodmont to pay their respects, was to banish Miss Mary Bloom and Miss Dorothy Darling from Woodmont. They were sent to live at the Circle Mission Church at the corner of Broad and Catherine Streets. They were the closest to Father Divine, they were the higher-ups. In the movement these two women yielded and wielded a power and a stronger word than Mother Divine did. Mother Divine, after all, was a trophy wife.

Like a scene out of Robert Graves' *I, Claudius*, after Father's death, Woodmont became the scene of many dramatic events and excommunications. Mother Divine would banish anyone who expressed doubts about her deity. She also exiled anyone who expressed doubts about her leadership or questioned her authority. If you crossed Mother Divine in any way, you were also banished. "If Mother Divine said, 'I want 14 purple roses arranged in that vase in 12 minutes,' if you didn't do it, you were banished," Lori Garcia said.

When I asked if Mother Divine had a secret side, Lori Garcia was quick to add: "There was a secret side to Mother that Tommy knows all about and because of that I know a lot that I cannot say just yet."

Mother Divine's life as a widow was marked with many public appearances at Philadelphia preservation society functions in which she would show up dressed in fine furs and jewelry. She appeared in the society pages of *The Philadelphia Inquirer* and *The Philadelphia Bulletin*. Tommy Garcia's story was also featured in many publications, although by this time he was living in Los Angeles. Even before his marriage to Lori, there were many questions about the future of the Woodmont estate. Mother Divine, as she aged, was becoming more and more remote, and the circle around her was becoming increasingly secretive. One common question throughout these years was, "Are you going to sell Woodmont?", to which Tommy Garcia would reply, "It's my house," inferring that the answer was no.

After Mother's death, Lori Garcia indicated that there was "a lot of activity going on in Woodmont" and that "somebody who has put themselves in a position of authority is doing things that shouldn't be done." An outgrowth of this, perhaps, is what I felt at the conclusion of my visit to Woodmont with Philadelphia artist Noel Miles, when I witnessed Mother Divine being led on her afternoon walk by a bevy of Rosebuds who somehow reminded me of polite prison guards. I told Noel Miles at the time that I did not get a good feeling about what I was seeing.

Tommy Garcia's relationship with Mother Divine was not at all traditional or conventional. "Good, bad, ugly or indifferent, that was his mother," Lori Garcia reminded me. "He would call her sometimes begrudgingly on Mother's Day because she would always ask him, 'When are you coming home?'"

But the grown up brown boy was not coming home, at least not yet. "They finally came to an understanding in 1989," I was told. "The understanding was that Tommy was not going to return home to run the Peace Mission movement until Mother passed away. This was because they had very different views concerning the movement. Tommy knew exactly what Father Divine expected of him." It is also true that Lori Garcia and Tommy had both talked about what they were going to do to continue the work that Father Divine wanted Tommy to do.

That work did not include the belief that Father Divine is God, was God, or will be God. On this point, Lori Garcia is adamant: "What Father Divine was, however, was an early champion for civil rights and racial equality." She revealed that Tommy has some ideas concerning this and told me that when Tommy was interviewed by a television news reporter and asked what he will do with all of Woodmont's resources, it was hard for the reporter to find a sensational spin when the adopted son replied, "With the resources I am going to take care of people."

Lori Garcia believes that Father Divine gifted Tommy with "foresight." Together, she and Tommy plan on preserving the good parts of Father Divine's philosophies so that Tommy will be seen to be the living legacy of his adopted father, not someone who would come forth and say, "My father was God, I am Jesus Christ—none of that," she asserts. On the other hand, she believes that controlling what people believe in their heart of hearts would not be possible to mandate. "If you believe that a turtle is God, and if that brings you comfort, then enjoy," meaning of course, that if some people chose to believe that Tommy shared in the Father Divine godhead that was on them.

When Tommy Garcia called Mother Divine from Los Angeles in 1997 and said that he would like to come home and introduce her to his wife, Lori, Mother Divine said, "Woodmont will always be your home, Tommy, but she cannot come with you." Lori, who was listening in on the phone conversation, heard Tommy say to Mother, "I picked Lori like Father Divine picked you." Mother Divine, undeterred, told Tommy, "I picked Father." She then reiterated, "She cannot come with you." Lori Garcia says this is when the relationship between Tommy and Mother Divine began to shift.

On Mother's Day, 2008, Tommy Garcia got a call from his best friend, Kenny, in Gladwyne, Pennsylvania, who told him, "Mother is pissed at you." Mother's anger stemmed from a visit that Kenny and another friend of his made to Woodmont. Mother Divine, who knew Kenny, at first thought the man with Kenney was Tommy. When she found out otherwise, she told Kenny, "I'm upset with Tommy because he hasn't been home in so long. He keeps promising to come home and I just know that he doesn't love me anymore."

After Kenny related the news to Tommy via telephone, Tommy resolved to call Mother Divine in the morning. Lori, who was in the house when her husband made the call, recalls the pained look on her husband's face after the conversation. "She doesn't sound right at all," Tommy confessed. He then mentioned the possibility of dementia, but he was not sure. He told Lori what Mother told him: "Tommy, they don't let me do anything anymore. They keep me locked in my room. When are you coming home, Tommy?"

"They keep me locked in my room." The phrase haunted both of them, and it made the necessity of returning to Woodmont all the more crucial.

"Mother," Tommy responded, hoping to get her to change her mind about bringing Lori, "We have to work through this. But I'm not coming home until you tell me I can bring Lori." In what seemed like an instant, Mother changed her mind and said that he could bring Lori Garcia to Woodmont. Naturally, after such a long separation, there was a general feeling of relief and celebration. Tommy was immediately on the phone to another friend in Philadelphia, a well-known florist, and asked him to deliver a magnificent arrangement to Woodmont. To add to the uniqueness of the occasion, the florist agreed to deliver the flowers himself. The bouquet included a card stating, "With love from Tommy and Lori." At Woodmont, the florist was met by a rosebud who told him that Mother was not available. The beautiful arrangement of flowers was placed on the floor of the Great Hall.

A few hours later, the florist received a call from Woodmont. The caller, another rosebud, said, "We will not accept these flowers. Come and get them." This development essentially shut down all further communication between Tommy Garcia and Mother Divine. All of Tommy and Lori's follow-up letters and cards to Mother Divine were "Returned to Sender."

Susan Garcia

Lori Garcia was aged thirty-four when she met thirty-nine-year-old Tommy Garcia. In 1992, she had known Tommy for a year as a casual friend she was always "running into" at parties and gas stations. Lori at that point lived in California's Woodland Hills and Tommy lived in the Agora Hills. She said she was first struck by Tommy's ability to "put a room at ease," as well as his demonstration of manners. "His manners always struck me," she said, "he would stand up when I left the table, for instance. They were formal manners. In those days I did not find people to be all that polite and well mannered.

His ability to put a room at ease without speaking, his sense of comedy—I'm not talking caustic sharp tongue comedy—but comedy that makes you laugh. Comedy, of course, almost always masks tremendous pain. But I knew nothing about the man until the second date."

The two enjoyed one another's company seeing films like *Aladdin*. All during the film, Lori says that Tommy was making cute noises, something she found touching and in keeping with the Disney motif. After the movies, they went out to eat. "It was a gourmet pizza and piano bar," Lori remembers. In the car on the way home, Tommy announced that he went to a boarding school in Paoli, Pennsylvania. This comment would have implications later but for the moment it just struck Lori as an autobiographical tidbit. For their second date, Tommy suggested a boating excursion. "If you can break away early Friday or Saturday we can go for a harbor cruise at sunset and have dinner on the beach." But sometimes the road to Shangri-La is paved with unexpected U-turns. On the day of the date, Tommy called Lori and said, "Lori, it's Tom, I'm not going to make it," and then abruptly hung up.

"There's something wrong," Lori thought. She immediately called his work number and left a message. Then she called a mutual friend and asked him if Tommy was there. There was a long silence and then the friend said that Tommy's sister, Suzie, was murdered the other day and that he had a lot to deal with. Lori took a step back. Who had she gotten involved with? Who was this man? "I really don't know much about him," she thought. "I've never experienced a friend or anyone who had lost a family member to a murder."

A couple of anxious hours passed and then Tommy called Lori and asked if he could come by. "He was an ashen man, he looked exhausted, haggard, his face had no expression and in his left hand he held a huge manila envelope," Lori said.

Tommy approached her. "Lori, there are things about me you don't know and when you know them you might not want to be involved with me." In the meantime, Lori's dog, PJ, a Maltese pedigree pup, was scampering about between their legs. Lori sat down with the envelope, opened it, and discovered a large article from the pages of *The Philadelphia Inquirer*, "The Lost Child of Mother and Father Divine." Subtitled, "Life After Heaven," Lori looked at it with confused curiosity. "I didn't understand it, and I had never been to Philadelphia," she said. She proceeded to read the article, but by the time she was finished, Tommy was sound asleep. Lori let him sleep but she was ready with questions and something to eat when he woke up.

"Why you?" she asked.

"I don't know," Tommy said. "Nobody has ever asked me that question. I only know what happened to my sister. She never had a chance. They took her soul."

"Are these really bad people?" Lori asked, thinking of the Peace Mission movement.

"No, Father Divine is wonderful," Tommy said.

"Did they kill your sister?"

"Oh no, no, no, they didn't have anything to do with it but they are certainly responsible because they took her soul."

Slowly, Tommy began to tell Lori the story of his sister and how he always knew that one day he would get that call. His sister had been found dead with a carton of milk and a container of Excedrin in a bag beside her. She had been sexually assaulted and shot. The coroner had called Tommy in the middle of the night. Besides the overreaching tragedy of losing a sister, the details of the murder reminded Tommy of his own sexual molestation by a Crusader as a child in the middle of the night on his second night at Woodmont.

Suzie's tragic life had its beginnings when she was separated from her brother and forced to live apart from him when she was almost four years old. After Tommy was dropped off at the Divine Lorraine Hotel on North Broad Street, Suzie was sent to the Peace Mission's International House for Girls, also on Broad Street, where she lived with residents Sonia, Laurie, Tina, and Linda. The caretaker was a woman named Cola, whom Lori Garcia says "didn't provide the girls with Mother nurturing. She was a disinterested caretaker."

Suzie was thrown out of the Peace Mission in 1974 or 1975 for having a sexual relationship with a Peace Mission plumber. Lori Garcia says it is more than likely that she got pregnant more than once and that all of her abortions were performed by Felix Spector, whose license was revoked many times for performing illegal abortions.

In April 2006, *Philadelphia City Paper* published the following report about Dr. Felix Spector:

> In the 1940s and again in the 1960s, he was found guilty of performing then-illegal abortions. Also in the '60s, a Philadelphia judge sentenced Spector to two years' missionary work in Africa. Then in 1997, *The Philadelphia Inquirer* indexed his numerous problems with the law, which included falsifying pharmacy records, billing irregularities and performing a castration of "grossly inferior quality."

The good doctor also specialized in castration. The article continues:

> For nearly 40 years, thousands of people have traveled here to have their testicles removed by Dr. Felix Spector, a retired osteopath who had offices in North and South Philly, and around the corner from the Pain Center in the Gayborhood.
>
> Unlike most trans-health professionals, Spector didn't follow the guidelines set forth by the Harry Benjamin International Gender Dysphoria Association, the regulatory body dedicated to the treatment of gender identity disorders. He never required that patients—transitioning or otherwise—undergo psychiatric counseling, take hormones or live outwardly as women.

The way he saw it, the Harry Benjamin guidelines created too many unnecessary hoops. By the time a person saved up enough cash to pay him a visit, they knew what they wanted. Spector believed his responsibility was to give it to them, "safely, correctly and with sympathy."

No questions asked, credit cards accepted.

Spector's Web site claimed he was "a founder of the field" and possessed "arguably more experience than almost any other doctor" in the treatment of trans people and men with overactive libidos. He even wrote a handbook on it—the $25 cost of which could be deducted from the price of surgery.

After her banishment from the Peace Mission, Suzie married a man with connections to Elvis Presley. The man's name was Max Shapiro, a famous West Coast dentist sometimes referred to as Dr. Feel Good because of allegations that he supplied patients with drugs. Lori Garcia says that Suzie met him at a party at Rod Stewart's house. She had gone at the special invitation from Tommy, who was also a musician. The year was 1977. Shortly after Shapiro met Suzie, he divorced his wife and proposed marriage. When Elvis Presley died, Geraldo Rivera did an investigative piece on all the doctors who had possibly supplied Elvis Presley with drugs, and Dr. Shapiro was included in the mix given that there was some speculation that codeine had contributed to Presley's fatal heart attack. One of the results of the investigation was that Shapiro lost his license and his practice was sold to someone with connections to LifeSpring and EST.

"When Suzie married Max, she had access to all this pharmaceutical cocaine," Garcia said. "She was an absolute mess. Max had unrestricted access to pharmaceutical cocaine, what was for Suzie all she needed or wanted."

Suzie grew up believing that Father Divine was God, and like all Peace Mission members, she had to find an outside job to pay her rent at the Divine Tracy Hotel. Residents of the hotel had to work at Divine Enterprises, located in the basement of the Divine Tracy. Many did secretarial work and others worked in the Keyflower Dining Room, but all members had to pay their own way. Suzie, however, had found a job with a doctor and soon got into the habit of taking home sample drugs. With the news of her sexual affair with the Peace Mission plumber, her abortions, and now her drug use, Mother Divine called Tommy into her office one day and said, "Suzie is no longer welcome. Make arrangements."

When Father Divine was alive, no one did anything without his permission. When he died, Mother Divine became the leader; the power and authority of Father Divine was passed to her. She controlled everything, especially all decisions concerning Tommy Garcia. Any decision made by Mother Divine concerning Tommy Garcia was carried out by a rosebud known as Miss Saint Mary Bloom (MSMB), now deceased. Lori Garcia says there is some discrepancy regarding MSMB's death date, although she stressed that both MSMB, who was black, and another rosebud, Miss Dorothy Darling (MDD), who was white, were no-nonsense businesswomen who were in charge of many Peace Mission projects.

MSMB, in fact, was in charge of a variety of issues for Tommy Garcia while Father Divine was alive. Father Divine even gave MSMB instructions regarding his adopted son that he wanted carried out.

"Miss Dorothy Darling and Miss Saint Mary Bloom were the highest of the high in the inner circle," Lori said. "They were Corporate Officers of several of the 501C3 entities—including President, Secretary, and Treasurer of The Circle Mission Church and Training School. Both were far more powerful than Mother was while Father was alive. As soon as Father died, Mother banished both MSMB and MDD from Woodmont—they were sent to live at the 'Sisters/Female' property at the corner of Catherine and Broad Streets. There were two buildings there—one for females and one for males."

Lori Garcia tells me how the Peace Mission's website, www.libertynet.orp/fdipmm, was eliminated after Mother Divine's death by two male Peace Mission higher ups, one named Roger Klaus and the other Christopher Stewart. "Clearly Klaus and Stewart's agendas necessitated they eliminate the site. There were hundreds of thousands of pages with information and photos. The original site was built by Tommy's biological mother, Georgia, who became Miss Harmony Faith, and was controlled by Philip Life, a white man, who was Father's chauffeur who hated that Tommy was more important than he was. When Father died, Life turned on Tommy, and in 2006, he sent a threatening email to him when Tommy inquired about his adoption paperwork. At this point, Mother was already in treatment for dementia.

"On the day that Tommy arrived at Woodmont, he was assigned a chauffeur/valet. He was also assigned a bodyguard by the name of 'Happy Love.' Of course, Lori Garcia asks, why would an 8yr old child need a bodyguard? The answer was that he was molested on his second night at Woodmont and Father Divine had a feeling that he needed to be protected." Happy Love was also the one to take Garcia to the King of Prussia Mall in suburban Philadelphia where the tailor measured him to make suits to match those that Father Divine wore. Happy Love was also instructed to get Tommy enrolled at Gladwyne Elementary School. Those school records state, "Child [Tommy Garcia] lives with Father Divine."

Lori Garcia says that MSMB was very fond of Tommy and that the boy was fond of her. "There was a real nurturing bond here and it was probably obvious to everyone at Woodmont," That bond was to become a memory, however, when during a visit to Woodmont in the mid-1980s, Tommy Garcia was shown the new "brothers quarters" by Roger Klaus. Klaus was showing Tommy the framework of the building when Tommy asked about MSMB. "Roger laughed an evil laugh and said, 'She died in a fire along with those important papers and their money.' Tommy was shocked by the news—but what Roger Klaus said barely registered until it came time to understand what he was really saying."

During his stay at Woodmont, Tommy got to see and experience "sides" of Mother Divine not many people would understand. "Mother was gracious to guests and visitors and to you [referring to the time when I visited Woodmont with Philadelphia artist Noel Miles], because you made her feel important."

At Father Divine's death, there was a scramble for positions of power. In order to remain in Mother's good graces, some followers wore masks. Some were upset when they saw Mother Divine changing what Father Divine stood for, that being treating everyone with dignity and respect. Some feared someone would be brought in from the outside world and given a high position of power and authority. After all, what was to prevent Mother Divine from going out and incorporating a male newcomer who she might then say was the reincarnation of Father Divine? "It was because of this that the Peace Mission staff viewed every person who came to Woodmont as a potential threat and rival. Less scrutiny was directed towards political leaders and preservation society officials who tended to validate Mother Divine, and allow her and her selected cronies to continue to live using the legend that Father created."

When Mother Divine invited Noel Miles and me into her private office for an intimate chat, I noticed a current of concern and disapproval from some of the Rosebuds who had just participated in the Holy Communion banquet. In retrospect, I can easily classify them as crossed looks or prolonged stares. One sensed secret sub layers here, like the uneasy but sinister smiles among the Great Dragon worshippers in Roman Polanksi's film *Rosemary's Baby*. Two Rosebuds accompanied Noel Miles and me into Mother Divine's office. They were there when Mother Divine piled us with Peace Mission books and pamphlets, encouraged photographs, and when she offered to arrange a second visit and interview in a couple of weeks. Miles was also eager to begin a series of paintings capturing the beauty of Woodmont's rooms, a project that Mother wanted him to do.

As we posed for photographs in Father Divine's office that day, I remember how the feeling of formality we felt at the banquet vanished as our bodies squished together in shoulder-to-shoulder, camera-ready camaraderie. It was also highly ironic how the same rosebud who had lashed out at me for daring to ask if I could take photographs of the interior of the house was now smiling, albeit uneasily, as she saw me clicking away with abandon. I recall asking myself at that moment what this rosebud must be feeling—resentment, humiliation, or both? Our conversation with Mother Divine lasted a good half-hour and included a good bit of laughing until it was announced that it was time for Mother Divine's afternoon walk. It was as if a nanny had suddenly entered the room and proclaimed with dour certitude that the party had to stop because it was time to walk the baby.

AN INVITATION CANCELLED

When Noel Miles and I contacted Woodmont to confirm our next visit, we were told in no uncertain terms by a rosebud that we were no longer welcome at the estate.

"You know, by the time you visited Woodmont in 2010," Lori Garcia said, referring to my visit with Miles, "Mother Divine was already well into her journey into dementia/Alzheimer's. During your visit they worried she might tell you some secret that they were keeping closely guarded."

In 2016, long after Mother Divine's dementia/Alzheimer's had set in, NBC 10, a Philadelphia news television station, interviewed Roger Klaus for a TV special on Woodmont and Mother Divine.

When Roger Klaus lived at the Divine Lorraine Hotel in 1956 with his Colorado-transplanted family, the rate was $2.50 a week.

He shook his head and smiled at the idea of someone paying as much as $2,500 a month, as high-end units will go for when the long-abandoned property reopens in the next year.

Klaus recalled the majesty of the North Broad Street apartment building in the heyday of Divine's International Peace Mission movement.

"In recent years, when they'd show the graffiti all over it, it made me sad," he said. "I don't like to think of it that way."

On the same day the new owner of the Divine Lorraine offered tours last week, Klaus gave us a tour of Woodmont, Father Divine's majestic estate in Gladwyne, where the long-deceased religious leader's 91-year-old wife, Mother Divine, lives with 17 followers.

The 72-acre hilltop property is tucked discreetly next to Philadelphia Country Club and above a steep wooded decline that falls to the Schuylkill Expressway at the Conshohocken Curve.

Not a blade of grass looked out of place on the recent visit. When asked who took care of the landscaping, Klaus looked around. As he spoke, two elderly women picked over the main house's blossoming flower beds. One woman, or "sister," as the women are known within the celibate religion, dragged a hose to water some bushes.

"We all pitch in," Klaus said

He gave me and my photographer a tour of the house's first floor—the high-ceilinged grand entrance hall, Father Divine's office, a sitting room, a drawing room off the banquet hall, the bright atrium. Wrought iron and carved wooden paneling dominate the window sills, door frames and trim. Known as Woodmont for its early 20th-century presiding family, a wealthy heir and follower of Father Divine ceded the property to the religious movement in 1953.

Mother Divine, who married the religious leader in 1945, was not able to talk with us, Klaus said.

When asked about her health, he said Mother Divine spends much of her time in her second-floor bedroom, but recently ate dinner with the rest of the Woodmont community, which gathers every Sunday for formal dinners. Mother Divine and all the sisters at Woodmont stay in the main house; the brothers stay in another house on the property.

The size of the Peace Mission movement is ever-dwindling, which seems inevitable with a stance that calls for lifelong celibacy.

BEHIND CLOSED DOORS

The so-called uplifting aspects of the Peace Mission cult might be compared to meat that has been left to rot.

"Some of the things that Mother Divine was about were never seen by the public," Lori Garcia informed me. "Everyone has a mask; we all have a public persona and then a private person, or what goes on behind closed doors." Garcia warned me that some of the things that she was about to share might reflect the distemper that Mother Divine did not show to the outside world. "You must understand that Mother Divine was the head, not the leader of the Peace Mission movement once Father Divine passed away. It's important to make the distinction."

Garcia explained that when Father Divine died there was no leader, proving that the Peace Mission was not a religion but a cult. "For many years no one wanted to use the word 'cult.' The word 'cult' is a frightening word. It insinuates that the people choosing a particular path are wrong. If it were a religion, when the leader or pastor died, they would bring in another pastor but they couldn't do that in this case because everything was Father Divine."

Garcia named an inner circle of Woodmont power brokers who have been prominent in controlling the movement since Father Divine's death. These include Roger Klaus, Evette Calm, Leon Jeter, and Elizabeth Kingdom, the former manager of Westminster Evangelical Home, a Peace Mission property on 41st Street in West Philadelphia. Westminster Evangelical Home had been cited several times over the years for misappropriation of funds involving the social security checks of followers despite the fact that Father Divine did not believe in Social Security. Mother Divine, however, is on record as having a Social Security number. "Leon Jeter was a mechanic, the only black man still around with any position of authority in the Peace Mission movement," Garcia said. "His name can be found among others on properties that the movement purchased. Through the years he has been able to maintain control unlike the rest of the followers."

Garcia went on to say that some of the things she was about to reveal might be disturbing:

Mother Divine did not like black people. She did not like old people. After Father passed, Mother would require that Tommy accompany her to inspect the kitchens at the various Divine properties like the Divine Lorraine, the Divine Tracy, the Circle Mission and the Unity Mission. She would inspect the entire property. There was a photographer, Kristin Bedford, who had received permission to live on the estate several years ago. She photographed life at Woodmont and wrote about her experiences but her writing displeased Roger Klaus and Evette because she happened to mention Mother Divine's real name, Edna Rose Ritching.

One of the photos that Bedford took was of a crippled woman who was hunched over, the result of a physical deformity or, as Garcia put it, "of having to spend years hunched over working on Peace Mission projects like making doilies for the table or cutting food in the kitchen." Garcia recalls how her husband, Tommy, told her how he had witnessed Mother Divine walking into this Peace Mission property and telling the woman to stand up to greet her. "She was crippled, she couldn't stand straight and Mother insisted—she was behaving as if she was The Queen—she was insisting that this woman rise and respect her, but the woman said, 'I can't straighten up.'" Garcia calls this "aspects of Mother Divine that were not very kind."

Then there was Tommy Garcia's visit to Woodmont in 1989, the result of Garcia having been contacted by *The Philadelphia Inquirer* to do an interview. After asking Mother for permission to do the interview, *The Inquirer* sent a reporter to interview him at the Beverly Hills Hotel. A few months later, Mother called Tommy Garcia and said that the newspaper wanted to publish photos to go with the interview, which would be published in *The Inquirer's* Sunday magazine supplement, *Today* magazine. The editors wanted photos of Tommy and Mother together.

Back at Woodmont during Garcia's 1989 visit, there were special banquets and announcements that the prodigal son had returned. Yet when Tommy and Mother got together, the mood was not so enthusiastic. Mother was concerned and told Tommy that the people in Woodmont, the followers, did not trust her and that she did not trust them. "At this point Roger Klaus was working security on the property but Mother's distrust extended to everyone, so much so that she asked Tommy to speak on her behalf at his welcome home banquet. After the banquet, Mother went to great lengths to speak to Tommy about the people at Woodmont," Garcia said.

"None of these people could put two nickels together and make a dime," she added.

The Peace Mission began selling off its various city properties in 2006. The selling of the properties began about the time that Lori says that Mother Divine was being treated for dementia and Alzheimer's. The medical records Lori was been able to obtain went back only to 2008 although she says that Mother had been treated by another physician before that. "Pennsylvania law states that without a court order medical records older than seven years do not have to be released. The records released in 2008 indicate Mother had been in treatment for several years prior to that date."

Throughout Mother Divine's medical treatment, there was some concern that the caretakers were not administering the medications as prescribed. "The whole thing smacks of elder abuse. Mother was a target for these people. As soon as Mother became a little too wordy or conversational, or if it seemed that there was something that could jeopardize what they were doing, which was certainly nefarious, they would whisk her away."

Garcia suggested that I watch the film *The Favourite*, a 2018 black comedy set in eighteenth-century England about two women in competition to be the royal favorites of Queen Anne. "See this film if you want to get a sense of the kind of life that Mother Divine led in Woodmont," Garcia said. "In the film, the queen is given massages. The massages begin at the legs and work their way up." She added that three important Woodmont resident/followers who were very fond of Tommy Garcia revealed that Mother Divine was the recipient of the kinds of massages one can see in *The Favourite*. The three followers were known as the Seamstress, the Dressmaker, and the Waitress and they are on tape as stating that they each walked in on Mother Divine as the massages were taking place.

"These were intensely private moments," she emphasized. "One person who walked in on a massage was put out for seeing what she saw. This means that she was thrown out of the movement because she was no longer needed."

The question of massages surfaced when I inquired what Mother did to relieve the stress of living in Woodmont with people she did not trust. "I think this was the only means that Mother had of releasing any tension," Garcia said.

Shortly after Father Divine's death, the Peace Mission movement started selling off many of the properties they owned throughout the city. These sell-offs were nefarious operations that did not take into account the number of Peace Mission followers whose names were on the leases for individual buildings.

When they started selling off properties, the people who were on the deed—in some cases there were hundreds of people on deeds and in one case that I personally uncovered on a public search, there were 75 names. Some of the people listed on the deed had died, some had not, but when the property was sold, the flowerers did not receive a dime. There were even people on the deed from Father Divine's early days in Harlem when he ran the Busy Bee Employment Agency.

The Busy Bee Employment Agency was for Peace Mission flowerers and believers alike. Here Father Divine made no distinction because he was very much aware that if landlords would not allow dark-skinned people to live anywhere they wanted to live, then it was the Peace Mission's responsibility to purchase properties that would enable that to happen. In all of these properties there was no undue mixing of the sexes, and when the property was sold, no money was distributed to the followers listed on the lease. How did this happen? How did the Peace Mission get away with such a thing? "A seller has to sign off on a property," Garcia said, "if there are multiple people on the lease then they have to sign off too."

Garcia points to Father Divine's personal attorney, Jay Austin Norris, a believer in Father Divine and the person responsible for convincing Father Divine to move the Peace Mission from Harlem to Philadelphia. Norris was also the publisher of the (now defunct) *Philadelphia Public Journal* and *Philadelphia Independent* newspapers. He was appointed to the Philadelphia Board of Revision of Taxes in 1936 and stayed in that position until his retirement in 1967. Norris was the executor of Father Divine's estate and died in 1976 at the age of 82. Father Divine died of a heart attack in the city's Graduate Hospital on September 30, 1965.

Garcia says that she spoke to one of Jay Norris' daughters, then in her eighties, in 2010:

> She was also a retired attorney. She remembered being a child when her father would take them to Father Divine's banquets in Harlem. She would also spend holidays with her father, who was then divorced, in Philadelphia, where they would go to the banquets at Woodmont. I learned that it was J. A. Norris who set Father Divine up in numerous non-for-profit 501 CE Church organizations. Of course, this is the problem. This eliminated the ability for anyone to question what the Peace Mission was doing. Norris was brilliant, but he also allowed people like Roger Klaus, Yvette Calm and Leon Jeter to hide behind the gates of Woodmont without any intrusion.

Garcia mentions the sale of the Divine Lorraine hotel on North Broad Street. "When they sold the hotel, it was all smoke and mirrors. They created different corporations to obfuscate and delay the final sale. This is why it took years and years to finalize the sale of the Divine Lorraine. It was sold and then sold to another developer and then nothing happened. This went on for a while. They knew it would take time to finalize the sale but they had time...nobody was in a hurry with those millions of dollars."

As the Divine Lorraine Hotel went from developer to developer, Mother Divine was beginning to exhibit signs of dementia. This was the cue for those forces inside Woodmont to begin their manipulation of her. First would come the death of Tommy Garcia's mother, Georgia. Lori Garcia, who has had many conversations with her husband about that time, recalled that when Georgia died in the Divine Tracy Hotel, Georgia's roommate insisted that she heard nothing despite the fact that it was noted that Georgia had passed away from an epileptic seizure. She said it took her ten years for her to get a copy of the police report on Georgia's death. "The Medical Examiner would not release a copy of the autopsy report," she said, noting that she was finally able to read it in 2010 when she learned that there was not any evidence that Georgia had epilepsy. The official police report that she received in 2001, however, did state that there was a bottle of Dilantin on a night stand (and in Georgia's name) in Georgia's room. In the extensive report that she read after that ten-year struggle, it was stated that Georgia's only medical treatments while she was at Woodmont involved two visits for the treatment of glaucoma. There was nothing about epilepsy.

In a scenario straight out of Angela Lansbury's *Murder She Wrote*, Garcia theorizes that the staff was paid to prescribe Dilantin. "Dilantin is used to treat epilepsy, however if you didn't have epilepsy and were given Dilantin it could cause an epileptic seizure. If you are given Dilantin because you have epileptic seizures and then have it taken away improperly without a gradual weaning, it will cause neurological disorders, which is exactly what they did to Mother Divine."

Garcia bases her allegations on the fact that throughout most of Mother Divine's medical reports, she read doctors' notes voicing concern that Mother Divine's medications were not being given as prescribed because the caretakers were saying that the meds were giving Mother Divine a body rash.

After Mother Divine's death, there was a memorial service that Lori and Tommy Garcia were not invited to. This was no surprise, given that, from 2009 to her death in 2017, Mother Divine was really no longer in control at Woodmont. After her death, Tommy and Lori traveled to Gladwyne, Pennsylvania, and appeared at the gates of the estate with the proper court documents. Tommy Garcia had been appointed administrator of Mother Divine's estate and they were there with their attorney and two childhood friends of Tommy Garcia's.

The group was met with threatening hostility.

J. F. Pirro, in an August 2017 edition of *Main Line Today*, describes the encounter between the Garcia's and Orwellian behind-the-scenes forces at Woodmont:

This past March saw the passing of 91-year-old Mother Divine—or Sweet Angel Divine—Father's second wife. Now, Garcia has been granted status as administrator of her estate. The day after the county's decision, he attempted to serve those papers at Divine's estate. He was unsuccessful.

Garcia last visited in 1989, and followers hadn't permitted him to speak to Mother in almost a decade—though outsiders told him she always asked for him.

But will the modern-day Peace Mission want him?

"Based on sufficient collateral evidence, the county considers Tommy to be the Divines' child, with the legal role of marshaling assets and making distribution of assets to people who may be entitled to them," says Garcia's Philadelphia-based attorney, Joel S. Luber. "The clerk didn't blink an eye."

And that's without any known formal adoption papers—or a will. "They lived in a bubble behind closed gates and did what they wanted," Luber says of the Divines.

Now, the challenge is determining what belonged to Mother Divine. Garcia's efforts could uncover that the 74-acre property and estate belong to the Commonwealth of Pennsylvania, a charitable or "shell" organization, or even the few followers the Peace Mission has left. "The answers are behind those iron gates and castle walls," says Luber.

Lower Merion Township Police Capt. Frank Thomas confirmed that the Garcias' requested police presence in June, when they tried to serve the administration papers with Luber and two of Tommy's boyhood friends from Gladwyne Elementary School. "The two parties didn't come together," he says, adding that the movement deferred to its Philadelphia attorneys at Blank Rome.

"We were on a peace mission," says Garcia. "But where has the peace gone? Father always used to say, 'Peace, peace.' Why are these people so angry? Back then, I asked him, and he said that they didn't get it. He told me he wasn't God, but that I had to keep that secret because it was all [the followers] had to keep them going. He talked to me like a dad."

Garcia and his wife, Lori, realize the complexity of the task ahead. Luber's initial phone call to Woodmont was met with a direct response from follower/spokesperson Yvette Calm: "We're not interested. We'll have him arrested."

Then she hung up.

Luber fully expects the Peace Mission's attorneys to challenge the register of wills' decision, along with petitions to delay or prevent the investigation. He spent "a very unusual" three months waiting for Mother Divine's death certificate—the one document required for the administrator application when there's no known will. Ciavarelli Family Funeral Homes in Conshohocken refused to provide it, but it came from the state eventually.

At press time, Luber was filing for the ability to serve papers with a sheriff present—even though he appears to be wavering on whether he'll continue to represent Garcia. "There has to be a proper accounting, and the Garcias are at least entitled to the truth," says Luber, who lives in the shadows of Woodmont.

Among followers, the question has always been why Father Divine—who died in 1965—doted on Garcia. "Even then, the thought was that the movement was dying," Garcia says. "Everyone constantly asked me, 'Why are you here? You don't even follow all the rules.' But Father grew to really care about me."

Concerned about Mother Divine's fading health, the Garcias began requesting wellness checks through the Philadelphia Police Department and Lower Merion Township. Each report indicated that she was fine, even three weeks before her passing. The certificate lists her cause of death as Alzheimer's disease.

Through his business, Cabo Magic Sportfishing, Garcia has raised the level of life for interested local Mexicans in a fishing fleet he's gradually sold off in Cabo San Lucas, Mexico. "I'd give up everything and move back to Philadelphia in a millisecond," he says. "If I could come back home, I will have come full circle."

With Woodmont and the remaining assets of the Peace Movement, Garcia says he wants bridge the nation's racial divide, nurture lost children, and apply Father Divine's ideals to elevate the lives of blacks. "I can't proselytize him as God, but I can use the millions to help people," he says.

"And not just the (estimated) six people left at Woodmont."

Years before Father Divine's death, J. Austin Norris, lawyer, editor and civil rights leader, was the main speaker during Woodmont's anniversary celebration in the Tea Room of the Divine Lorraine Hotel. On that day, September 11, 1958, Norris noted:

Peace, FATHER: (Father replies, "Peace!") Peace, MOTHER: I'm taking advantage of the opportunity of sitting in here to speak in this room for the first time. I think I have had the privilege of speaking at most of the auditoriums in or near Philadelphia bur this is the first time that I have had the opportunity of being in this most sacred and personal dining room.

FATHER invited me here just an hour or so ago, and, of course, HIS Invitation is a command as far as I am concerned. I have often said in all the eighteen years that I have been associated with the Movement I have never asked FATHER to do any favor that HE has turned me down about; so if it's midnight, if it's morning, if it's noon or afternoon, HIS Request is always a command to me.

I thought here that I might tell you some of the questions and thereby you can measure the concern of the public for the concern of the Movement here—some of the questions that they have asked me because they know that I am FATHER'S Attorney. I think this last year I have had even more questions directed to me than probably any previous year.

The questions run like this: "What kind of Personality is FATHER DIVINE?" Well, I tell them, and I almost know it by rote, my answers to these questions, because they are asked weekly. "What kind of Personality does HE have?" Well, I say here, I don't know of anyone that's more genteel that handles as much power as HE does. I don't know if there's anyone that is more cultured and refined. I have never heard HIM raise HIS Voice in anger at anyone; have you? ("No," came the prompt sanction.) I don't know of anyone who is more considerate of the feelings and the thoughts of others than FATHER DIVINE. I don't know anyone that's more humble than HE. I don't know anyone that puts one person above another less than HE does. Everyone is on the same plane with HIM whether they are big, mighty, or whether they be humble and lowly. I have seen HIM, and I have spent a day just observing these things—a full twenty-four hours—and I have never known anyone that worked continuously so hard as HE does; do you? ("No," again came the sanction.) And so I tell them the story of the Personality of FATHER DIVINE.

This past year I have been busy almost weekly rebutting the rumors of HIS enemies that HE's dead. You know, more constantly every week there's someone even as far as west of Chicago, that calls me to say, "Why, we heard of the demise of FATHER DIVINE." My answer to that is, HE has never looked better during all of the seventeen, eighteen years that I have known HIM! (Loud applause sanctions this.)

Then the second question they put at me is this: "HE is very rich. HE has all of the money that's Croesus', that's attributed to Croesus." I said, you're wrong there. FATHER DIVINE doesn't have a penny. And HE could be very rich if HE traded HIS Services for wealth; HE could be wealthy, couldn't HE? ("So true!" came the reply.) And all of these other Christianities and all of these other religious sects, where the money goes to the head. HE reverses the order. It goes to the people! (Loud applause sanctions this.) And they ask me about HIS income tax. I said I don't know about that but I'm sure HE doesn't have any because HE has no income.

There's not a week that goes by that someone doesn't try to get me to persuade FATHER DIVINE to buy something. Not a week! And I think Miss D. will tell you and certainly FATHER and MOTHER will tell you, that I never transmit those messages to HIM. I say that here, I only handle those matters which HE in HIS Wisdom and HIS Own Divine feelings might feel that I should handle and only those things that HE turns over to me.

2

The Cultic Lure of
Philadelphia Psychics

Is it possible for people who consult psychics on a regular basis to come to regard them as the primary source for spiritual subsidence? Can consultations with individual psychics take the place of a much larger spiritual institutions? Can well-known psychics become the go-between spot for spiritual seekers? Are they a different kind of guru?

In Philadelphia, the place to go when you belong to the Cult of the Psychic, which also includes the Cult of the Crystal and the Cult of the Tarot and the Cult of Incense Burning, is the Garland of Letters New Age bookstore on South Street.

The Garland of Letters has been described as a magical bookstore that has been on South Street at the same location since 1972. Most people find it to be a unique shop specializing in spiritual materials of the "New Age" sort, carrying books, crystals, jewelry, statues, chakra wands, Tibetan Singing Bowls, sage for smudging, lots of incense, soaps, journals, and more. It is all you need to build your little personal church.

In the 1960s, there was a plan to connect I-76 and I-95 by cutting across the city with a new highway. This highway was to replace South Street, demolishing a healthy shopping corridor below 10th Street. A number of historic properties were on the chopping block, many of them dating to the 1700s.

When the highway plan was chartered, many established businesses panicked and moved away, leaving empty storefronts. "Hippies," artists, and free spirits saw an opportunity to live cheaply and make a small living while there was still time, theorizing that they could get out before demolition. The area soon became the home base for Philadelphia's punk scene, as well as great arts and cultural venues like the Painted Bride Arts Center.

The increasing popularity of South Street became so high that the idea of a highway cutting it up into surgical bits was no longer feasible. Unfortunately, the downside of extreme popularity in this case meant that the once authentically bohemian corridor became a magnet for chain stores and standardization. Garland of Letters survived all of these changes and still very much resembles what it was decades ago.

My association with, and investigations of, various Philadelphia psychics began some years ago.

As 2016 drew to a close, many people complained that it was an awful year and that they were glad to see it go. When 2017 arrived many people began thinking about what the coming months would bring, especially with a new president in the White House.

Among some, there was a lot of fear regarding the issue. If you were to go by posts on Facebook then, you would come away thinking that the world was doomed and that "peace" in the United States was over. A friend of mine at that time was so worried about the incoming administration that he wound up seeing two therapists, his regular therapist and a special "Trump presidency" therapist to help him deal with Donald Trump in the White House. My friend was convinced that the world would end on January 20, 2017. He often spoke of being hauled off to a concentration camp because he is African American.

I have not witnessed this much fear since I was a boy during the time of the Cuban Missile crisis. At that time, our parents gathered us in a circle before bed and asked us to pray hard because we might not wake up in the morning. My parents rarely minced words and tried to tell us the truth about the world. To this day, I thank them for this honesty.

In 2016, I thought that people could do one of two things about the incoming presidency. We could contribute to the never-ending stream of negative energy that nothing good will ever come from the new president, or we could retain some hope that something positive might come out of it despite dire warnings of doom and gloom. At the very least, give the new president a chance before threatening to take to the streets, or move to Costa Rica while screaming "Apocalypse Now!"

In my search then to find out what might happen in the next four years, I discovered Spiritman Joseph, or Joseph Tittel, a talented clairvoyant who hails from Levittown, Pennsylvania. Tittel is a tall blond tattooed guy who grew up wanting to become a police officer but then discovered that he had a psychic talent that he had to put to use. Listening to Tittel's videos is a little like listening to an articulate, unpretentious homeboy in a Philadelphia-area Dunkin' Donuts (he loves the Eagles). Tittel's predictions, unlike the predictions of mildly talented psychics, have a good accuracy rate. At least this is what his followers say.

So what did Tittel say about 2017?

Tittel made it clear that he did not vote for Trump because he believes that the man is a psychopath. Harsh words indeed for a psychic intent on building his customer base, but then he says: "I don't like him but he's president-elect and we have to put positive energy around his presidency. I'm only a Trump supporter for the moment. Trump's a bully, but there have been many leaders of countries who have been complete psychopaths who have done great things for their country."

I thought of my friend with the Trump therapist who fears that World War III is coming, but Tittel says that World War III was avoided in 2012 when indigenous Native American tribes and others, such as monks and nuns, prayed, meditated, and did all sorts of ceremonial stuff to avoid that catastrophe. While we will have to take Tittel's word on that, the psychic did say that Donald Trump will not start World War III but will have a great opportunity to cement a peaceful relationship among China, the United States and Russia. Tittel saw Trump going to Russia and he even saw Russian president Vladimir Putin coming to the United States, but probably not to Hollywood or to Rosie O'Donnell's house.

If partisan ideologues hate psychics, it is because good psychics see what they see with little or no regard to party loyalty. Partisan, ideologically driven psychics rarely make the grade.

Tittel predicted that Trump would be one of the most well-traveled presidents in U.S. history, going to the most obscure places on the globe. He also saw Trump calling more spontaneous news conferences than any other president in U.S. history. This prediction makes sense when you consider Trump's propensity for instant communication (Twitter), even though Barack Obama was the first president to Tweet. Tittel also predicts a Trump win in 2020.

Tittel said that President Obama had less than great intentions when he supported the Russian hacking charge. Obama did this, Tittel says, to discolor Trump's relationship with Russia. "Obama is part of the Clinton-Bush Washington establishment whereas Trump is not establishment at all."

Russia is not the problem, Tittel insisted, China is. China is also headed for a big economic crisis. As time passes, it will become evident that China is the real threat to world peace.

As for the summer of 2017, Tittel predicted intense demonstrations and riots especially in the summer months and not only in the United States but the world over. Tittel seemed to score a hit on this one.

He also predicted that we should be prepared to see established leaders being overthrown or kicked out of office and embassies attacked by ordinary citizens fed up with the status quo. He also saw multiple assassinations and assassination attempts as never before. There will be an attempt on Trump's life but it will mirror the unsuccessful attempt on President Reagan's life. Even the most talented psychics in the world have trouble with timelines when they are not just plain wrong.

Tittel predicted a U.S. economic crisis in July, but after that, the economy will rebound in a big way, thanks to Trump.

It does not take a psychic to know that the people Trump has surrounded himself with are generally problematic. In the beginning of Trump's presidency, Tittel called the Trump Cabinet a "dark energy source" who were really not Trump's friends but who would secretly work for his demise. Here is where Tittel's predictions begin to sound like a novel by Dan Brown or a chapter out of Robert Graves' *I, Claudius*. Trump's insider enemies will seek to do him harm in the next four years, Tittel said, including attempts to poison his food and hurt his family. Tittel is adamant: "Trump is an independent non-establishment type who is surrounding himself with the wrong people."

I thought of a musical version of *The Cabinet of Dr. Caligari*, when Tittel said that Trump will claim another historic presidential first when he begins to fire and hire new Cabinet members with amazing frequency. Tittel says: "His Cabinet firings will be like his reality show, *The Apprentice*. You're fired!"

The scary people that Trump surrounds himself will attempt to turn him into their puppet, but they will not succeed, Tittel maintained, while mentioning that there would be strange occurrences happening in the White House, like a person being taken out in a stretcher with a blanket over his face. He does not believe that the person will be Trump but perhaps a reporter who suffered a heart attack while attending a news conference.

"Both the United States and China love money before they love their own people," Tittel said, and then our tattooed clairvoyant suggested that people not invest in the stock market, IRAs, or "anything on paper."

Tittel went full blast when he said he looks forward to the coming earth shift, when the two poles will shift and cause the earth "to be purified," meaning that the darkness now on the planet will be "flooded off." He points to 2020 as being a significant date when "secrets and lies will no longer have merit." 2020 to 2028 will be a time of great change. (The so-called "earth shift" will also have unpleasant physical ramifications, but Tittel did not elaborate. In one vision he saw many people wearing face masks in 2020).

His other predictions include:

1. Before the pole shift, Europe will be devastated by terrorism, especially France, which he sees as being wrecked into almost total oblivion by an atomic like blast, but not bombs from the sky but bombs planted underground, such as in sewers or in tunnels. Trump will unleash full fury after a failed 9/11-style attack on American soil. Although the attack will be thwarted, Trump's anger and his response will help to eradicate ISIS.

2. Pope Francis will be that last pope of the Catholic Church though he cautions that the next pope might be the last pope. (Pope predictions of this sort are mystifying because no one ever mentions who will lead the Catholic Church after the so-called last pope. Is Tittel saying the Catholic Church will end?) In an even more shocking prediction, Tittel says that Pope Francis

will be killed by someone in his inner circle and that the death will be made to look like an illness. (A similar story about the death of Pope John Paul I was "confirmed" by an article in *The New York Post* in October 2019.)

3. The summer of 2017 will result in sea and lake front beach closures to the public because of toxic water. Dead fish will be washed ashore and beloved, legendary beaches will be shut down—forever. (Failed prediction, apparently.)

4. Trump will complete the first term of his presidency although there is a chance he could be impeached sometime in the third or fourth year.

5. People should stay away from Walmart where he sees mass shootings.

6. He advises against traveling to Israel and the Middle East after May 2017.

7. He advises travelers to avoid booking hotel rooms in Trump-owned businesses, especially overseas where they will be the target of terrorists.

8. The Mexican wall will be started but it will not be completed, and in time it will become apparent that where we really needed a wall was along our northern border.

THE HOUSEWIFE PSYCHIC

Some psychics are in the "word of mouth fame" category. This brings me to Arlene Ostapowicz, a Philadelphian who died in 2018 after a long illness.

Though not an attorney, singer, artist, or writer, Arlene had been a guest on many television and radio shows. In fact, she was once offered a guest spot on Bill Maher's show, *Politically Incorrect*, but had to decline because the live show was on too late at night. For several years, she worked at *The Courier Post* of New Jersey and as a monthly commentator on an Atlantic City cable T.V. station. In the 1980s, she was in high demand with City Hall politicians and judges.

Her life as a City Hall consultant started when Philadelphia Councilwoman Joan Krajewski (now deceased) stopped at Arlene's place one day for a session. Krajewski had heard about Arlene's talents via "word of mouth," the most powerful advertising tool in the world, and decided it was time for a reading. After the session, Krajewski became a fan and wanted to see Arlene on a regular basis. She liked what Arlene told her, not because it was what she wanted to hear, but because it was accurate stuff. Very soon, word of Arlene's talents, thanks to Krajewski, spread among the vast network inside City Hall, especially among the judges, some of whom contacted Arlene and asked for appointments.

The judges were so eager to see Arlene that they sent limos to her humble house in the city's Wissinoming section to pick her up and drive her back to their chambers. For the judges, the process must have been like ordering a delicious take-out lunch. Once delivered to their chambers, Arlene did her thing, after which she was quietly chauffeured home again. After a few months of this, Krajewski came up with an idea. She asked Arlene if she would see former mayor Frank Rizzo, who was then set on running for a new term as mayor. This was in the 1980s, when Rizzo had his famous local radio talk show. Arlene agreed, and met Rizzo and Krajewski in a South Philadelphia house where the consultations began.

A little segue here: I met Frank Rizzo in the 1980s and remember being awed by the size of the man. The man was a giant, with hands the size of waffle irons and shoulders as wide as a Broad Street intersection. I was there to interview him for a downtown newspaper and was seated in a waiting area at the radio station when Rizzo walked in the room. When I first saw him, I assumed he was part of the in-house security team because what I saw resembled a WWE wrestler. Yes, he was that big. After we shook hands, he led me to a sofa where we sat for the interview. Within minutes, we were eyeball-to-eyeball, with the ex-mayor slapping my shoulder and calling me by my first name.

"So this is that magic charisma I've always heard about," I said to myself. The interview was a success despite the fact that I had written unflattering things about the man for years.

Arlene never told me what Rizzo asked her, or even what she said to him, but what went down must have impressed him because the next time he saw her, he said, "If I get elected, I'm going to get you an office in City Hall and put you on the payroll."

How is that for instant enthronement? Arlene was worth it, however. When she was on T.V. during the Wilson Goode administration and the city was on the verge of bankruptcy, she was asked by a reporter if the city would sink or swim, and she said swim, meaning that the federal government would come to the city's rescue at the last minute. She provided other details, of course, and when the prediction came true, there were more limos at her door.

Naturally, you would think that a woman this talented would charge the moon for consultations, or if not that, then she would certainly move into an exotic penthouse with busts of Egyptian gods and goddesses, get her hair done every few minutes, and start to act like a diva. She would also have to have a press agent who screened calls and booked customers, and then she would have to hit the lecture circuit, all for a very big fee of course. Our culture, up to its ears in gross materialism, overflows with corruption, whether it is how Philadelphia (house) Sheriff Sales are conducted, how local firehouses are funded, or how "important" people put on airs. Had Arlene allowed her head to swell, she might even have started her own religion, *à la* psychic Sylvia Brown, who was a frequent guest on the Montel Williams show.

Arlene continued to live in her humble Northeast home with its ramshackle porch while doing consultations for the high and mighty, but also for her so-called "little people," who she said were just as valuable to her.

"I never wanted to be famous," she told me. This was true even when she studied metaphysics in England in 1972 and became an organizer of the Atlantean Society, and then came back to the U.S. to start a chapter here. The chapter studied things like auras and everything related to the paranormal, including possession and exorcisms.

A good many people equate people who have a natural gift of prophecy with the dark side. I do not know where this equation comes from. Instead of something good, they see sinister shades of Aleister Crowley, Anton Lavey, black magic, or Satanic stars. Arlene told me that she venerated a number of Catholic saints, like Saint Thérèse of Lisieux. When she was alive, she liked to say how she had a special devotion to the Sacred Heart, and to the rosary; she also noted that her belief in angels was strong, and that she sometimes made believers out of skeptics. She was fond of saying that St. Thomas was the medium for the 12 apostles, and that the gift of prophecy has always been with the world, from Moses on, and did not suddenly disappear with the death and resurrection of Christ. This is why she was able to attract people who would not otherwise venture into these realms. I like to compare her to world famous Jeanne Dixon, who was also a devout Catholic.

Arlene insisted that she saw no spiritual danger in her work. Her wish was to exercise her gift for the good of people, even if she needed to get paid, but not too much, since a lot of money inevitably attracts corruption.

All types of people came to her: real estate agents, jaded businessmen battling out ugly deals, worried moms and dads, nurses and physicians, judges, politicians, and even other talented people who see the future. Some of them asked her how she could be so humble and charge so little when she could be sitting on Easy Street.

The Philadelphia Police Department came looking for her, usually in the form of a detective knocking on her door, asking for help to solve a murder or a missing person case. She has worked with the police on many crimes, such as the infamous Dolores Della Penna murder in 1972, the Candace Clothier killing in 1968, and far more recent cases.

She told me about her experiences in a possessed house in the Bridesburg neighborhood near All Saints parish. The malevolent presence was so bad that when the home owner tried to get the pastor of All Saints to come by to do some prayers, the poor priest could not even get up the steps. A force kept pushing him back. With her Atlantean Society friends, Arlene said that she went into the house and to the troubled room in question where her group formed a circle, held hands, and began some prayers when something unbelievable happened. She says that she was pushed all the way across the floor, as if gliding on ice, to the very edge of the stairs.

While there is no way to prove to skeptics who laugh or sneer at the paranormal, those of us who have had an "Ostapowicz" moment know better.

When clairaudient Carolann Sano appeared at Philadelphia's (now defunct) Astral Plane restaurant, the people waiting to see her gathered by the restaurant's staircase and noted their place in line with hawkish dedication. That is the way it is when a talented medium gives away psychic counseling sessions for free. It was certainly the method for the two women who jumped ahead of a friend of mine who was due to be read after me. The women seemed to appear out of the woodwork; perhaps they had been lurking behind a column or one of the restaurant's huge wicker chairs. But suddenly there they were, breathless in Philadelphia, seating themselves at Carolann's corner table lit only by two handsome candlesticks that gave it the feeling of Theosophy and Madame Blavatsky.

Proving that her mind is no sieve, Carolann remembered the order of the line and left her corner table in order to find out whose turn it really was. Order, needless to say, was restored.

The mild mayhem that Carolann's sessions caused that night as the Astral Plane celebrated its annual "Best of Philadelphia" awards is a testament to humanity's hunger for information beyond the pale.

As she later told me in the swanky garden of the Rittenhouse Hotel where we had gone for high tea, "When you offer something for free, everybody wants to try it even people who say they don't believe—especially people who say they don't believe."

As a veteran psychic traveler—I can recall readings and dinners in psychic Valerie Morrison's home in Roxborough, and pizza, beer, and good times while hanging out with syndicated astrologer Jacqueline Bigar—I pride myself on usually being able to spot a paranormal fake. In the world of the paranormal, fraud is rampant. In many ways, finding a good psychic can be as difficult as finding a good plumber. The classic storefront gypsy card reader who cons the naïve into giving them cash to dispel curses is only the tip of the iceberg. Although I have never consulted a medium, like most people in the past, I have watched television sessions with John Edward. Edward seems like the real deal, although with mediums one is always inclined to think of those Victorian melodramas where the medium, sans turban and crystal ball, works a set of trick contraptions under a tablecloth.

"Forty-one saints in the Catholic Church were clairaudient. Oh my goodness, it's not that I'm looking to get on the charts, I'm just looking to do what I'm supposed to do," Carolann tells me after biting into a particularly moist scone.

She says the messages she gets when reading for a client come from "them," or energies she refers to as angels, but they can also be called spirit guides. The guides, she says, are "a more highly evolved intellect than humans, serving God, the universe, but they are not God." "They" are also not 100 percent accurate all the time because only God can be accurate. These energies exist where time does not, therefore, timing can be delayed.

She channels through automatic writing. A person asks her a question; she hears a response in her right ear. She calls the process "immediate," and says that it is similar to dictation. When the message she gets is over, the words she is transcribing, or the message for the client, suddenly stops. Immediately before she records the message, she says that her writing arm goes numb and then comes an almost involuntary movement of her arm as she begins to write.

Questions can be asked through dead loved ones. When asked this way, the messages come back in the style or emotive feel of the deceased. My mother, who died in 1993, "reminded" me during my session with Carolann how she used to pull and snap my suspenders when she wanted to make a major point. I had forgotten all about this childhood memory but Carolann brought it back with a loud snap. Suddenly, I could see my mother snapping my suspenders— yes, how could I have forgotten that she used to do this?

In the Rittenhouse Hotel, I asked Carolann three additional questions and watched as she scrawled her replies on a blank sheet of paper. What she wrote was not intelligible—the writing often appears as a scrawl—although the accompanying verbal messages that Carolann delivered were clear. One of my questions concerned a deceased friend who was killed in 1993; suffice to say that the message delivered to me answered a lingering question regarding the death of this friend. Generally, the messages are stream of consciousness monologues. "They," the spirit guides or angels, have a tendency to call men of any age "young men," a habit that may have something to do with the fact that on the other side we are all supposed to be thirty-years old.

But do not call Carolann "psychic." "I tend to think of psychic as people who feel. Psychics tend to put a lot on themselves, 'I can tell you this,' 'I can tell you that.' whereas I can say to someone, 'I can tell you nothing. I just deliver a message that is given to me.'"

She says the information contained in the messages is garnered to help people make better choices in life. "It is to help you with directions. It isn't to predict so that you won't have to think on your own. If someone says, 'What do I need to know about what's going on in my office, the boss is acting very aloof, am I on the list to be terminated?' then the message will give you background information."

Although our conversation in the well-appointed Rittenhouse Hotel had all the appearances of a charmed life, Carolann's life has been anything but a tea party.

Years ago, a marriage thought to last forever fell apart. Her idea of marriage was that which God joins together, no man shall put asunder. Yet suddenly she found herself having to raise two adopted children on her own. "I had issues with God," she told me. "I couldn't understand how this could happen. I asked God, 'How could you allow two children to be adopted into a family that would break up, being an all-knowing God?'"

For her, such a thought was a radical concept. As an Italian, she is "twice Catholic," not to mention that she was brought up in the pre-Vatican II Church on the Baltimore catechism, a stricter Catholic Church to be sure.

She said she lost it one day when she smashed all her ugly 1960s earth tone color dishes. Her cries were tense as she asked God, while smashing the plates, "How could you do this?"

"Then I realized what I did and I held my breath. I didn't know what I was waiting for—was the floor going to open up, was I going to be struck?"

The realization hit her that with unconditional love, one can have their moments and be so angry with a person but when that anger has passed the love has not changed at all. "The love hasn't diminished, and not a single thing has changed," she said.

"In day-to-day earth life, whether it's a friend who has betrayed you, a family member who disappoints you or a partner who leaves or whatever; no matter what you do, no matter how angry you get, you're allowed to be you. God is not going to love you any less because you revert into being you."

Years ago she was national sales manager for a major hotel chain based in Arizona. She came to Philadelphia in the late 1990s to make sales calls and fell in love with the city. "You could get a lot done in a short amount of time here because of the way the city is laid out," she said. Then there was the culture, the ambience, and the diversity of the city. Philadelphia reminded her of New York when she worked in that city as a supervisor in Kennedy Airport for Pan Am, a job that she says helped her understand and appreciate different cultures and beliefs.

Her Pan Am job helped her to learn the importance of getting the hatboxes of Hadassah-Jewish women on the planes to Tel Aviv. Hadassah Jewish women had to have their hatboxes because they contained the wigs of their religion required them to wear. The Pan Am job also forced her to use what she calls her "less than perfect Spanish."

She admits that when she started channeling, she did not know how she would work or whom she should address. Then she says she remembered that there are guardian angels or entities around us for protection, and then she said she started to ask questions, despite disbelief and laughter among some people she knew.

"You know," she said, turning towards me so that her shoulders seemed to square one of the cherubs on the Rittenhouse Hotel wall behind her, "I didn't know how this interview would go, so I decided to ask the angel of interviews what to expect."

The angel of interviews? I wondered if I had heard her correctly. Beneath her notebook was a typewritten script, words from the angel, forecasting the nuances of our talk. Later that day, she sent me a copy of that forecast via email.

"I feel sad for people who don't think there's anything beyond this life," she said in response to a question I asked about vitriolic attacks by skeptics. "More people are asking about loved ones or friends who have passed on. The word 'mission' is used a lot. They (the deceased) have missions or assignments and that's interesting. I was always moved to ask people who have passed over that had a particular strength in life to help me out here."

That help comes in many forms, including lessons in grief from the deceased who have told her that a good way to wean yourself from sorrow is to devote two days a week and just an hour a day for visiting the room of the departed. "Fell my presence, touch my jewelry, touch my clothes, and you're invited to cry. Set the timer and at the end of the hour go back out to the family and do what you need to do. Do this for two months. Each time you go into the room you won't be feeling as anxious. You're going to feel peaceful knowing you're going to go in there."

Sano, a charismatic Catholic, credits her religion with allowing the manifestation of "this whole spirit kind of stuff." She has been to Medjugorje and says that she has stories about the place. "Really I do," she told me, "but let's save that for another time." (Medjugorje has been downplayed by leading Catholic thinkers, including Pope Francis, as having little value).

After tea, we took a tour of the Rittenhouse, going upstairs to the restaurant and bar. Over and over she kept remarking on what a wonderful day it had been and how good it was to sit in the courtyard and talk about things that mattered. I had to agree that it had been a prefect afternoon, reminiscent somehow of the classic 1972 Lou Reed song, "Perfect Day:" "Just a perfect day/Drink Sangria in the park/And then later/When it gets dark, we go home/Just a perfect day/Feed animals in the zoo/Then later/A movie, too, and then home."

SOMEWHERE IN TIME: MY LIVES AFTER DEATH

In the 1980s, I was friendly with a Protestant minister. Periodically, we would discuss religion or politics, smiling or shrugging off our disagreements. But when I wanted to discuss subjects like the psychic world, reincarnation, and the writings of Edgar Cayce, an unmistakable frown replaced his smile.

"If you continue to discuss this subject," he announced suddenly, "I will have to ask you to leave"—his own version of excommunication.

That experience forced me to ask myself what makes the subject of psychic phenomena anathema to so many people, most notably evangelical Protestants. In this instance, my minister friend never explained his objections; he just did not want the word "psychic" uttered in his house.

I read all I could on reincarnation after an intense experience in the 1970s. Though the literature on reincarnation is substantial, I was never convinced that what is termed a "past life regression"—*vis-à-vis* hypnosis—possessed much merit. Nevertheless, when I was asked if I wanted to be hypnotized and regressed to one of those possible lives, I jumped at the chance.

Unfortunately, by this time, I had read much of the work of Dr. Ian Stevenson, a research assistant at the University of Virginia who had published several volumes on past-life experiences as recalled by children under the age of six. His meticulously researched data (covering two decades and tracking the recollections of children worldwide) impressed even the skeptics. I had also read the extensive interview with Dr. Stevenson in *Omni* magazine—an interview in which Dr. Stevenson claimed that reincarnation can be verified in a scientific fashion, but that the data from hypnosis-regression is merely the work of the imagination—in short, the stuff of historical novels.

I wanted to know what hypnosis felt like: was a person really conscious during a hypnosis session? When you speak under hypnosis, is it like another person talking for you or are you aware that you are forming your own sentences? Is ordinary consciousness clouded, as if a veil had been placed over it?

The hypnotist, Philadelphian Marianne Waylock, a former Roman Catholic nun, had written a book, *The Physic Habit* (Apollo Books, 1983), detailing her seven years in the convent and her psychic experiences there. Her past-life hypnosis practice was originally in New York before she transferred it to Philadelphia

Years before my session with Dr. Waylock, however, I experienced something like a past-life experience while riding Amtrak from Philadelphia to Boston. I was reading the poetry of W. B. Yeats when suddenly the poetry on the page changed from "normal" printed matter into a kind of living, breathing organism. While skeptical about reincarnation, the words of the poem seemed to breathe, revealing all their surface and hidden meanings simultaneously.

The force of this "living" poem was so intense that I had to put the book down. No poem had ever affected me like this.

In the seat behind was an elderly couple, very well dressed, with white hair. As I read the poetry, I would occasionally think to myself, "They are thinking and looking at me, and they are important to me somehow. But they make me extremely nervous."

As the train pulled in to New York's Pennsylvania Station, the steam from the engines came into the car, first in little whiffs, then in great clouds. As I watched it pour in over the conductor's seat, it thickened considerably. Then I noticed an odor—an odor not of New York rust and steel, but of gas, pungent and life-threatening. It was none other than concentration—camp gas. It increased in volume until it became hard to breathe.

Then ordinary reality did an about face. It was as if I had plunged into the celluloid abyss of an old movie: The train became an old 1940's passenger car, and the people around me—men, women, and children—assumed the dress of that time. All of us were Jews—tricked into believing we were taking a train ride when in reality we were about to be killed.

The sense of that time and place was not muted or dream-like; it was as real as my walk to work everyday. And though the elderly couple behind me had departed, they left me with a "thought"—this came to me as a blinding illumination: In the '40s, as a German, I had killed them; in fact, I had participated in this mass killing as a soldier and was now, as karmic punishment, about to undergo a similar experience myself.

Sheer terror paralyzed me as I waited to die, and "real" reality did not return until after the train moved.

Was this sheer madness?

Today I cannot watch a Holocaust movie without thinking of this Amtrak episode, which came and went like a bolt of lightning and has never returned. Whenever I take Amtrak to New York, a part of me flashes back to that day, just after the Thanksgiving holiday, when I was given a too-authentic taste of history.

When I told Dr. Waylock about this experience, she listened with some interest. However, her concern was to bring me, in the most gentle and pain free manner possible, to a past life that could be taped on her Sony recorder. As such, she brought me into the regression room and told me to lie down on a mat. Soft new age music—the sound of waterfalls and harps, the cry of seagulls—helped transport me mentally out of new downtown office.

I was told to relax—to close my eyes and imagine myself merging with the music. I counted backwards and forwards, lulled by the music. Suddenly, before I knew it, I felt extremely relaxed but still strongly conscious and aware of my surroundings. It was so unlike old movie versions of hypnosis, in which the client stares transfixed like a Kriya Yogi.

The feeling of lightness and relaxation was so powerful that I felt it possible to levitate myself in the style of the grandmother in Pasolini's film *Teorama*.

After guiding me through various stages of life—teens, childhood, and even the womb—Dr. Waylock told me to imagine the door to my past lives as the door to a cave that I now imagined on the side of a hill. At this, a flood of feeling, unrelated to anything in the present, seemed to gush forth like a liquid held for centuries behind a wall. Involuntary tears then began to flow. Embarrassed, I tried to hold them back, but doing so proved difficult.

Dr. Waylock asked me to say the first things that came to mind and to describe any shadows or images that I saw in my mind's eye. (Saying the first thing you think, she said, is the language of the subconscious, or the truth of a past life emerging.)

What I said was this: I was a Native American boy in fourteenth-century America. I lived alone with my mother in a dense forest. Soon, I felt suffocated and trapped by the isolation, and at the age of fourteen I ran away. While exploring the countryside, I met a girl from a neighboring tribe. We fell in love and I joined her family (in one of those shadow images, I saw my own mother weeping in the forest.) I married the girl and stayed with her family until I was aged twenty-four; then the trapped feeling I had felt with my mother returned.

I planned an escape, but the girl's family, aware of my plans, engineered a stampede of horses and had me killed.

Throughout the session, I was aware of making the story up, of deciding between alternate courses of action. In some instances, I would mention the second thought that crossed my mind and not the first, or I would go back to the first thought after considering a third. The only thing that seemed real was the pressure I felt on my chest when I "saw" an image of running horses. And the tears were real; I do not know where they came from—maybe from a hidden, far-away place we all have stored in us somewhere.

Goethe said, "Those are dead even for this life who hope for no other. But an able person, who has something to do here, and must toil and struggle and produce day by day, leaves the future world to itself, and is active and useful in this." No wiser words have ever been spoken.

His abrasiveness aside, perhaps this is what my minister friend was attempting to convey to me when he ordered me to stop talking about psychics in his living room.

3

When the Secular Meets the Religious: Earth Day and the Rise of the Secular Guru

In 1999, *The Philadelphia Inquirer* magazine writer and poet Maralyn Lois Polak wrote an article entitled "Meditation on a murderer: Ira and Me."

"Where have all the Hippies gone?" she asks.

On the surface, Ira was King of the Hippies, a paunchy paragon of Radical Chic, Mr. Peace-and-Love-and-Flower-Power-Personified, a pot-smoking, LSD-popping, sex-happy counter-culture activist. Poet. Philosopher. Physics person. Psychic phenomenologist. Became a New-Age networker with CEOs and rocket scientists and whiskey heiresses and rock stars like Peter Gabriel. Sold them informational blueprints of the future. Launched Philadelphia's Earth Day celebration. Ran for Mayor of Philadelphia as a self-proclaimed Planetary Enzyme, a catalyst for global change. Lost. Even was a Fellow for one semester at Harvard's prestigious Kennedy School of Government. This was after a stormy five-year relationship with "The Unicorn," when Helen "Holly" Maddux had been missing more than a year. Ira claimed she simply went to buy some tofu and sprouts at the food coop and never returned. And then Holly's 37-pound partially mummified corpse was found decomposing in a padlocked steamer trunk in his Powelton Village apartment after neighbors complained of an ungodly stench from icky fluid oozing down the walls ... the Hippie deity stonewalled to Detective Michael Chitwood on March 28, 1979, insisting he was the innocent victim of an international CIA plot, framed maybe because of his rumored deep involvement in Mind Control projects for US Intelligence. $4,000 fronted by one of Ira's richest friends, Mrs. Edgar Bronfman of the Seagrams whiskey family. Naturally, Ira jumps bail and flees!! Missing for the better part of two decades, the fugitive was traced to Ireland as "Ben Moore," briefly sighted with still another girlfriend in Dublin, and then Stockholm, eluding everyone. Eventually he's discovered June 12, 1997 under an assumed name in France's wine country with a statuesque strawberry-blond Swedish wife, Annika

Flodin, living picturesquely in a converted moulin bankrolled by her parents.
InterPol and Philly's DA office had joined forces to track him down, and he was
arrested. "Unsolved Mysteries" claimed credit, too. Though Ira had been tried
in absentia here in Philadelphia and convicted, back in 1993—guilty of murder
in the first degree and sentenced to life imprisonment—France initially waived
extradition. The trial-in-absentia went against their legal grain. After several
months in custody in a French jail, still insisting he was "Eugene Mallon"—a
Trotskyite bookstore-owning buddy from Dublin—Ira was set free, and France
gave a gigantic Gallics.

Philadelphia's era of the secular-political guru can be traced to the 1960s
counterculture. Countercultural types not inclined to put their faith in a guru
claiming to know the truth of existence from a spiritual perspective were more
than willing to consider gurus who addressed more tangible issues. These issues
included drugs as a way to expand consciousness, macrobiotics, vegetarianism,
remote viewing, the use of crystals as a method of healing or soothsaying, the I
Ching as daily oracle (replacing priest, rabbi or minister), the use of feng shui or
Tarot cards as spiritual guides (replacing old grandma notions of opening the Bible
and randomly selecting a passage meant just for you).

In the late 1960s and throughout the '70s, only exotic Eastern religions made
inroads into the army of patchouli oil wearing counter-culturists. Religion or
spirituality was otherwise dead. For the spiritually indifferent, total submersion
into other aspects of the scene—politics, revolution, rock 'n' roll, drugs, or
the films of Jean Luc Goddard—were all that was needed to keep body and
soul intact. People spoke of being raised in "this" or "that' denomination with
the faraway detachment of someone talking about a thing they used to do in
infancy, like wetting the bed.

When LSD first appeared on the scene it was as a consciousness raising tool rather
than a party drug. Users were not looking to get a cheap high but to experience a
series of breakthrough moments that might aid them in their understanding of the
riddle of life. A Harvard professor friend of mine at the time who was an avid LSD
advocate advised me: "Raising your consciousness the normal way can take years
but LSD provides a shortcut." A fast cut express to enlightenment sans meditation,
mantra intoxication, fasting or the pleasure-denying orthodoxies of Hare Krishna.

My professor friend offered no answers to life's riddles—why we live, why
we die, what if anything happens after death. He rarely if ever spoke on these
topics. LSD was about colors and seeing "into" people; it was about learning
to appreciate the present moment, contemplating a tree and being able to see
it as a living, "breathing" organism. It was about being able to "get off" while
seeing the tree. It was about being able to see and feel the truth of the unity and
the "oneness" of all created beings. This "sacramental" albeit limited approach
to LSD was short lived. In no time, LSD became the new high-wire party drug.

Want to see the inner working of a mushroom that will remind you of jelly fish? Or how about experiencing the wallpaper in a room expanding in and out like a pair of human lungs? "Wow, dude, let's do it," became the mantra of the day. Life became a kaleidoscope of sensation.

Overnight it seemed people were taking LSD for its color-wheel sensations, popping it in their mouths the way they would a box of Chicklets. An artist acquaintance of mine when I lived in Boston took LSD and became convinced that he could fly, so he promptly jumped out of the window of a high-rise apartment building. His death came as a shock to his bohemian circle of friends, but it did not deter others from experimenting with the drug.

Philadelphia's High Priest of psychedelics, Ira Samuel Einhorn, was born in 1940 to Bea and Joseph Einhorn. A second son, Stephen, would be born later, but the parental favorite was Ira, a lover of books, who as a boy would read far into the night despite the fact that his uncontrolled precociousness was often a problem for teachers and family. Steven Levy, in his iconic book *Unicorn's Secret: Murder in the Age of Aquarius*, which documents Einhorn's life up to and after Einhorn's murder of his girlfriend Holly Maddux in the 1970s, wrote: "Once in school, Ira's restlessness would be disruptive. He would yell out in class, get out of his seat, and wander. His report cards reflected the problem quite specifically. For his subject grades, there was a line of O's for outstanding. But his marks for conduct were always P for poor."

"All seems possible," Ira Einhorn wrote in a letter in 1963. "Nothing is too difficult when I occupy this rarefied atmosphere—I exalt in the expectation of my future dreams as I encompass all I touch. In these moments when one reads Chinese like a native, zips through the quantum theory without a pencil, and explains Wittgenstein to his dog, the mind seems to be an enemy that is able to digest data faster than an electronic computer."

Einhorn entered the University of Pennsylvania in 1957 but, according to Levy, his university education was almost entirely self-directed. He attended very few classes but graduated from Penn in 1961. In the mid-'60s, he moved to a century-old building called the Powelton Apartments, nicknamed "The Piles." "This moniker was earned by its stone edifice and perpetual disrepair; the building was entering a state of intentional neglect that would worsen over the years until the city ultimately condemned it," Levy writes. But Powelton Village was a prime real estate area for the city's bohemian elite.

"Powelton was Philadelphia's Bohemia," Levy explains, "the place that housed its outcasts, fringe characters, mavericks, counterculturists, and lunatics, along with a number of people—possibly the majority in 1963—who were just plain poor. Located only a few blocks north of the University of Pennsylvania and virtually abutting the growing campus of the Drexel Institute of Technology, the Powelton was an amiable enclave of declining Victorian homes on quiet tree-lined streets, with a dash of ghetto tenements mixed in."

Guru Einhorn had large groups of people visit him, sitting in a semi-circle around his elevated position on a window seat while he expounded on LSD, cellular consciousness, pre-paradigmatic issues and Marshall McLuhan. His reputation as a seer was growing and people listened to him as they would listen to a medium. Einhorn survived by borrowing money from friends and family and then dealing a little marijuana on the side. Later, corporations and organizations would pay to hear him speak on the coming new age and its impact on technology, or they would treat him to daily expensive lunches at the French eatery, La Terrasse, in University City. The treatment accorded Einhorn mirrors the treatment accorded Hare Krishna's Śrīla Prabhupāda when the latter issued directives to his devotees to humble themselves and serve him, the guru, in all things. In Einhorn's case, it was not about directives or anything related to a Godhead, it was all about giving Ira his due because he was Ira and just as deserving as a political Swami.

Called "The Mayor of Powelton," Ira knew everybody: Allen Ginsberg, John Cage, Julian Beck of the Living Theater, Alan Watts, Jerry Rubin, and the Mothers of Invention rock group. A *Philadelphia Magazine* writer who profiled Einhorn then commented: "He was a terrible writer. His poetry has been described as Whitmanesque yawp and he wrote in block capital letters." When Don De Maio started the *Distant Drummer*, Philadelphia's premier underground newspaper, in 1967, Einhorn went to the newspaper's office on Pine Street and demanded a column. De Maio, according to Levy, felt intimidated by him. "He was very aggressive, but at the same time he was a very nice Jewish boy."

Einhorn got his column, "The Unicorn Speaks," but De Maio was shocked at the quality of the first submission. "It was sloppy, incoherent, everything uppercase, no punctuation." Almost immediately there was a *Drummer* staff revolt to dump the column, so Einhorn was relegated to freelance status but that was okay by him because he wanted publicity for himself at any cost.

When Einhorn visited California in 1966, he reported that "California is definitely a product of the twentieth century in a way that New York or Philadelphia will not possibly be for years to come." Einhorn taught at Temple University and conducted night courses on the Penn campus. As the guru of the psychic paradigm shift, he became an expert on Marshall McLuhan, Herbert Marcuse, and Wilhelm Reich. Levy writes that he also taught classes in his apartment at the Piles where sometimes the sessions turned into parties where joints were passed around and Einhorn took off his clothes and danced around.

In the 1970s, there were many pop-up, albeit minor, gurus in Powelton Village. I knew of one such guru, a gay naturist who held his own brand of nudist, marijuana-laced consciousness raising parties in which the all-male participants took off their clothes, sat in a circle on the floor, and, when sufficiently stoned, submitted to the guru's sexual peccadilloes and commands. A guru must be obeyed in all things, after all.

Einhorn became a countercultural celebrity. Described as verbal, pushy, and forceful, many said that he used his body bulk the same way that (then) Mayor Frank Rizzo used his towering body bulk. When the first Earth Day was instituted on April 22, 1970, Einhorn rushed the podium and controlled the microphone for fifteen minutes, forcing keynote speaker Senator Edmund Muskie to delay his speech.

While it can be argued that Einhorn had a lot to do with Philadelphia's Earth Day celebration in Fairmount Park, according to Ken Anderson of the *Hawaii Free Press*:

> The history of environmental activism's biggest day is as cloudy as the ozone layer so many activists are fighting to save. Far more embarrassing than Einhorn? The fact that Earth Day was initially promoted as a way to fight global cooling. "The world has been chilling sharply for about 20 years," prominent ecologist Kenneth Watt told an audience at Swarthmore College in 1970, noting that if it continued, "the world will be about four degrees colder by 1990 and 11 degrees colder by 2000."

In 1970, Stanford University biologist Paul Ehrlich predicted worldwide famine by 2000. Another prediction was that gas masks would be required in big cities by 2010, and that American life expectancy would drop to forty-two years old. (Perhaps what Ehrlich was really seeing was face masks generated by 2020's COVID-19).

Most people know Ira Einhorn as the murderer of his girlfriend, Holly Maddux. Einhorn and Maddux lived together in another Powelton residence, 3411 Race Street. Maddux disappeared in 1977 and her body was discovered decaying and mummifying in a truck in a closet at 3411 Race Street about a year and a half later. People did not want to believe that the venerable guru and favorite Philadelphia celebrity could do such a thing so his bail was set at $40,000 (he had to pay a mere 10 percent). Einhorn escaped to Europe for twenty-three years until his extradition to the United States in July 2001.

Philadelphia-based novelist and journalist Maralyn Lois Polak, quoted earlier, read poetry with Einhorn at the old Bandbox Theater in Germantown. She also interviewed him at his Race Street apartment before the death of Maddux.

In a piece for *WorldNet Daily* in 1999, an online news site, Polak recalls the following:

> He had the worst body odor in the history of the entire world. When I was a student, and he was a professor, he patted me on the head. We sat in his class, even if we hadn't registered. He had a profile like a hawk, aquiline nose, raven hair. Smoked in the classroom, which was illegal. And flicked his ashes into the radiator, which was insouciant, or incendiary, I'm not sure which.

Ira loved Holly and knew she was alive, but already he had a new girlfriend. Though he was the worst-smelling man you would ever meet, he never was short of new women, standing in line waiting to be abused.

His mother still believed in him. She mortgaged her house to pay for his lawyers. When he fled and vanished, she still believed in him.

Once Ira asked me out, but I didn't go. Naturally, Ira jumps bail and flees!! Missing for the better part of two decades, the fugitive was traced to Ireland as "Ben Moore," briefly sighted with still another girlfriend in Dublin, and then Stockholm, eluding everyone. Eventually he's discovered June 12, 1997 under an assumed name in France's wine country with a statuesque strawberry-blond Swedish wife, Annika Flodin, living picturesquely in a converted moulin bankrolled by her parents. InterPol and Philly's DA office had joined forces to track him down, and he was arrested. "Unsolved Mysteries" claimed credit, too.

Finally, on Feb. 18, 1999, the French court granted extradition for accused murderer Ira Einhorn with the proviso he must get a new US trial if he asks for one and must not receive the death penalty. In his months of intermittent "freedom" between his June 1997 capture and his most recent extradition hearing, Ira attempted to resume his normal, which is to say, abnormal bucolic routine interrupted by two weekly visits to the French police station. As always, he had a worshipful woman and no job, amid whispers of her family's wealth. She effervesced about his genius, great books in the making, hints of prodigious Internet activity, his inevitable recognition as a thinker and visionary. And yet, for all his vaunted smarts, Ira has consistently demonstrated an apparent inability to master even rudiments of the most fractured French, or most other foreign languages, for that matter. She was the stylish, convivial European who conversed openly with villagers and charmed shopkeepers with her allure.

MOVE

The most important and controversial alternative religious group to come from Powelton Village was the back-to-nature group, MOVE (not an acronym), founded by John Africa (born Vincent Leaphart), who adopted the name Africa because all of life originated there. Co-founder Donald Glassey was the Caucasian son of the Boy Scouts of America national vice president and a student activist at the University of Pennsylvania.

Writer Paulina Malek of Philadelphia's *University City Review* described MOVE as being originally called the Christian Movement for Life when it was founded with fifty members in Powelton in 1972 by Leaphart and Donald Glassey:

This radical movement drew escalating attention from authorities, as well as police who were summoned into action by its amplified, profanity laced demonstrations against the bourgeoisie,

On August 8, 1978 the conflict came to head when the police attempted to enforce a court order to vacate the property at 311 N 33rd Street. A shootout ensued, killing one police officer and injuring seven other police officers, five firefighters, three MOVE members and three bystanders.

Nine MOVE members were each sentenced to a maximum of 100 years in prison The organization eventually relocated away from Powelton Village, to nearby Cobbs Creek, at 6221 Osage Ave. where in 1985, after increased tensions in the neighborhood, the City dropped a bomb on their house, killing 11 people, including five children, as well as, devastating the entire neighborhood.

Philadelphia's Powelton Village neighborhood during the MOVE years, from the late 1970s until the 1986 bombing, was a contentious place. I remember walking through the neighborhood and hearing the bullhorn shrieks of MOVE members shouting obscenities. Word clarity was not always a component of these presentations so everything came across as gibberish-turned-to-static because of the microphone. MOVE claimed to be revolutionary but it was out of step with most of the popular-political movement's current at the time, such as the burgeoning gay rights movement, which had an important ally in the University of Pennsylvania. The Gays at Penn lecture series, for instance, was a popular seasonal event that brought many prominent gay and lesbian thinkers and activists to the Penn stage. Several of the lectures were raided by MOVE members who stormed the stage while chanting obscene chants about homosexuals. Through the years, MOVE protesters also raised their voices against a wide range of persons, including the Rev. Jesse Jackson, the Quakers, and the Communist Party. This unhinged ideological hodgepodge made the group hard to fathom. The passage of time, however, has erased many of MOVE's blatant assaults against the city and the Powelton Village neighborhood, resulting in a kind of revisionist view of MOVE as well intentioned in essence despite these assaults.

MOVE members took great pride in living close to nature by spurning electricity, leaving their garbage outside on the ground for natural earth recycling, advocating vegetarianism, not taking baths, and growing their hair in dreadlocks common to the Rastafarian religious movement in Jamaica. John Africa expected each member to take the last name of Africa.

Chicago Tribune writer George E. Curry wrote in 1985 that, instead of soap, MOVE members use an herbal mix that includes garlic:

They routinely take in stray dogs, also considered one of nature's gifts, and feed rats that assume the status of co-tenants in their dwellings. Although they claim to be against technology, the group dropped its early non-violence creed and began arming themselves with automatic weapons and enrolling in self-defense courses during the mid-1970s.

Ron Javers, editor of *Philadelphia Magazine* in the 1980s, said that MOVE's members always seem to be on a death trip. "It's a group that needs to feel the world is imploding on them to have inner group solidarity."

The *Los Angeles Times* in 1985 reported: "And despite an avowed pacifism, police said Tuesday that MOVE's followers were skilled in building sophisticated fortifications, including bunkers with half-inch steel walls in their nondescript frame row house on Osage Avenue in West Philadelphia."

The Times also reported:

Glassey, the white co-founder, was a social worker for six months in suburban Cornwells Heights before moving into a Powelton Village commune. When MOVE grew more militant, he became a government informant.

Most current MOVE members hold menial jobs or are on welfare. Fifteen are currently imprisoned on various charges.

Nine have been imprisoned since 1981 for their resistance when police stormed a headquarters of the group in August, 1978, when Frank Rizzo was mayor.

That siege left a Philadelphia policeman dead and 13 persons wounded in exchanges of gunfire between the radicals and SWAT team sharpshooters. When it was all over, the three-story row house that the group had occupied under allegedly unhealthy conditions was demolished with the use of a derrick and a bulldozer.

Twelve persons were arrested in the 1978 raid, including five MOVE sympathizers who hurled rocks and bottles at police after the shooting stopped.

After the bombing, Mayor W. Wilson Goode defended his actions when he described MOVE as a "terrorist group."

On Tuesday, Mayor W. Wilson Goode described MOVE as a "terrorist group" that had to be removed from its neighborhood.

"This community knows MOVE," he stated. "It knows them as a group dedicated to the entire destruction of our way of life." The mayor added that MOVE had threatened the lives of the President, the police, judges and even their neighbors.

"The MOVE members wanted a desire to have a violent confrontation," Goode said. "We should not allow any group to hold an entire city hostage."

While the loss of life in the MOVE bombing was immensely tragic, the gross mishandling of the situation should not be cause to sugar coat the threat that the group posed while it was active in West Philadelphia. In 2015, after a preview of *Let The Fire Burn*, a film about the Osage Avenue tragedy, writer Dani Burlison wrote for KQED Arts:

Yet, before the shootout, the MOVE house was typical of the post-1960s experimental, consciousness-shifting times. Founded by John Africa in 1972 with the intent to simply life, the MOVE house was a commune of black families focused on unplugging from media and advocating for green politics and social justice. What started as a peaceful, anti-establishment revolution slowly turned violent as police used force to settle conflicts and MOVE members started collecting guns to defend themselves.

Sugar-coated revisionist history like this does not begin to match the real-life experiences of Philadelphians who lived through this time.

THE CULT OF YOGA

In my Fishtown-Northern Liberties Philadelphia neighborhood, many of the young women in their twenties and thirties wear tight black yoga pants. Yoga pants have become a uniform of sorts, like bell bottoms and love beads in the 1960s. Many but not all of the women who dress this way have incorporated yoga into their daily lives. Yoga has become big business, big enough to accommodate hundreds in a rehabbed warehouse near the Market-Frankford El station at Frankford and Girard in Northern Liberties. The sign Amrita Yoga graces the front of the building like the identifying framed information board outside the city's Cathedral Basilica of Saints Peter and Paul.

The Fishtown-Northern Liberties neighborhood is also home to Grace & Glory Yoga, MotherHeart Yoga Sangha, and Pacific Yoga. For many, it is Yoga Heaven. The Yogic Encyclopedia states that "Ananda Sangha also provides people with two options for formal renunciation as Brahmacharis or Sannyasi. Brahmacharis renounce family ties in an inward path of realization."

On Girard Avenue not far from Amrita Yoga, you are likely to spot smiling yoga proselytizers handing out colorful booklets entitled *Yoga*. This is a relatively new development in the neighborhood. The proselytizers tend to be young, some from Indian backgrounds and some not, yet every time I have encountered these yoga missionaries, they have always been deeply engaged with one or more passersby unlike the stoic but bored looking Jehovah's Witnesses standing under the Market-Frankford El by their portable rack of *Watch Tower* magazines. Because yoga has broken the stratosphere of "Super Cool" status, the yogic street missionaries are almost always found in deep sidewalk conversational huddles.

The online video advertisements for these yoga workshops usually feature young women talking about yoga in that unique millennial way of ending each sentence with a question mark. Observing these trends, one is tempted to ask: are these angelic-looking proselytizers advocating yoga as a form of physical exercise, or is there something else going on here?

Hatha yoga is mostly an umbrella term for all the branches of yoga that emphasize yoga's physical practice. Other branches of yoga, like kriya, raja, and karma yoga, are more meditative and interior. All yoga, of course, is at the heart of the New Age movement, and it all comes from India. Yoga, it might be said, is the heart of Hinduism despite the many different schools of practice. Hatha yoga promises mental and physical health. At the outset in many of these yoga-as-exercise industries, there are no mantras involved or instructors who appear to be wannabe gurus in waiting (called geshes in the yoga world.)

I have read of instances of how some yoga instructors assume more and more power among class attendees so that eventually the student practitioner comes to see the instructor as something much more than someone who shows them how to flex or stand on their heads. They become total life teachers with specific guidelines on how to live your life—food-sex, fasting, etc.—outside the yoga class. This personal invasion happens so gradually it may not be noticeable at first, although the first red flag may be when the exercise instructor suggests a light mantra to accompany exercise.

One mantra leads to two mantras and after that might come a repetition of "OMs," and before you know it, you have a yoga class that is tipping into the tenets of Hinduism.

Besides the types of yoga already mentioned, there is Baby Yoga; Mama Yoga; Laughing Yoga; Superbrain Yoga; Beer Yoga; Drunk Yoga; and Yoga and Wine. Yoga covers the waterfront, so in the future, there is likely to be additional yogas added to the list.

Articles and books on yoga regularly claim that there are more women than men enrolled in yoga classes, although that does not mean that men have any objections to observing the high numbers of women walking around the city in yoga pants. Numerous articles on yoga point out that yoga started with male sages 2,000 years ago and that male leaders dominated the world of yoga until the 1990s. Today, however, it is mostly a female-dominated practice. And while there has been a tiny upswing in male participation, the truth is that yoga is perceived as being much more conducive to the female body with its built-in ability to twist in pretzel-like body discombobulations. Most men are just not that flexible and do not see yoga as providing a sufficient workout routine. One *Huffington Post* article explained that men "might also be turned off by various spiritual aspects of the practice, such as 'OM' chanting or naming poses in Sanskrit."

But why are young and older women in yoga pants chanting "OM" anyway? If yoga is supposed to be merely exercise and a way to loosen up, how does chanting "OM" fit into the equation? One could say that the repetitious chanting of "OM" puts one in a transcendental state much like any chant, be it Hare Krishna, Make America Great Again, or Mary Had a Swarm of Bees. "OM" is said to approximate the vibrational sound of the universe, which might be perceived as a very neutral thing, but yet there are fervent Christian practitioners of yoga who avoid saying "OM" because they say it lends itself to more questions than answers. They might as well be saying that "OM" opens the vestibule door to Hinduism.

The chanting of "OM" has a venerable history, especially in the annals of contemporary American literature. In a 1998 *New York Times* piece entitled "Chanting on Homage to Allen Ginsberg," Dinita Smith wrote:

> It was a typical, raucous Allen Ginsberg event, with chanting and music and blunt speeches on gay rights and the nuclear threat, as some 2,500 of his friends and fans gathered at the Cathedral of St. John the Divine on Thursday evening to pay tribute to this poet, who died in April 1997 at the age of 70.
>
> Most of his friends were well into middle age: Patti Smith, the singer, who was with Ginsberg when he died; Dave Dellinger, Ed Sanders and the Fugs, Philip Glass and Anne Waldman, the poet.
>
> But the audience was mostly young, packing the Gothic reaches of the cathedral even though it was the night of the last episode of "Seinfeld" and the streets of the Upper West Side were filled with distractions, including police officers and television cameras there for the Seinfeld celebration at Tom's Restaurant.
>
> Ginsberg's secretary, Bob Rosenthal, an organizer of the tribute, which was called "Planet News," opened the event with his version of a Buddhist chant.
>
> "Hum, Hum, Hum: that's our attention!" he cried. "Ah, Ah, Ah: that is our breath! Allen Ginsberg taught us to breathe in the poison and breathe out the nectar."

Few would disagree that the multidimensional aspects of yoga also includes "The Uniform" and "The Look."

A 2018 Op Ed in *The New York Times* explained "Why Yoga Pants Are Bad for Women." The writer questioned the necessity of going out and buying a uniform in order to "do" yoga. "Seriously, you can't go into a room of 15 fellow women contorting themselves into ridiculous positions at 7 in the morning without first donning skintight pants? What is it about yoga in particular that seems to require this? Are practitioners really worried that a normal-width pant leg is going to throttle them mid-lotus pose?"

The one-must-have-a-uniform-infection virus has even contaminated the world of bicycling and running so that participants in these once *ad hoc* casual activities now find it necessary to spend serious money on the right clothes in order to engage in the sport. Grown men have even taken to the "soy boy" practice of shaving their legs because they think that shaving off a few hairs will give them additional speed while pedaling or running.

Robert Hurst, in his book *Cyclist's Manifesto: The Case for Riding on Two Wheels Instead of Four*, writes:

> And then there are the bicyclists who wear the clothing for reasons having virtually nothing to do with practicality. They dress up in bike clothes so they feel and look like "real" cyclists, because that's what "real" cyclists wear. A lot of unnecessary

leg shaving occurs for this reason as well. There are those who are attracted to the look-at-me factor of a shiny, bright colored outfit.

Aerobics, popularized in the U.S. by a physician named Kenneth H. Cooper, swept the City of Philadelphia in the 1980s, inspiring men and women alike to take classes so they could dance in the form of exercise to music by Pat Benatar, Kool and the Gang, and Michael Jackson. For a couple of years, I took regular aerobics classes at Philadelphia's (now defunct) Maywood Dance Academy near 17th and Sansom Streets. The exhilarating hour sessions led to a heightened state of physical being so that all I wanted to do after class was continue dancing at a local disco. There was no "OM" in aerobics and there was certainly no meditation

The push with yoga today is to move it "off the mat" and to discover "a deeper understanding of who you really are," at least according to Darren John Main, a yoga teacher. Main uses quotes from *The Yoga Sutra*, the *Bhagavad Gita*, and the *Upanishads* to bring "these ancient Hindu texts to life in contemporary cities."

Alexandra Stein, a scholar of social psychology of ideological extremism, writes that a cult is "A group that violates the rights of its members, harms them through abusive techniques of mind control.... Or, a group that is adverse to adherents' best interests."

IS YOGA A CULT?

Pope Francis, who is liberal on many issues, including his acceptance and blessing of the controversial "Pachamama" statues (referred to as pagan goddesses by traditionalist Catholics) on prominent display at the October 2019 Amazon Synod held in Rome, holds the line at yoga.

"You can take a million catechetical courses, a million courses in spirituality, a million courses in yoga, Zen and all these things. But all of this will never be able to give you freedom," Pope Francis stated in a homily in 2915. The Greek Orthodox Church, reacting to the U.N.'s decision to designate June 21 as International Day of Yoga in 2014, reminded its adherents that the postures of yoga were created as adulation to 330 million Hindu gods. The postures are viewed in the Hindu faith as offerings to gods that in Christianity are considered to be idols.

In today's world, however, idols may be yoga's stellar selling point.

In the book *Seven Schools of Yoga*, author Ernest Wood writes about Hatha yoga. Wood cautions:

I must not refer to any of these Hatha Yoga practices without sounding a severe warning. Many people have brought upon themselves incurable illness and even madness by practicing them without providing the proper conditions of body and mind. The yoga books are full of such warnings…. For example, the Gheranda Samhita announces that if one begins the practices in hot, cold or rainy weather, diseases will be contracted, and also if there is not moderation in diet, for only one half the stomach must ever be filled with solid food…. The Hatha Yoga Pradipika states that control of breath must be brought about very gradually, "as lions, elephants and tigers are tamed," or "the experimenter will be killed," and by any mistake there arises cough, asthma, head, eye and ear pains, and many other diseases. I should like to make it clear that I am not *recommending these practices, as I hold that all Hatha Yogas are extremely dangerous.*

In a blog entitled "Hidden Fire: Orthodox Perspectives on Yoga," Joseph Magnus Frangipani writes that the literal meaning of yoga is the word "yoke."

It means tying your will to the serpent kundalini and raising it to Shiva and experiencing your "true" self. All paths of yoga are interconnected like branches of a tree. A tree with roots descending into the same areas of the spiritual world. This is evident in the ancient books the Bhagavad Gita and the Yogic Sutras of Patanjali. I learned that the ultimate goal of yoga is to awaken the kundalini energy coiled at the base of the spine in the image of a serpent so that it brings you to a state whereby you realize Tat Tvam Asi.

Of course, yoga may facilitate exceptional experiences of body and mind. But so does the ingestion of mind-altering drugs, and flavorless, imperceptible poisons. Through yoga, little by little, one is harnessing shakti, which yogis refer to as the Divine Mother, the "dark goddess" connected with other major Hindu gods. This energy isn't the Holy Spirit, and this isn't aerobics or gymnastics. Attached to this entire system are bhajans and kirtans—pagan equivalents to Orthodox Christian akathists, but for Hindu gods—as well as mantras, which are "sacred" formulas, like calling cards or phone numbers, to the various pagan gurus and gods.

It is said that Hinduism does not refer to a specific religion but a term given by the British to refer to the numerous shamanistic religions of India. While one Hindu may believe in a Creator God, another one might tell you that you are God. Hinduism has been compared to a Russian nesting doll: you open one philosophy and within it are 10,000 more.

I personally discovered the "ten thousand" more glitch when I read Yogannada Paramahansa's classic, *Autobiography of a Yogi*, as a teen. I was struck at that time by the inclusion in the book of the story of Catholic mystic and stigmatic, Therese Neumann. Neumann (1898–1962) was a German mystic born in the village of Konnersreuth, Bavaria, to a poor family. In 1918, the young Neumann experienced a series of horrendous falls that debilitated her and that caused her to lose her eyesight. A devout young woman, Neumann prayed to St. Therese of Lisieux, and on the day of St. Therese's beautification in Rome in 1923, Neumann's eyesight was mysteriously restored. Two years later in 1925, Neumann's other physical maladies, paralysis and bedsores, were cured on the very day that St. Therese of Lisieux was canonized a saint in Rome.

March 1926 would change everything for Therese Neumann. That is when a wound appeared above her heart on the first day of Lent. Several days later, she claimed to have a vision of Christ at Mt. Olivet as the wound above her heart kept appearing and disappearing. On March 26, a wound appeared on Neumann's left hand and by Good Friday there were wounds on her hands and feet. At Easter, Neumann states that she had a vision of the Resurrection after having experiences the full Passion on Good Friday. During these bleeding episodes, observers remark that she often spoke Aramaic, Greek, and Hebrew. By the time of the Third Reich, Neumann's fame had swept throughout Germany. The Third Reich considered her a mortal enemy and often attacked her home, her parish church, and her parish priest, although the mystic was never personally harmed. Neumann urged personal resistance to Hitler and for this she was put on a watch list.

Hilda Charlotte Graef's (1907–1970) book *The Case of Therese Neumann* is considered by many to be the seminal work on the mystic, whose cause for sainthood is still under consideration in Rome. As a boy in suburban Philadelphia, I recall hearing family members from my mother's County Tyrone, Ireland, side remark how after a visit with the mystic they were given specific prophecies about the City of Philadelphia and that the prophecies concerning the city were "worrisome."

The chapter on Neumann in Paramahansa's book is a curious study of objectivity and non-judgment. Newmann seems to accept the yogi's visit without a censorious nod, and judging from the yogi's account, there was no attempt to convert him to Catholicism or Christianity. This is an especially curious thing when one considers certain writings from Scripture, such as the first Epistle of Saint John when he writes: Dearly beloved, believe not every spirit, but try the spirits if they be of God (4:1).

Paramahansa writes of his visit with Therese Neumann:

Though the bishop has asked me to see no one without his permission, I will receive the man of God from India.

Deeply touched at these words, I followed Dr. Wurz upstairs to the sitting room. Therese entered immediately, radiating an aura of peace and joy. She wore a black gown and spotless white head dress. Although her age was thirty-seven at this time, she seemed much younger, possessing indeed a childlike freshness and charm. Healthy, well-formed, rosy-cheeked, and cheerful, this is the saint that does not eat!

Therese greeted me with a very gentle handshaking. We both beamed in silent communion, each knowing the other to be a lover of God.

Dr. Wurz kindly offered to serve as interpreter. As we seated ourselves, I noticed that Therese was glancing at me with naive curiosity; evidently Hindus had been rare in Bavaria.

"Don't you eat anything?" I wanted to hear the answer from her own lips.

"No, except a consecrated rice-flour wafer, once every morning at six o'clock."

"How large is the wafer?"

"It is paper-thin, the size of a small coin." She added, "I take it for sacramental reasons; if it is unconsecrated, I am unable to swallow it."

"Certainly you could not have lived on that, for twelve whole years?"

"I live by God's light." How simple her reply, how Einsteinian!

"I see you realize that energy flows to your body from the ether, sun, and air."

A swift smile broke over her face. "I am so happy to know you understand how I live."

"Your sacred life is a daily demonstration of the truth uttered by Christ: 'Man shall not live by bread alone, but by every word that proceedeth out of the mouth of God."

Again she showed joy at my explanation. "It is indeed so. One of the reasons I am here on earth today is to prove that man can live by God's invisible light, and not by food only."

"Can you teach others how to live without food?"

She appeared a trifle shocked. "I cannot do that; God does not wish it."

As my gaze fell on her strong, graceful hands, Therese showed me a little, square, freshly healed wound on each of her palms. On the back of each hand, she pointed out a smaller, crescent-shaped wound, freshly healed. Each wound went straight through the hand. The sight brought to my mind distinct recollection of the large square iron nails with crescent-tipped ends, still used in the Orient, but which I do not recall having seen in the West.

4

Cults That Have Become Mainstream

In a world where yoga instructors, dog parks, and weekly therapist appointments are king, how can there be anything of value in a big, gilded fiberglass angel?

When it comes to church or temple architecture, Mormons have it all over Catholics and mega-church Protestants, whose modernist churches frequently overemphasize cold, hard lines and sterility.

The Mormon temple at 18th and Vine Streets near the Benjamin Franklin Parkway does not look like a utilitarian warehouse. The design is one of many temple designs currently in use throughout the Mormon world. The Philadelphia Temple has two spires, one hosting an image of the Angel Moroni, the angel whom, according to Mormon belief, appeared to Mormon founder Joseph Smith in Palmyra, New York, sometime after Smith asked God which church he should join.

The angel, as the story goes, directed Smith to dig in a certain spot where he would find golden plates containing a new scripture. The translated plates became the *Book of Mormon*, also the name of the current Broadway hit. The full story of Smith's discovery of the plates can be found in Fawn M. Brodie's 1945 bestseller *No Man Knows My History*.

When I contacted the Mormon Church for a little bit of background on the new temple, I was put in touch with Ahmad S. Corbitt, of the LDS New York Office of Public and International Affairs.

"For Mormons," Corbitt told me, "the angel Moroni symbolizes the 'flying angel' in Revelation 14:6."

"The flying angel is what the ancient apostle John saw, 'in the midst of heaven, having the everlasting gospel to preach unto them that dwell on the earth, and to every nation, and kindred, and tongue, and people.'"

Serious angel motifs are rare in the world of architecture. Contemporary culture, in fact, has reduced angels to Cupids or saccharin girlie images when the reality is quite the opposite: in historic, traditional Christianity, angels are sexless but assume a male form when they "appear" to human beings.

The Philadelphia temple spires reach over 200 feet in height, providing an impressive point of reference in a sky-scape filled with crosses and steeples. The 68,000-square-foot building houses a separate visitors' center, a family history center, a financial service office for LDS communicants and an employment services office. Renderings of the proposed structure show an eclectic mix of Greek classicism and federalist eighteenth- and nineteenth-century styles, the antithesis one might say of the work of current architectural legends Frank Gehry and Zaha Hadid.

The Philadelphia design is one of the more basic temple templates, chosen from a wide range of styles in use throughout the world. The two spire temple is in fact one of the more recognizable Mormon temple styles and blends harmoniously with the Benjamin Franklin Parkway's neoclassical structures.

Other Mormon Temple styles, such as the so-called Bountiful, Front Tier, Native American Grecian, or even the ultra-Disneyland-conjuring six spire temple in San Diego, have become impressive city landmarks. One reason why Mormon temples become instant landmarks is because they are commonly built in isolated but high visibility sections of the city, such as near freeways. While the Center City location does not afford quite the isolation of a freeway ramp, the temple's Parkway presence has a landmark feel nevertheless. The signature capstone, of course, is the towering gilded fiberglass Angel Moroni, trumpet in hand, which competes with the cross atop the Catholic Basilica of Saints Peter and Paul. This juxtaposition is not as theologically jarring as the mix of minarets and crosses now popping up all over Western Europe.

Like Islam, Orthodox Judaism, or Eastern Orthodox Christianity, Mormons do not want to fit in as just another religious denomination. The design of Mormon temples tends to reflect this view. One will always find traditional elements in Temple design; a Mormon Temple will always be recognizable as a Mormon Temple despite occasional flourishes into modernism. Mormons, in fact, seem to have a sense that too far a stretch into modernism might invite a reinterpretation of the faith. Can a religion be altered through architecture? If the alternations can be accomplished through a massive reconstruction of its liturgical life, as in post-Vatican II Catholicism, bricks and mortar may also prove to be a powerful influence.

The Mormon temple in Mexico City is still recognizable as "Mormon" underneath its modern Mayan design, a far cry from, say, the multi-million-dollar Catholic cathedral of Our Lady of the Angels in Los Angeles, which seems to twist post-Conciliar Catholicism into a discombobulated box wreck, an appropriate symbol perhaps for a Church in crises. While the Catholic architectural reformation began years before Vatican II, the Council gave modernism its wings. In architect Richard Meier's Jubilee church in Rome, for instance, worshippers are reminded by the architect that this church of concrete-clad shells and glass, allows the "rays of sunlight to serve as a mystical metaphor for the presence of God," the same way perhaps that indirect sunlight streaming through any generic structure allows for a sense of the mystical. In the Jubilee church the absence of traditional Catholic references (icons, statues, etc.) has been replaced by the power of the sun to induce feelings one may also just as easily get by looking into the Grand Canyon or by experiencing a Waikiki beach sunset.

The sun as sole mystical component is a pagan idea.

Consider the new Catholic Church built alongside the decades-old shrine in Fatima, Portugal. The new structure is a banjo-shaped, low-level building capable of holding 9,000 worshippers. Dominating the outside courtyard is a towering crucifix that looks more like an ode to a preying mantas impaled on a stake. Designed by Greek Orthodox architect Alexandros Tombazis, the church is the antithesis of Orthodox Church architecture, which so far has managed to keep out- of-control modernism at bay. Tombazis, however, has given the design a little bit of his own tradition with the large wall-to-wall fresco behind the raised altar, which resembles a reverse-order iconostasis. The massive mural is dreamlike in form and color—as if it stands on the edge of evaporation like cloud formations in the sky. Looking outward into the congregation from the altar area the building could just as easily be a basketball gymnasium. Perhaps future worshippers will go looking for the locker rooms.

The Vatican, which under Pope John II seemed to have turned a blind eye to both liturgical abuse and modern church architecture, is now striking back in the formation of a commission to discourage the building of ugly churches. The Italian daily *La Stampa* reported that Cardinal Antonio Cañizares Llovera, Prefect for the Congregation for Divine Worship, and Pope Emeritus Benedict XVI, "considered this work as 'very urgent.'"

"Too often, architects do not use Catholic liturgy as a starting point and thus end up producing avant-garde constructions that look like anything but a church," *La Stampa* reported.

Regarding Philadelphia's Mormon Temple, critics say that the design contains elements of the confectionary, as if buildings built today must never hearken back to another age.

Hidden City Philadelphia, for instance, found nothing attractive about the structure.

"No one wants to discuss the appalling design of the 70 million dollar temple—if we ignore it, it just might disappear, folks seem to say—but it points up real tension in the decision about the role of new buildings. Should they blend in or boldly pronounce the values of our day?"

But what are the values of our day? Hidden City's criticism seems to suggest that religions update their values as the culture "progresses." After all, in a world where yoga instructors, dog parks, and weekly therapist appointments are king, how can there be anything of value in a big, gilded fiberglass angel?

The temple architect, B. Jeffrey Stebar of Perkins + Will, an Atlanta firm, is also a Mormon bishop in the Jonesboro Georgia Stake. The firm is generally noted for its Prairie-style modernism, except of course when it comes to the design of temples.

Mormon temples historically have had a heavy granite look, a carryover from the days of anti-Mormon prejudice when temples, such as the one in Nauvoo, Ill., were burned to the ground in 1848 shortly after being abandoned by Mormons heading west to Salt Lake City. Mormon Temples, according to Paul Anderson, a curator of a show on Mormon architecture at BYU, "aim for a delicate harmony between the Church's desire to appear reassuringly Christian, while at the same time proudly advertising its separation from Catholic and Protestant dogma."

Salt Lake City's Mormon Temple, perhaps the most famous in the world, was finished in 1893 (it was designed by Brigham Young's brother-in-law). A little known fact is that before its completion Church leaders made sure that it was astrologically aligned. Earlier temple designs also contain symbols you are unlikely to find in modern temples. Besides the absence of crosses, older temple models are filled with Masonic handshakes, moon phases, suns, Big Dipper Constellations, and Inverted Pentagrams. Critics of Mormonism love to point out that such symbols are proof that the religion is from "the dark side," but sometimes, as has often been said, a symbol is just a symbol and nothing more.

I participated in a press tour of Philadelphia's new Mormon temple. As I made my way to the opening event, I thought of my introduction to Mormonism as a teenager.

After a Mormon family moved into our neighborhood, I quickly read the only Mormon book in my high school library, *No Man Knows My History.* Joseph Smith, the founder of the Mormon Church (established in 1830), claimed to have had a visitation from an angel who showed Smith where to dig up the ancient religious history of American civilization on a hill near Palmyra, New York. That history was engraved on metal plates and became *The Book of Mormon,* which purports to be the story of Jesus Christ's presence in the Americas after his death and resurrection in Jerusalem.

Another memory this visit evoked was that of a trip I made with my family as a small boy to the 1964–65 New York World's Fair. Here I saw a number of religious sites, such as the Vatican Pavilion, a Russian Orthodox chapel, and the Mormon Pavilion. What stood out for me in the Mormon Pavilion was the famous copy of the Thorvaldsen's *Christus* statue in Copenhagen, Denmark.

The tall, imposing white statue of Christ was conceived by the Mormon Church for the $3 million pavilion. Its sheer size and dominance not only commanded attention, but also helped put the Mormon Church into the popular consciousness. The *Christus* statue followed the accepted Mormon practice of representing Jesus as striking and extraordinarily handsome. The Mormon Jesus was not a dark and swarthy Rembrandt likeness, but a cleft-chinned, blue-eyed, well-built, golden-haired gladiator. This is the Jesus of Jeffrey Hunter in the film *King of Kings*. not the thin, ascetically inclined Jesus in Pier Pablo Pasolini's wonderful *The Gospel According to Saint Matthew.*

The New York World's Fair, in fact, was a pivotal moment for the Mormon Church.

"...The huge leap forward initiated by the Mormon Pavilion must be considered a seminal event in the evolution of the Church's use of media in spreading the gospel message to the world," wrote Brent L. Top, dean of religious education at Brigham Young University. "From that time to the present day, the Church's outreach through its use of technology and media has increased steadily and exponentially."

This fact was clearly in evidence during the Philadelphia Temple's first media tour.

The press group of about twenty-two people included members of both the print and broadcast media. A Fox News reporter was there along with her camera crew. There were other unidentified camera crews and a number of photographers, although no pictures were permitted inside the temple itself since it is considered the House of the Lord. The press met in the less than inspiring Robert A. M. Stern-designed Meeting House, the place for Mormon Sunday worship, since the Temple is reserved for marriages (and the "sealing" of those marriages for eternity) and for baptisms of the deceased. The tour was to last two hours, with light refreshments at the end.

At the time of the tour, it was announced that there were 112 operating Mormon temples worldwide. At times, the building of such a temple or a Mormon institution has caused some controversy. In 1984, when ground was broken in the Mount Scopus area of Jerusalem for the Brigham Young University Jerusalem campus, all hell broke out. Ultra-Orthodox Jews saw this invasion of Mormons from Utah as a proselytizing threat and sought to have construction halted. The Mormon Church had to hire security guards to proceed with the project. Mordechai Ben David, a famous Orthodox pop star, even composed a hit single titled "Jerusalem is Not for Sale:" "Jerusalem is not for sale!/Voices, crying, thundering throughout our cities/You better run for your life, back to Utah overnight/Before the mountaintop opens wide to swallow you inside."

Today, the BYU Jerusalem campus hardly raises an eyebrow, although students there must sign a contract promising not to missionize non-Mormons.

Our Philadelphia Temple tour guide was the Harvard-educated Larry Y. Wilson, who serves as Executive Director of the Temple Department in Salt Lake City.

The silver-haired Wilson had a sleek "father-knows-best" demeanor about him. He took us from the Meeting House to the Temple entrance where coverings were put over our shoes. The shoe coverings were to keep street dirt off the meticulously clean Temple floors and rugs.

Inside the Temple, Wilson described the furnishings and the commissioned art on the walls, including several original murals. He also explained how the Temple's features were aligned to fit a southeastern Pennsylvania and Philadelphia theme, right down to the temple's main door and frame with its bas-relief mountain laurel "Pennsylvania" blossom design. "We believe that the founding of this country was divinely inspired," he said.

The interior of the temple was an extravaganza of quality craftsmanship. There were no traces of the flimsy and cheap construction materials that you see in new construction all over town. There are no thin walls or doors that weigh a few ounces. One astonished journalist asked how the temple was able to ward off the sound of outside traffic. Wilson replied, "With very thick walls."

Press questions about the Mormon religion began early on. This was to be expected, given that much of the tour included references to Mormon theology and doctrine. These references were woven into descriptions of the temple's Ionic, Doric, and Corinthian columns, the decorative lighting, flooring, the outside fence, walkways, and the landscaping. "We believe that this is the Lord's House," Wilson reiterated, something that many Christian denominations might ascribe to in theory, but that in practice sometimes falls short, especially when one considers those Protestant sanctuaries that are used for services on Sunday are transformed into jazz festival arenas or concert halls on other days of the week.

Emaneul Swedenborg, a Swedish scientist, mystic, and founder of the Swedenborgian Church, wrote that heaven is filled with cities and houses of many different types. There are mansions and simple homes, lavish communities, and humble neighborhoods. We reap in heaven what we sow in life, meaning that those who were terrifically good in life live in afterlife mansions of marvelous splendor, while those who lived mediocre lives on earth inhabit less than spectacular heavenly neighborhoods.

In Mormonism, there is a belief that non-Mormon ancestors in the afterlife are free to accept or reject the offer of baptism into the Mormon faith by living relatives or friends. A "yes" answer, however, would transfer the deceased to a Swedenborg-like "greater" heaven.

In the Philadelphia temple, each floor is designed as a stairway to heaven. As one goes higher, the furnishings and the chandeliers on each floor become more elaborate until one reaches the apex, or the Celestial Room. This chamber is the most scared and beautiful room in the temple. The Celestial Room features a hanging chandelier that fans out into the room like an exploding comet. Visiting Mormons in good standing (Mormons must get a recommend pass from their bishop or stake leader in order to enter the temple) pray and meditate here despite the fact that this room, as well as the entire temple, tends to resemble a lavish Ritz Carlton Hotel with a lot of pictures of Jesus.

The press' fascination with Mormonism came to a fore at the Baptismal Font. Generally, a concerted design effort would be necessary to transform a baptismal area into a secular-looking space, but one can see elements of that here. It is not hard to imagine someone perceiving this space, despite its sacred nature, as a hot tube of the highest quality, perhaps a *faux* Disney recreation of the baths of ancient Rome. Still, "spectacular" does not begin to describe the font area, which had journalists gazing into the pool of water as if lost in the bliss of hypnosis. Like characters in a Robert Altman film, we journalists formed a long line along the circumference of the curving marble barrier that overlooked the oxen accented pool as questions about Mormonism ricocheted back and forth like tennis balls. The Baptismal Font, to me, was the highlight of the tour.

Later on in the tour, in the marriage sealing room where couples kneel facing one another across a small altar to have their marriages sealed for all eternity, things got a little dicey. A journalist, inappropriately dressed in shorts, a tight T-shirt, and a frayed baseball cap, asked Wilson if same sex marriages are performed in the sealing room.

The question seemed to come across as a triggering device for other members of the press, designed to set off a series of consecutive explosive comments and questions all related to same-sex marriage and engineered to put Wilson on the defensive.

Perhaps it was possible that a reporter had no clue about the Mormon stance on same-sex marriage. Americans, after all, are tremendously ignorant about religion. This is why the wife of one visiting Mormon elder told me that people who should know better mistake her for a Mennonite or Amish.

"But would an Amish woman wear these kinds of heels?" she asked me, showing me her feet ensconced in the brightest of the bright Frederick's of Hollywood heels that would attract a thumbs up at a *Philadelphia Style* magazine party.

As for that baseball-capped reporter, his question did set off a few same-sex marriage follow-up comments, although the ever-savvy Wilson was able to defuse whatever small bomb lay hidden in the reporter's initial inquiry.

In October 2018, the president of the Mormon Church, Russell M. Nelson, announced that he had had a revelation from God. "The Lord has impressed upon my mind the importance of the name He has revealed for His Church," he said, meaning that the common and ever popular name Mormon Church, which began as a derogatory term in the nineteenth-century after the church's founding by Joseph Smith, was now on the chopping block. "Using the term 'Mormon' is a victory for Satan," President Nelson added.

Nelson's comment was more Church Lady-Saturday Night Live-routine than anything related to sound theology.

The word "Mormon" can almost be said to be in the DNA of this uniquely American religion with its epic story of a cross-country wagon train and its

Hebrew Bible-like miracle story of how flocks of seagulls saved the early Salt Lake City settlement from a plague of locusts.

After President Nelson's revelation, *The New York Times* ran the headline: "Stop Saying 'Mormon Church,' Leader Says. But Is the Real Name Too Long?" For once, the *Times* got it right. The real name is too long and it is highly likely that journalists and secular writers will not be using it in print anytime soon. Even good Mormons are not going to use it, and why should they? The church's holy book, *The Book of Mormon*, bears the name proudly (without, presumably, any contamination from Satan).

The elimination of the word "Mormon" is really a victory for modernism. In a weird "gotcha" kind of twist, this could also be considered to be a victory for "Satan." One might say that President Nelson got it all backwards. In trying to be hip or contemporary or more with the times, he may have inflicted permanent damage on the Church of Joseph Smith.

Rather than the word "Mormon," the Church of Jesus Christ of Latter Day Saints is the preferred identifier with the shortened the Restored Church of Jesus Christ listed as a possible alternative. But the latter name is as bland and as inauthentic sounding as any of the zillions of storefront pop-up churches in the inner city. Why would an iconic American religion want to dumb itself down in this way?

Also on the "out" list is the term LDS Church, which to me seems like a perfectly fine identifier and one I have heard since I was a child even though LDS comes awfully close to LSD. If the Mormon Church had serious concerns about the label LDS, it should have scrapped it fifty years ago at the height of the hippie counterculture era when the drug culture was beginning to rear its head.

The question still begs: Why did the Mormon Church change its DNA powerful name at the height of what appears to be its worldwide missionary (and temple building) success?

The same question has been asked of the Roman Catholic Church when it convened the Second Vatican Council in 1963. Why did the Roman Church convene Vatican II at the height of its own worldwide success, when its convents, monasteries, and seminaries were full, when its parish churches all over the world were filled to capacity? Vatican II was organized to bring the Roman Church into the modern world, but it had the opposite effect: those same filled-to-capacity convents and seminaries emptied out as its ancient liturgy was changed beyond recognition: guitars replaced chants and old hymns, nuns changed their traditional habits for "Nuns on the Bus" feminist garb, and churches were stripped of their altars and traditional iconography until at last Catholicism became to resemble the low church Episcopal church on the other side of town.

A Mormon convert friend of mine says it took him a long time to stop using the word "Mormon" to describe himself after President Nelson's announcement. In many ways, I can see that he is still trying to deal with it.

This is not the first time the Mormon Church has attempted to change its name. In 2002, during the Winter Olympics in Salt Lake City, the church decided to use its full formal name rather than "Mormon" when describing itself. The result was a disaster. Rocky Anderson, the mayor of Salt Lake at the time, commented that the new nomenclature was "so awkward."

But President Nelson has been pushing for the name change since 1990, just as in the Roman Catholic Church reformists and iconoclasts were working behind the scenes decades before Vatican II.

In 1955, the Roman Catholic Church established a Commission for Liturgical Reform that went to work on changing the rites of Holy Week. Many believe that this was a kind of trial balloon for the Novus Ordo Mass of 1969. The Commission suggested that everything should be short and simple and that essential rites be performed by the priest with his back facing the altar.   Mormons worldwide seem to have an inkling that getting rid of the word "Mormon" will lead to bad things, and because of this, their voices are beginning to be heard. One Mormon writer quipped, "Don't mess with the name ever. (New Coke = Bad Idea. Do we learn nothing from history?)"

Mormon blogger Jana Riess wrote: "Any time you require a journalist to employ multiple clumsy words when just one was working fine and ask them to embrace obfuscation rather than clarity, you have a problem.... It is not legitimate to suddenly insist that the word 'Mormon' not be used even to refer to the people who follow that religion."

To get the "feel" and power of the word "Mormon" one must consider the media hype surrounding the Mormon pavilion at the New York 1963 World's Fair.

The New York World's Fair, in fact, was a pivotal moment for the Mormon Church.

"...The huge leap forward initiated by the Mormon Pavilion must be considered a seminal event in the evolution of the Church's use of media in spreading the gospel message to the world," writes Brent L. Top, dean of religious education at Brigham Young University. "From that time to the present day, the Church's outreach through its use of technology and media has increased steadily and exponentially." Exponential growth, however, need not become a name-eating mania, or change for the sake of change.

As of 2019, there were 51,954 members of the Church of Jesus Christ of Latter-Day Saints in Pennsylvania. The number of Mormons living in Philadelphia was put at 6,400 in 2016.

The future of the Mormon Church in Philadelphia came under scrutiny in an article written by David Krueger in *Religion Dispatches* in 2016:

> The formation of a Mormon enclave will likely be critical to the church's ability
> to retain members, especially in a city that can be unfriendly to many widely-
> held Mormon values. Mormons identify with the Republican party at a rate of

80%, but in Philadelphia Democrats outnumber Republicans 7 to 1. The church's stance in opposing same-sex marriage in particular will be unappealing to many of Philadelphia's millennials. Time will tell if experiments in Mormon urbanism will spark a surge of enthusiasm among millennials, but the odds are against them.

CHRISTIAN SCIENCE, THE RESPECTABLE CULT

The First Church of Christ, Scientist, Philadelphia, extends the following message to all newcomers:

> Whether you are a visitor to Philadelphia, or a new or longtime resident, you are invited to attend services, bring children to Sunday School, visit the Reading Room, and learn more about Christian Science.
>
> This is a Bible-based, Christian church focused on healing and based on the word and works of Christ Jesus and the teachings of Christian Science.
>
> Thousands of individual accounts of Christian Science healing can be found in our Reading Room.
>
> In our Sunday School, children learn the Ten Commandments, the Lord's Prayer, and the Sermon on the Mount, and how to apply their lessons at school and home.
>
> Our church services share the teachings of the Bible and Christ Jesus and their application to daily life.
>
> The history of First Church of Christ, Scientist here in Philadelphia dates back to the early years of the 20th century. After its preliminary years of organizing, First Church of Christ Scientist, Philadelphia held its initial services in June 1910 in a large new edifice at 4012 Walnut Street. The building was designed by Carriere and Hastings. One year later, dedicatory services were held.

With a growing membership, members saw the need for branches in other sections of Philadelphia, and members began to withdraw to organize other branch churches. In October 1919, twenty-six members (including one teacher of Christian Science and seven *Journal*-listed practitioners) withdrew from First Church in order to form Fifth Church in Center City. Fifth Church flourished and in January 1930 purchased Christ Church (Episcopal) Chapel at 1915 Pine Street. The Chapel had officially opened on June 9, 1877, as an outreach of Christ Church at Second and Market Streets. Philadelphia architect James Peacock Sims (1849–1882) designed the church. The organ, made by Hook and Hastings of Boston, was installed when the church was sold to Fifth Church of Christ, Scientist. The thirteen original memorial windows, some of them by Tiffany, were removed when the church was sold to Fifth Church of Christ, Scientist. After modifications to the structure, Fifth Church held its first service in the new location on May 25, 1930.

The church history section goes on to explain that in the mid- to latter part of the twentieth century, as suburbs grew and the demographics of Philadelphia changed, so did the memberships of the churches. By the early 1990s, both First and Fifth Church branches had been looking to their respective futures, studying their missions, and relationships to the community.

Each was facing challenging problems that required action. First Church was considering the sale of its distinguished edifice at 4012 Walnut Street, which had become too large for the members. Both churches were seeing annual operating expenses exceeding income in greater amounts than endowment income could supply indefinitely. Both branches were exploring options independently.

What do Christian Scientists believe?

1. Sin is an illusion.
2. Sickness is also is an illusion.
3. Sick people must be convinced that they are not sick then they will get well, since sickness doesn't exist.
4. Death is an illusion. A person gets old and dies because they believe that is what is supposed to happen.
5. The Christian Science god is not the personal God of the Bible. The whole universe is falsehood—an illusion.
6. Christian Science does not heal. What heals is denying the disease itself, e.g., "*I am not sick. I do not have cancer.*" This is not prayer but an affirmation.
7. Women can become pregnant by a supreme effort of their own minds; men are not needed for procreation.
8. Man is not made of the dust of the earth as in Genesis 2 because matter doesn't exist - therefore Mrs. Eddy calls Genesis 2, "*a lie*". Mrs. Eddy's word trumps the Bible.
9. Jesus is not God. He was the highest human concept of the perfect man, but not to be worshipped.

In 1999, a writer for Salon.com, Laura Miller, wrote a piece entitled "The Respectable Cult:"

Picture a relatively new American religious sect founded by a charismatic, paranoid, authoritarian leader. The church has a set of secret doctrines, and it threatens legal action against those who would reveal them. It vigorously pressures journalists, publishers and booksellers who attempt to disseminate anything but the officially sanctioned accounts of its deceased founder or its current autocratic leadership. It has a handful of celebrity followers and some really weird beliefs. It's also a potential threat to the well-being of many of its members.

"Physician, heal thyself" is the quote that I hear in my mind's eye whenever I pass a Christian Science church. It is not that I put sock in faith healers, it is just that, as a former operating room technician, I have seen my share of unnecessary and excessive surgical procedures: patients hacked to steak tartar, then stitched up just so they could have a few more minutes of life; life support measures and corrective remedies that caused more pain then the diseases they sought to eliminate. I have witnessed the horrors of exploratory surgery before the days of MRI and CAT scans, of watching surgeons cut open patients from the chest to the lower abdominal region.

I have witnessed the fallibility of doctors as they experimented on patients too numb and shell-shocked to protest. I have held frightened men and women as they were given spinal anesthesia blocks where the anesthetist repeatedly missed the mark and had to repeat the injections many times over. Spinal blocks were painful and often the patient screamed in agony while they held on to me for support. I held hundreds of patients during my two-and-a-half-year sojourn in the operating room; if I close my eyes I can still see some of the faces of these patients. The nurses thought I had a knack for calming people so I was in demand as "a holder."

Surgeons were the supreme CEOs of the operating room. They ruled with iron forceps. God help the scrub nurse who made a mistake during the course of an operation, the most common being the passing of a wrong instrument. The offending nurse was dressed down in the manner of a lowly peasant. Many were expelled from the operating room in tears. The "refugee" scrub nurse was then assigned to another operating room or sent away to sterilize instruments.

Some surgeons acted out by throwing instruments across the room. These experiences were quite common. The tantrums could be long or short, depending on the "offense," but the idea—indeed, part of the job description of the scrub nurse—was to prevent these outbursts from happening in the first place. The surgeons, considered by the nursing administrators as above reproach, were coddled in every way; rudeness and arrogance from them was accepted as a byproduct of the stress they were going through as the "gods of life and death."

Years ago, I read a book by Martin Gardner on the life of Mary Baker Eddy. Gardner's book is anything but an objective account of this spiritualist and medium's life. In fact, the book mounts a heady attack early on without allowing the reader to come to his/her own conclusions regarding Mrs. Eddy.

Gardner explains how Eddy adopted the healing techniques of Phineas Parkhurst Quimby (1802–1866), a former clockmaker turned mind healer and clairvoyant who had some success in healing individuals through hypnotism. "Almost every bodily ill is the result of wrong thinking," Quimby wrote.

Eddy hooked on to Quimby's belief that human beings are not matter because matter is an illusion. Since spirit lives forever, illness and death have no effect on humans; it is our belief in their power to overcome us that ages us and that gives disease its power and ultimate victory.

If we believe we will grow old and die, we will grow old and die. If we refused to let this belief influence us, we might never age.

Eddy often talked about a mountain woman in Eastern Europe who lost track of her age and so never celebrated birthdays. Doctors determined she was seventy-five years old, but she looked about twenty-six. Her belief system, Eddy tells us, never had a chance to tell her she was getting old, so the aging process was stalled. (It should be noted that in old age, Eddy saw physicians, wore spectacles, and even got false teeth.)

Dying is another matter. If we are really spirit, and matter is a total illusion, then our bodies are temporary transport vehicles and nothing about us dies when we pass over. Gardner insists, however, that Eddy really believed that she would live forever in the physical body.

When this was obviously not happening, Eddy, Gardner says, attributed this to her beliefs not being strong enough, as well as to something called "Malicious Animal Magnetism"—or negative thoughts/vibrations projected on to her from other people, namely enemies.

According to Gardner, Eddy was a religious tyrant, excommunicating people she was jealous of or felt threatened by. She would not allow church members to read any metaphysical or spiritual books but the Bible and *Science and Health*. When she enshrined herself in the regal "Mother Room" in the big church in Boston, Mark Twain attacked her taste for opulence. The criticism affected Eddy so much that she later dismantled the room.

Had I been allowed to come to my own conclusions about Mary Baker Eddy, I might have agreed with Mark Twain, who in a 1903 satirical essay on Eddy described her as "grasping, sordid, penurious, despotic, arrogant, illiterate, shallow, and immeasurably selfish."

Former Christian Scientist Caroline Fraser tells the story of the rise and fall of Christian Science in her book *God's Perfect Child*.

Unfortunately, Eddy's forceful personality sometimes turned downright bizarre. She lied freely about her education, her age, her marriages, her role in the emancipation of slaves. She believed that she could control the weather ("I have heard our Leader describe in a number of instances how she has dissipated a thundercloud by simply looking upon it," one employee reported). She spoke to followers in what Fraser calls "oracular biblical patois," channeling messages from the Almighty that confirmed her holy mission: "Oh, blessed daughter of Zion, I am with thee.... Thou art my chosen, to bear my Truth to the nations." A host of fears and hatreds—of sex, weakness and death, of Catholics and Jews—consumed her, apotheosized in her terror of "malicious animal magnetism," an invisible, poisonous force that befouled her food, impaired her health and, in the form of "mesmeric magnetism," was used by her enemies to murder her third husband. Scandals plagued her and her followers; to this day, as Fraser painstakingly details,

Christian Science has been rife with dissent and now teeters on the brink of "a massive institutional nervous breakdown."

Philadelphia was once home to an extraordinary Christian Science church, comparable almost to the church's mother church in Boston, a cathedral-like edifice built in 1911 and designed by Beaux Arts architects Carrere and Hastings of New York, architects of the New York Public Library in 1897, and the Arlington Memorial Amphitheater in Washington, D.C., in 1920. The church design has been compared to early Christian spaces such as Santa Sabina in Rome. Located at 4014 Walnut Street and now called The Rotunda, the space is now used for a variety of community-based arts initiatives.

5

Philadelphia's Pop-Up Messiahs

The best qualification of a good prophet is to have a good memory.

Lord Halifax

The New Jerusalem, when it comes, will probably be found so far to resemble the old as to stone its prophets freely.

Samuel Butler

The phenomenon of the Cult of Philly Jesus is apparent to anyone who happens upon numerous YouTube videos of Philly Jesus going about his "mission" in the city, including "baptizing" a man in LOVE fountain near City Hall. How could anyone, one might wonder, be so gullible as to believe that a baptism by a fake Jesus was somehow more real than a baptism in a church? No sooner did I ask this question than I understood the reason: Everything in this society is about appearances. Philly Jesus, a.k.a. Michael Grant, was a hot media commodity at the time of the YouTube baptism filming. People who buy into celebrity culture want easy answers, and Philly Jesus is the perfect man for that.

It is easy to imagine how it all started for him: A close friend probably told him, "You know, your face and eyes, and the way your beard hangs, you are a Jesus clone. You should take advantage of that look. Ditch the Philadelphia Flyers shirt and the Phillies cap and put on a robe. Then walk around the city and see what happens."

It was a brilliant move, the kind of maneuver that public relations people love. Where can the world of marketing and public relations find a better story than Grant's? An admitted ex-heroin addict, what has Mr. Grant not seen on the mean streets of the city? Rejection, starvation, dirty needles, homelessness, dirty clothes, and days without a shower, not to mention, as the drug culture goes, unseemly ways to make money. It is a certainty that Philly Jesus has been to hell and back, but now that he is resurrected and clean, his beard fluffed up and his piercing eyes aflame, he is a real showman. And yes—no doubt about it—he is hit on a new career path and he might even get a movie role down the line.

The day that Michael Grant put on Jesus robes, the city opened up for him. The local paparazzi went crazy because they were hungry for something new and different. If your job is photographing people, you can only snap so many pictures of ladies in strapless evening gowns at parties before boredom sets in. Since Philly Jesus was not just another night crawler sucking on Martini olives, his picture was soon everywhere. He went from ex-drug addict status ("Got spare change, Miss?") to media icon celebrity. The effect of all this publicity was that soon people were going to Philly Jesus for spiritual counseling. In a series of online photographs by CBS3, for instance, one can see Philly Jesus praying with the homeless, counseling strangers, conversing with addicts, praying in the Parkway Catholic cathedral, and walking through North Philly carrying a huge wooden cross. In other photos, he is skateboarding or playing hockey—because, you know, Philly Jesus is cool.

In Philly Jesus' "counseling the weak" photos, he looks very sage-like with his arm around a homeless man sitting on the sidewalk. What words of wisdom was the savior imparting? In this photo, one can see that he has ceased being an actor but is beginning to take himself seriously. He thinks he is Jesus. As Philly Jesus told one interviewer (it astounds me, frankly, that journalists even interviewed him), "I have to grow. I have to take it to the next level," but the next level meaning what? To become Jesus, of course.

Appearances mean everything in the world. If you want to make your mark in life but have no particular talent—you do not know how to draw, cure diseases, design buildings, or write music—you can always create a gimmick or find a hook to catapult yourself into the world of doers.

Find the right gimmick and the paparazzi will be at your door. If Philly Jesus has any talent at all, it is the "power" with which he believes in himself. Let us say, for instance, that Philly Jesus lost that air of self-confidence and showed visible traces of embarrassment or doubt while dressed in robes. That ambiguity would be noticed and felt by observers, and his career would begin to unwind.

Philly Jesus reminds me in many ways of the famous *New York Magazine* art critic Jerry Saltz. Some months ago, Saltz spoke at the Barnes Foundation about his being a college dropout and never having had a formal education in art, although his interest in art led him to study art books and art criticism. Employed as a cross-country truck driver at the time, one day Saltz decided that he was going to call himself an art critic. In an instant, he became what he had always believed about himself. Over time, this belief led to an esteemed position at *New York Magazine*. Saltz's story calls to mind the many people who say that they are going to spend time "making art," certain that just because they call it art it is art, no matter what the critics may say. If you believe that what you make is art, then it is art because your belief makes it so. But does it, really? Writers, of course, are much less prone to this kind of grandstanding. They do not say, "I'm going into my house to make literature." Writers, perhaps, are humbler than visual artists.

Philly Jesus has been arrested about a dozen times, mostly for loitering and trumped-up charges like "theft of services." Anyone who has traveled extensively outside of the United States realizes that in Europe people "loiter." They sit on benches; they hang in cafes for hours; they sit or stand by rivers. In many parts of the United States, such behavior might attract attention, the logic being that you can "loiter" in a public space but it must be in a park or in a place where buying something allows you to "loiter." Public spaces in the U.S., with the exception of parks, have become "hang out" suspicious, hence the slow disappearance of the public bench.

The police officer who arrested Philly Jesus because he accepted a tip from a prayerful stranger at LOVE Park is an example of this "new world order." Philly Jesus did not solicit tips, but he was arrested anyway. True to the classic Jesus formula, he went willingly in handcuffs to his trial before Pontius Pilot. But he also got a lawyer. The incident also won him a lot of publicity and fans.

If Michael Grant thought it would be fun being Philly Jesus, he was in for a rude awakening. When you stroke the mane of the paparazzi, you have to do certain things right to keep them coming around. You can ruffle feathers, but they have to be the right kind of feathers. You have to be the kind of Jesus that does not exclude anybody.

During the Gay Pride month of June, Philly Jesus lent his support to the fiftieth anniversary of the historic gay rights protest at Independence Hall. The paparazzi photographed him smiling and waving among a mostly LGBT crowd. In one photo, you can see him standing near a drag queen and Henri David, Philadelphia's Mr. Halloween. When the Supreme Court voted in favor of same-sex marriage, Philly Jesus said that the ruling was a very good thing and that he approved.

Did the religious right backlash against the Supreme Court ruling on same sex marriage inspire strict fundamentalists to contact Philly Jesus for a spiritual rehabilitation? The self-righteous among us love to point out the sins of others; in this case, did they tell Philly Jesus that God's love is not unconditional? The prospect of alienating conservative Christians was not something Philly Jesus wanted to do. That was certainly his right. After all, he had his future fundraising efforts and his Jesus ministry project to think about. What would happen to his financial contributions, and to his goal of expanding Philly Jesus into an American, nationwide Jesus, if he alienated the wrong people? Being Jesus is a bit like walking on egg shells.

Philly Jesus, in a quick turnabout, announced that he was sorry for his positive comments on same-sex marriage. "I wanna publicly apologize to all of you," he said, "and ask for your forgiveness. I repent in Jesus' name." On his Facebook page, he spewed a harder dose of medicine: "Gay Pride is why Sodom got fried."

The instantaneous change baffled many of his fans. The real Jesus from Nazareth never had to correct himself, never had to say that he was wrong when he said something the first time.

In one fell swoop, Philly Jesus' love affair with the media seemed to evaporate. With his "Love one, love all" message now in the trash bin, the paparazzi made themselves scarce. His star was taken from the media heavens. There would be no more flashy media interviews, such as the Q&A he did with Simon Van Zuylen-Wood and Bryan Butler in 2014 for *Philadelphia Magazine*. In that piece, Grant told the magazine that he was always an eccentric type of guy. "I grew up doing musical theater, plays. My mom is an actress, so she always brought me to auditions. I bring the story of Christ to the street. Like William Shakespeare said, all the world's a stage. I use this as my stage." The magazine wanted to know what a typical day was like for "Jesus." Grant told them that he washed his wardrobe every day. "I bleach the robe to make sure it's nice and crispy white. It takes me about half an hour to get my hair right. I don't use a comb. I just use my fingers. Then I head to the subway. Takes me about 20 minutes to get downtown."

Grant is a neighborhood Philly boy who grew up in the North Philly areas between East Oak Lane and Olney. "When I went to high school, I was really incorrigible. Got involved with the wrong crowd, smoking marijuana, one thing led to another, started drinking a lot, started partying too hard. I said, Eff school. And then at 19 I got run over with a car by my ex-girlfriend. It's a crazy story. She was cheating on me." It's then that he got hooked on painkillers. "They were giving me anything I wanted," he told the magazine. "Morphine, opiates, Percocet." In a drug treatment program he found religion. It was a turning point in his life. "You either got to go to the Narcotics Anonymous meeting or you go to the Bible study. I was like, Yo, let me follow the narrow road." When *Philadelphia Magazine* asked Grant if he ever got bored ("Real Jesus had disciples"), he replied that sometimes his human nature, his fleshy desires kick in. "People think I'm nuts, you know? How am I ever going to meet a woman? 'Cause I'm a weird guy. I dress like Jesus."

Regarding his arrest in LOVE Park when he refused to leave the premises when asked by a police officer and then later alleged mistreatment by the police, Grant said: "I just wanna tell them all is well. This is just pushing me towards the best of me. You're always gonna have your haters. People are not gonna like what they don't understand. I love the hate. Keep the hate coming. Be patient, because the war is coming."

THE CULT OF UFOS AND EXTRATERRESTRIALS

In an article entitled "The New American Religion of UFOs," *Vox* writer Sean Illing wrote, "It's a great time to believe in aliens."

> *The New York Times* published an article that went viral about reports of UFOs off the East Coast in 2014 and 2015. It included an interview with five Navy pilots who witnessed, and in some cases recorded, mysterious flying objects with "no visible engine or infrared exhaust plumes" that appeared to "reach 30,000 feet and hypersonic speeds."
>
> No one is quite sure what they saw, but the sightings are striking. And they're part of a growing fascination with the possibility of intelligent alien life.
>
> According to Diana Pasulka, a professor at the University of North Carolina and author of the new book American Cosmic, belief in UFOs and extraterrestrials is becoming a kind of religion—and it isn't nearly as fringe as you might think.

The subject of UFOs remains a non-issue for most people until they see an unidentified object in the sky. But since most people never get to see a UFO, the question, "Are there UFOs or flying saucers from other planets?" has very little relevance except as cocktail party fodder or as the punch line of jokes.

The do-you-believe question is perplexing. On one hand, you have people who claim to have seen triangular, round, or cigar-shaped objects hovering or orbiting or racing at speeds unheard of in the known world, but their personal stories almost always seem to lack what Carl Sagan called "empirical evidence." Many personal photographs of unidentified objects raise similar questions: were they doctored or artificially produced?

It does not help that the field of UFO research has become overpopulated with people who have turned the phenomenon into a cult. From random sightings, people have gone on to extrapolate that these are our ancestors; that they brought civilization to earth; they may be "us" in the future coming home to take a "looksee;" or maybe they are here to save the planet. Then again, they may be the gods who sent Jesus and Moses, built the pyramids, did weird things to the Sphinx, etc.

It is one thing, perhaps, to go on record as witnessing a sighting, quite another to construct a Scientology-like religion to explain the mysteries of the universe.

Military and commercial air pilots are perhaps the best and most credible witnesses to come forward in recent years. A ground-breaking book, *UFOs: Generals, Pilots, and Government Officials Go On the Record* by Leslie Kean, has been called "the most important book on the phenomenon in a generation." Kean's work skips "theology" and Henry Potter myth-making and gives the evidence that there probably is something out there, but what?

The preferred replacement term for UFO among credible sources is UAP, or unidentified aerial phenomena, meaning (as defined by NASA senior scientist

Richard Haines), objects "which do not suggest a logical, conventional flying object and which remain unidentified after close scrutiny of all available evidence."

While many objects in the sky are misidentified as UAPs—from weather balloons, the planets Venus or Mars, to satellites and ice crystals—Kean reports that "roughly 90 to 95 perfect of UFO sightings can be explained." The author advocates a kind of agnosticism when it comes to UFOs. Agnosticism or skepticism helps, Kean says, because "the UFO debate fuels two polarities, both representing untenable positions," meaning the two camps of believers and total debunkers. "This counterproductive battle has unfortunately dominated public discourse for a long time, only heightening confusion and creating more distance from the scientific…"

Major General Wilfried De Brouwer headed the Operations Division in the Belgian Air Staff and helped investigate a rash of sightings over Belgium in 1989. For two years, hundreds of people in Belgium saw what Kean describes as "a majestic triangular craft with a span of approximately a hundred and twenty feet and powerful beaming spotlights." The craft moved at a snail's pace and made no noise but it could accelerate instantly. The situation was so serious that Belgium's defense minister, Guy Coeme, asked De Brouwer to handle the sightings. The consensus then was that something was invading Belgian airspace. During his investigation, De Brouwer interviewed hundreds of eyewitnesses.

One of De Brouwer's interviewees, Colonel Andred Amond, a former director of military infrastructure for the Belgian Army, reported seeing a craft flying close to the earth while driving with his wife. Colonel Amond filed a report as well as drawings of the object to Coeme. Suspicions that the wave of UAPs were American B-2 or F-117 military aircraft engaged in a secret mission over Belgian territory were quickly dismissed by the U.S. Embassy in Brussels.

De Brouwer, in his investigation, describes what two police officers saw: "They [the policemen] described a dome on the upper structure with rectangular windows, lit on the inside." There were two crafts, one of which was "emitting red light balls." These same policemen encountered one of the crafts sometime later, but by that time, the craft was "immobile and silent, but it suddenly transmitted a hissing sound and reduced the intensity of the lights." Both officers then saw a red light ball exit from the center of the craft, proceeding along vertical and horizontal paths until it eventually disappeared. De Brouwer reports that a total of thirteen police officers reported seeing "the craft at eight different locations in the vicinity of Eupen."

"Of the approximately 2,000 reported cases registered during the Belgian wave, 650 were investigated and more than 500 of them remain unexplained," De Brouwer writes.

In 1982, Portuguese Air Force pilot Julio Guerra was flying solo in a DHC-1 Chipmunk at about 10:50 a.m. when he noticed an airplane without a fuselage flying below him. "It didn't have wings and it didn't have a tail, only a cockpit! It was an oval shape. What kind of airplane could that be?" he recounts in his essay, "Circled by a UFO."

When Guerra steered his plane to the left in order to follow the object, "the object climbed straight up to my altitude of 5,000 in under ten seconds." Guerra recalls that the object stopped in front of him, "at first with some instability, oscillations, and a wavering motion, and then it stabilized and was still." He reported a metallic disc with two halves with a brilliant band around the center.

For a few moments, the object seemed to engage in a game of show and tell, flying at incredible speeds in left-leaning elliptical orbits.

Guerra called the tower and reported the object, but was told it was a weather balloon ("How could a weather balloon ascend from the ground to 5,000 feet in a few seconds?" he asked). Eventually he was joined by two other Air Force pilots who saw the same object. "It came toward me and flew right over me, on top of my aircraft, and stopped there, like a helicopter landing but much, much faster, breaking all the rules of aerodynamics," Guerra wrote.

At Chicago's O'Hare Airport on the afternoon of November 7, 2006, Kean reports: "For about five minutes, a disc-shaped object hovered quietly over the United Airlines terminal and then cut a sharp hole in the cloud bank above while zooming off." On January 1, 2007, the story was front-page news in the *Chicago Tribune*. Numerous people saw the disc: pilots, terminal managers, and U.S. mechanics. Kean reports that even "pilots waiting to take off opened the front windows to lean out and see the objects for themselves. There was a buzz at United Airlines."

Unfortunately, the many witnesses of the O'Hare disc opted to remain anonymous, afraid for their job security, and Kean reports that the FAA "tried hard to ignore the incident despite its safety implications." The FAA later went on record as explaining the incident as the result of "bizarre weather," something Kean calls a lie because she was able to hear the airport tower tapes when the disc was first spotted. "Official distaste for dealing with the UFO phenomenon is entrenched to the point of being not only counterproductive, but possible dangerous," Kean concludes.

NATO coordinator of Allied Air Services General L. M. Chassin has also warned that by refusing to "recognize the existence of UFOs, we will end up, one fine day, by mistaking them for the guided missiles of an enemy—and the worst will be upon us."

In 2007, commercial airline pilot Ray Bowyer and his passengers saw two large UFOS while flying over the English Channel. The plane was cruising at 150 mph and headed to Alderney, England, from Southampton.

"Both objects were of a flattened disk shape ... they were brilliant yellow with light emanating from them," Bowyer reported. After calling the tower, Bowyer says that the passengers began to notice the objects and were asking about

Above: Mother Divine and Woodmont staff (Rosebuds). (*Courtesy of the author*)

Right: Father and Mother Divine Booklet.

Peace

REV. M. J. DIVINE, Ms.D., D.D.   MRS. S. A. DIVINE
Better known as
Father Divine   Mother Divine

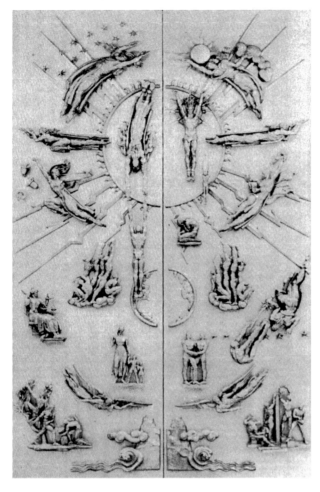

Left: The Shrine at Woodmont.

Below: The *New Day Newspaper*, newspaper of the Peace Mission movement.

Invitation — 21st Woodmont Anniversary 3; The Word of God Revealed (11th section) 17-20
Father Divine's Messages; To Live In Divine Hotels 12; Mortality's Hold on Persons 10

The NEW DAY

The Flag of the Free
Shall Be Seen In Every Land,
Americanism, Christianity, Democracy.

Published in Philadelphia — The Country Seat of the World
NATIONAL & INTERNATIONAL — Featuring the Works of FATHER DIVINE

★
WE REPRESENT
ONE RACE
INDIVISIBLE —
UNDIVIDED
✻

Vol. 38 No. 35   REG. U. S. PAT. OFF.   SATURDAY, AUGUST 31st, 1974 A. D. F. D.   10 CENTS

This Is Not "Churchanity" Formality or Mortal Organizations — Father Divine

The People Follow ME Because I Free Them and Do Not Materially or Legally Bind Them

Right: Tommy and Lori Garcia with their pet dog.

Below: Political protest, streets of Philadelphia. (*Courtesy of the author*)

Left: Mother Divine in fur. Not much is known about this photograph, but it was obviously taken early in her marriage to Father Divine. The image is evocative of a 1965 "praise poem" written by a fan of Mother Divine's shortly after Father Divine's death. In that poem, the fan calls Mother Divine, "Queen of the Angels." The poet adds: "Death is rapidly going out of style/You'll read about it in *Life* magazine soon..." (*Courtesy of Lori and Tommy Garcia*)

Below: Mother Divine directs the dining room activities in a Philadelphia Peace Mission house. (*Courtesy of Lori and Tommy Garcia*)

Above: Arlene Ostapowicz,
psychic. (*Courtesy of the
author*)

Right: The Unicorn's Secret:
Ira Einhorn

THE UNICORN'S SECRET

MURDER IN THE AGE OF AQUARIUS

A TRUE STORY BY

STEVEN LEVY

Above left: Modern Catholic cathedral after renovations, Vienna, Austria. (*Courtesy of the author*)

Above right: Mother Divine standing in front of the Woodmont estate. (*Courtesy of Lori and Tommy Garcia*)

Traditional Orthodox Christian chandelier. (*Courtesy of the author*)

Catholic Traditionalism, St. Paul's Church, South Philadelphia.

Philadelphia homeless. (*Courtesy of the author*)

WAWA: Where the homeless hold doors for customers. Some of the homeless are from Lancaster County and a few have been Mennonite and/or Amish.

The Dollar Tree store in Philadelphia's Port Richmond Shopping Center is where many of the homeless panhandle or hold the doors for customers. (*Courtesy of the author*)

them. "I decided not to make any announcement over the intercom so as not to alarm anyone, but it was obvious that some were getting concerned ... the two identical objects were easily visible without binoculars."

Bowyer reports that he landed the plane safely and that there had been "no interference with any of the aircraft systems or instruments, and radio communications were likewise unaffected."

In September 1976, a "*War of the Worlds*" of sorts occurred in the city of Tehran, Iran, when an unknown object began to circle the city at a very low altitude. Iranian Air Force General Parviz Jafari (now retired) was a major and squadron commander then and was one of the pilots charged with pursuing the object. "It was flashing with intense red, green, orange, and blue lights so bright that I was not able to see its body. The lights formed a diamond shape. Jafari attempted to fire at it when he says, 'my weapons jammed and my radio communications were garbled.'" Then he noticed "a round object which came out of the primary object," which he says came at him at intense speed, "almost as if it were a missile." "I was really scared," he reported, "so I selected an AIM-9 heat-seeking missile to fire at it."

Not only was Jafari's weapons control panel out, but his instruments and radar were as well. The object was headed straight towards him, but at the moment of projected impact, it disappeared, reappearing behind him.

"To this day I don't know what I saw. But for sure it was not an aircraft; it was not a flying object that human beings on Earth can make. It moved way too fast ... this needed very, very high-level technology," Jafari stated.

Closer to "home," I had the opportunity to interview five Pennsylvania-based UFO witnesses, most of whom have talked about their experiences on television news shows as well as CNN's Anderson Cooper. I present their stories as evidence of the wider pool of personal UFO experiences that occasionally slip into esoteric areas that debunkers often use to dismiss the entire phenomenon.

Levittown, Pennsylvania, resident Denise Murter grew up in Lansdowne. In July 2008, Murter, a former optical lab supervisor, had an experience that changed her life:

> It was in the middle of the night and I was asleep with my husband and our dog. Suddenly our Yorkie was growling. He never does that. I thought somebody broke into our place. He wouldn't stop growling so I figured I'd better get up and see what's going on. I figured since I was up I'll take him out to go potty, so I took him out back and a light caught my eye. I thought it was the moon, but it was a craft overtop a treetop to the left of my backyard, about 1,000 feet in the air. I was staring at it trying to figure out what it was. It wasn't a helicopter because there was no noise, everything was absolutely silent and you could see these three giant white lights underneath this thing in the sky.

Murter watched it shuffle across the sky. "You'd blink and it was in another position," she said. When it finally did disappear, she went back to bed but could not sleep.

One month later, the craft was back. Murter's little Yorkie woke her up again at 3 a.m. She went out back, and saw the object much closer to her this time, a little distance above the trees. "I got my camera but every time I took a picture the camera kept going off. I just kept snapping but it kept going off."

The craft returned for a third visit, only it was much closer to Murter's house this time:

> It was a little off to the right when it began dumping stuff on two trees. It was during the month of July and the stuff looked like snow. I open and shut my eyes to make sure I wasn't sleep walking, but once the stuff hit the trees it was sparkling like a show. I felt that I was paralyzed. As I watched the stuff come down something in my head said, "Don't be afraid, we're not here to harm you."

Murter says the entire episode lasted about twenty minutes, and that the "snow" poured down from the craft in an inverted "V" shape and was then sucked back up gracefully in regular "V" formation. "When it was finished, it was just gone in a flash of an eye," she says. After going public about her experiences through the MutualUFONetwork (or MUFON), Murter says she got letters and emails from people around the country stating that they saw similar things. One letter stood out among the rest: it was from a scientist who told her that he had the same experience with his father when younger.

"The trees in my backyard that were sprayed with white stuff were tested by three different scientists and found to contain huge amounts of Boron and magnesium. It's as if someone took a microwave and radiated the tree," she said.

After Murter told her story on T.V.'s *UFO Hunters*, and on the History and Discovery channel, the radiated trees in her backyard began to attract the curious. This stopped when she and her husband took a trip to Florida to bring back her son's family who were moving back to Pennsylvania.

> When we returned home we saw that the apartment complex had chopped down the tree. They said it was their property. I was devastated. The other tree, which is further back, is falling apart now. The scientists who took samples from the tree earlier came back after the complex chopped it down to investigate this weird growth coming out of the remnants of the tree—it looked like celery stalks, but they took it all. They also took samples of the tree down the road and found boron and magnesium in that one too.

For Rich Ferello, a Northeast Philadelphia accountant, seeing a UFO has meant questioning everything he has been taught.

On a summer's evening in 1992, he and Jo Anne were walking towards Verree Road when suddenly something appeared before their eyes.

"Oh my God," he said to Jo Anne, "What's that?" According to Rich it was "a large oval-shaped vehicle, like an orange color with a bulge around the mid-section, and underneath that it had like portals." The craft appeared to be drifting north along Verree Road.

The Ferello's watched the craft hover over the intersection where there was a large tree. "As this thing slowed along," Rich says, "I separated from my wife and headed to the other side of the tree to see it pass along, but nothing appeared. I called back to Jo Anne and said 'Where is it?' and she said, 'It went behind the tree.'"

The craft had been just several hundred feet above their heads before it disappeared behind the tree, as if slipping into another dimension.

As soon as the Ferello's got home, Jo Anne called the Northeast Airport and Philadelphia International and asked if they had a record of any blimps floating around. Both airports said no.

The couple told their respective families about the encounter. "This was in 1992, when people who said they saw UFOs were thought of as complete idiots," Rich says. "We got a lot of that from our families."

Eighteen years later, in 2008, in a new home in the Hatboro area near the Willow Grove Air Force Base, Rich took his dog for a walk when he saw four bright lights flying in formation coming towards his home. "I figured they were Black Hawk helicopters because of the nearby base, but then I realized that four big helicopters should be making a hell of a lot noise. The helicopters also don't fly after 7:30 p.m. because of the neighborhood." The lights then seemed to make a right turn and headed north.

Rich took the dog inside and slipped into the bathroom before heading off to bed when he told his wife he thought he had another sighting. No sooner did he say this then he turned the lights off and opened the window blinds, and there were the lights again. "They're back," he told Jo Anne. He recalls that this time they resembled a police or military action. "Two of the craft held back and hovered, while two rotated around and seemed to search for something."

Rich describes the lights as looking like a floating star of Venus. He says the two rotating craft stopped circling and joined the other two and then the four of them flew North in formation, disappearing behind trees. The entire episode lasted about fifteen minutes.

In 2011, while walking the dog, Rich saw what looked like a star moving very fast across the sky. "I'm watching it, there were two stars in the sky and the light was going between them. I called my wife; she came out. The light going between the stars makes a U-turn and disappears."

"Is that what you mean?" Jo Anne said, pointing to the end of the street. Rich looked and saw three to four orange globe objects that just seemed to pop up over the trees and then flew away over the southwest. "I'm thinking to myself, the ones up in the sky made a U-turn because of these things."

Unexplained phenomena like UFOs can cause many people to rethink old beliefs. For Rich and Jo Anne, this meant the end of regular church going. "We used to be regular church goers. I was a lay minister, but seeing these things got me to reassess even the birth of Christ and the role of the Virgin Mary," Rich said. "I now think outside the box."

For Radnor, PA, resident Jennifer W. Stein, an independent documentary filmmaker, founder and director of Main Line Philadelphia MUFON, and a trained UFO investigator, reports of UFOs have not gotten adequate coverage in the United States. "We are entertained to death in this country," she says:

> In terms of getting the news especially on the UFO phenomenon, we are much more hushed. And our files are much more closed than other countries. Russia has been much more open. In Tehran, Iran, in 1976, there was a huge UFO event that made world news and it was all over the front page of the newspapers in Iran…that would not have happened here in the United States. It would be hushed immediately, as it was in the Roswell case. Roswell was our 1975 Iran.

The story behind Roswell is that an alien craft crashed in Roswell, New Mexico, in July 1947 and that alien bodies—the size of children—had been recovered. "By the time the newspapers were printing the Roswell story in California, Washington had already been in touch with them and said it was a weather balloon, so the papers had already recanted and had the original story killed," Jennifer says.

Stein reminds me that every American astronaut that has gone up into space has seen UFOs, including astronaut Edgar Mitchell who founded Noetic Sciences in 1973.

Stein believes that Americans are as sheltered from the truth as the Soviet Union was in the Iron Curtain, Cold War days. "There is filtered news in the United States. The government is aware that we are not alone in the universe."

Her one sighting happened when she was nineteen years and asleep in her room in her parent's home in Kulpsville, Pennsylvania, known as scenic Mennonite farm country. At 5:30 a.m. she awoke from a nightmare, a dream in which she says she was falling, and proceeded to reach for her dream book to write the dream down when outside her window she noticed a rectangle of white light about 1,500 feet in the air. At first she thought it must be light from an airplane that only appeared to be static but that any moment would begin to move, but that was not the case.

"I was thinking 'What the heck is that?' when the thing skipped or jumped in 3 quick seconds, then disappeared, reappeared, disappeared and reappeared, and before I knew it, it was smack in front of me over this big tree."

While hovering motionless above the tree, she was able to estimate it to be about 90 feet long. "Its brilliant undulating white light undulated the way early screen savers did; there was no propulsion system, no sound, no beings, no big grey alien heads, except I am totally shocked and I am paralyzed. I want to get up and run out of the room because I have the sense that some sort of consciousness is looking at me."

Stein says she started to cry when the craft "communicated" to her that it was leaving. "In leaving, it did almost the same movements but in an opposite direction."

She says that after the craft left she woke her mother up and asked if she saw it. "That was feasible because our house was almost all floor to ceiling Frank Lloyd Wright-style glass, designed by her father, an architect, but all my mother could ask was, 'Are you on drugs?' and 'Why are your pajamas wet?'"

Copious tears caused the wet pajamas, and there were no drugs of course, but there was missing time.

"I went back to my room and the clock said 7 a.m. but I knew it was 5:30. That's when I realized that something happened that didn't make sense." Physically and emotionally exhausted, she says she collapses into bed.

The stereotypical question: Why, if UFOs exist, don't they just land on the White House lawn or in City Hall Courtyard and announce, "We're here, we're alien, get used to it!"

John Ventre, Pennsylvania state director of MUFON, a science fiction writer, and the state director of security for Pennsylvania (UPS), thinks he has the answer to that: "I don't go in my backyard and try to build a better any hill for the ants and I don't try to communicate with the squirrels."

He may be right. What would the ignorant among us do? Get out their guns and shoot?

Ventre, who resides in Pittsburgh, describes himself as an inveterate reader who has never seen a UFO, but at the age of twelve, however, he says he had an out-of-body experience in which he flew out over his neighborhood. The sensation was so real he says that he could see the top of his parents' house. Another OBE, this time in 1999, had him floating above his house where he looked down and "saw my green Cherokee in my driveway."

These two experiences became important to Ventre after he read a passage in Whitley Strieber's book *Communion*.

"The one passage in that book that scared me is the one that talks about out of body experiences not being what you think they are. The passage said it is not the soul that leaves the body, like people believe, but they are abductions. When I read that I closed the book and said, 'Oh my God, I've had two.'"

Ventre believes that about 80 percent of the cases that MUFON gets are just misidentification. "We'll go on a tracking site and find that a meteor passed at that time, or the space station passed over, but the 2008 case (Denise Murter) was the really first thorough case that I had."

Whoever and whatever they are—demons, glimpses of ourselves in the future, visitors from outer space—he knows that they "are not entirely benevolent beings."

"For a long time I thought that they were not harmful, that they were benevolent, because logically I thought if they wanted to take over the planet for the resources they could get rid of us very easily—like a virus in the air or water."

Ventre tells me to look inside the FEMA-approved booklet, *Fire Officers Guide for Disaster Control*, where there is a section on UFOs and the Enemy Threat.

"The guide warns against coming into contact with UFOs or their occupants," he says," because of their psychological effects, such as radiation. People who have gotten under UFOs have gotten radiation poisoning. There are good solid examples of not walking up to them and raising your hand to be taken. Nobody comes away from an abduction experience with a positive experience." Sightings in Pennsylvania have jumped since 2008 with an average of 275 to 300 cases a year. MUFON holds regular conferences in Philadelphia and Pittsburgh, while encouraging people who experience sightings to come forward.

Ventre, however, shies away from a person when they say they were abducted. "In my mind they may need professional help, but MUFON is not qualified to counsel people on abductions."

He considers it strange that people today are seeing different sizes and shapes of crafts. "How can they be so different?" he asks, "sometimes right in the air they change or morph into something, first their circular then cigar shaped, that's an aspect I don't understand. How can they be so different?" Could they be beings from another dimension? "Could be," Ventre says. "They could be doing this as a way to trick people. The devil was a powerful angel; maybe this is his way of creating disarray."

The question of demonic beings is an old one. In the book *UFOs: Operation Trojan Horse*, researcher John Keel maintains:

> [The UFO world] is one of ghosts and phantoms and strange mental aberrations ... an invisible world which surrounds us and occasionally engulfs us ... a world of illusion ... where reality itself is distorted by strange forces which can seemingly manipulate space, time, and physical matter—forces which are almost entirely beyond our powers of comprehension.... The UFO manifestations seem to be, by and large, merely minor variations of the age-old demonological phenomenon.

Iowa professor Brad Steiger, in his study on the Air Force "Blue Book" files has concluded, "We are dealing with a multi-dimensional paraphysical phenomenon, which is largely indigenous to planet earth."

Writers from antiquity, namely St. Symeon the New Theologian (A.D. 949–1022), have warned seekers of God "to rarely look into the sky out of fear of the evil spirits in the air. These miracles," he attests, "have no good, rational purpose, no definite meaning, ... they are monstrous, malicious, meaningless play-acting, which increases in order to astonish..."

But according to Chris Augustin, a Philadelphia MUFON member and paranormal researcher, the unidentified crafts are absolutely "nuts and bolts real."

"I'm not saying there are no gray areas," Augustin says, "they could be some type of spirit or energy, but some of the phenomena seems to be nuts and bolts craft."

In 2009, Augustin claims that he and his wife had a shared abduction, the second of two for him, the first occurring in 1996 when he saw a large triangular craft over land in New Jersey. Augustin describes that first sighting this way: "There were three lights, one on each corner and a dim light pulsating in the center." At the time, he says, he was extremely interested in UFOs and had an intense desire to see one, causing him to consider the possibility that he willed the experience to happen to him.

In 2002, Augustin experienced a missing time episode, attributable, he thinks, to the 1996 sighting.

After the 2009 sighting, he says he began to "experience a lot of synchronistic type things," but things really got strange when a foreign object, an alien implant, he says, was found by ultrasound. Although the object in Augustin's leg has not been removed, he cites a case showcased by UFO Hunters in which an object giving off two radio frequencies was removed from someone.

Augustin believes that the implants are not tracking devices but some type of monitoring to measure health, blood pressure, and sugar levels in the body. "But anything is possible. I don't think it is a controlling device."

Sightings, according to Augustin, tend to follow multiple generations of the same bloodline. "These experiences are probably much more widespread than people realize, but the thing to remember is, certain people become activated, something changes and their awareness is expanded ... and then they suddenly remember all of these things happening."

What does he think about abduction stories?

We capture a species, we clip wings, we do tests on their bodies, and then we release them into the wild. In many cases we are doing this to save the species, so I don't see abductions as an invasion thing at all. It's our own fear, our close mindedness and the "You can't do that to me" mentality. How could a more advanced civilization convey their motives to such a primitive mammalian brain and be understood?

Augustin faults the United States with playing ignorant when it comes to UFOs:

Since this philosophy was adopted at the end of Project Blue Book at the end of 1969, the United States has been stonewalling the information and disclosure process, while at the same time through the power of the Internet the rest of the world is still exploring it and talking about it, and eventually it's going to come out.

And come out it must—not as Harry Potter theology—but as clear cut answers related to what happening in the sky, and why so many people are seeing these things, from former President Jimmy Carter to Fife Symington III, the former governor of Arizona, to major generals and four-star brigadier generals, to your next-door neighbor who happens to glance at the sky, at the crack of dawn, while on her way to work.

CULTS OF THE ALL-SEEING SWAMI

Philadelphia in the 1980s and 1990s was a hotbed of New Age philosophers and do-it-yourself Swamis. Popular at that time was a magazine called *New Frontier*, which covered the waterfront when it came to New Age esoterica. This was well before Philadelphia's "alternative press" reading public adopted atheistic humanism as their intellectual badge of honor. In *New Frontier*, one could read about reincarnation and Edgar Cayce, the healing power of crystals, holistic foods, and the power of Reiki. There were ads for visiting yogis or Indian godwomen (they usually made appearances at the Unitarian church at 21st and Chestnut Street).

The editor and founder of *New Frontier* was Swami Nostradamus Virato, formerly Joseph Bacanskas (some bios list his last name as Banks) but also known as Slimy Tomato. Born into a Lithuanian family in Brooklyn in 1938, he was a smart kid with an introspective and scholastic bent. He first realized that he was able to tap into mystical realms at the age of nine while praying in a Catholic church in Brooklyn. At that time, he said that he saw Jesus Christ come to him in "spiritual physical form."

After completing college, the future Swami entered the corporate world, married, and had three children. His biography states that he was even a member of the local Junior Chamber of Commerce. This is all solid citizen stuff; it certainly had the makings of a future Philadelphia City Council member. Then something happened. Banks walked out on his family in 1972 and adopted the life of a cosmic drifter, a vagabond in search of truth. In 1976, he recalls how he was struck by "two flashes of light from above" while walking in New York City. The experience, he says, allowed him to enter into a "fulfilled state of consciousness" where his intuitive abilities and his attitudes towards life changed. The experience caused him to leave the corporate world in 1979, after which he traveled to India where he studied meditation and eastern philosophy. A year later, he was initiated by the famous guru Osho (Bhagwan Shree Rajneesh) and accepted the new name of Virato.

The name Bhagwan Shree Rajneesh was also making the rounds in Philadelphia at that time. One could go into the homes of astrologers and tarot readers and see Rajneesh's books displayed on book shelves and coffee tables.

This was the time when many people were also chanting *Nam Myōhō Renge Kyō* at Buddhist centers around town. For a while, I tried this myself, practicing the chant at home and then going to meetings, but in the end gave it up because, as the French poet Arthur Rimbaud once noted, we are all a slave to our baptism. Buddhism just was not in my blood.

Osho's Ten Commandments can be summed up at follows:

1. Never obey anyone's command unless it is coming from within you also.
2. There is no God other than life itself.
3. Truth is within you, do not search for it elsewhere.
4. Love is prayer.
5. To become nothingness is the door to truth. Nothingness itself is the means, the goal and attainment.
6. Life is now and here.
7. Live wakefully.
8. Do not swim—float.
9. Die each moment so that you can be new each moment.
10. Do not search. That which is, is. Stop and see.

Osho's biggest teaching tenet was tantric sex, but he also emphasized meditation, mindfulness, love, celebration, and humor. In his tantric sex workshops around the world, his followers engaged in psychotherapeutic orgies where everything was allowed. Incidences of brutality, rape, and death sometimes marred these Lee Strasberg-like method acting sessions, although when a devotee died in a violent workshop, their body was quickly cremated to get rid of the evidence.

Osho was famous for his luxury cars and lush lifestyle, and he often said that if he could not supply the world or his followers with luxury, he could at least make himself happy with luxury. In 1984, Osho predicted that three-quarters of the world would die from AIDS and advised his followers to wear latex gloves and condoms when having sex, but to refrain from kissing. Osho did not subsist on meditation and sex alone but was known to have taken 60 milligrams of valium a day; he was also addicted to nitrous oxide.

Osho's disciple, Virato, was involved in EST and Lifespring, major consciousness raising movements of that era that demanded large sums of money upfront. Although not specifically categorized as religions, EST and Lifespring adherents often did covert missionary work in Philadelphia, even going into gay bars to make "dates" with people they thought would make good followers. When it came time for the "date" to take place, the unsuspecting victim would be driven to a Lifespring meeting. This was also a common practice among some evangelical, fundamentalist Christians at the time.

Virato liked to say that there was "no Tantra school," that Tantra was just a matter of waking up and learning the art of letting go. He once told an interviewer that one could be falling from a tall building and heading past the 32nd floor and if he/she "let go in the Tantra fashion," it would be a wonderful experience. Tantra could also be eating plant-based foods, and its meditation techniques, he claimed, could cure addictions to food, alcohol, and heroin. Virato was against the wearing of colognes or perfumes and was fond of expressing his delight about something by saying, "It was really trippy." He did a lot of work in Russia where he met and married a much younger, slender, long-haired girl named Ludmila Bacanskas, also known as Dhiraja.

Virato often said that there were four kinds of Tantra. "White Tantra" was the Sikh traditional; "yellow Tantra" was Tibetan or Buddhist Tantra; "black Tantra" was the worship of death, sado-masochism, and voodoo; and "red Tantra" was the Tantra of sensuality, of taste and smell. Vitro said that he was a red Tantra fellow, adding "Most of the work I did was very sexually oriented for thirty years."

"Tantra doesn't tell you to control your sexual urges to reach God," Virato wrote, "but rather the opposite. It supports the development of this vital energy to achieve union with Divinity. The essence of Tantra is the full expression of existence … a merging with, rather than a withdrawing from. It is the ultimate yoga which is Sanskrit for union…"

"What about God?" Virato asks in one online video. "I do not believe in God! All beliefs for me are mechanisms by which people are controlled unconsciously or are self-controlled because they are mentally dysfunctional." Then he adds: "How does one believe in the sun? How does one believe in a little puppy dog or a flower? There's nothing to believe. Belief is the blasphemy of truth."

Virato lived on South Street before his departure to Asheville, North Carolina, in 1994. His work at that time included the management of a holistic detoxification and meditation retreat 20 miles outside of Asheville. He felt that Philadelphia was overly crowded and that the region in general was falling victim to dangerous "sprawl." While he seemed to find some peace and comfort in Asheville, he once complained that he had a car stolen one block away from the public access television station where he worked as a producer. He was afraid that Asheville, now that it had been discovered as a rustic mountain sophisticated hide-away, would in time be ruined by its own popularity. In 2007, he complained that "you can't even walk the streets of Philadelphia or New York City."

Virato hated crack smokers and was not a fan of smoking marijuana in the street, so he probably would not be happy with today's Philadelphia where you cannot go anywhere without smelling the brain-cell-destroying odor of marijuana.

"I'm not necessarily in favor of the Iraqi war," he said in 2007, "but I'd like to see some wars in some of the United States of America, like New York, Brooklyn, Philadelphia and Detroit, because everything is about money now."

"We should continue to support AIDS," he told said in 2007, "not AIDS research but support getting AIDS [as a method of population control]."

Virato died on February 2, 2013 in a hospice in Asheville with his wife, Dhiraja Luda, by his side. In one photograph, he is shown lying in repose with a feather in his hand, a happy expression on his face. In one online obituary there were comments both pro and con about his life and legacy.

"Virato was the first person to open my eyes about Tantra back in Philly in the '70s," one woman wrote. "I loved *New Frontier* magazine. He was a bit fake with his approach to Tantra and women including me ... just wanted to seduce whatever he could and pretend to show what Tantra really was. But I am grateful that he opened my eyes to it ... it was actually the beginning of my path..."

OTHER YOGIS AND AVATARS

The question "what does it mean to be a sorcerer and how does a sorcerer differ from a saint?" is a real one. Dionysios Farasiotis, in his book *The Gurus, the Young Man, and Elder Paisios* (St. Herman of Alaska Brotherhood, 2009), elaborates:

> They both work miracles, but who is telling the truth? Who is right? The purpose of my trip to India was to answer these questions by examining matters firsthand. My intention remains fixed. I had gone to the Holy Mountain [Mount Athos], now it was India's turn. I wanted to speak with her holy men face-to-face and be shaped by them, giving them the same opportunity I had given the monks of Athos.

Farasiotis traveled to New Delhi, Haldwani, a small town at the foothills of the Himalayas, in search of holy men. He wrote about the difficulty in traveling in India. He mentioned people crammed into buses, eating, smoking, and sleeping inside. He met swamis who told him that Jesus Christ was a great guru, "whose final ashram and chosen resting place, 'New Jerusalem' was in the Himalayas, to which Christ traveled after preaching in Palestine." His journey, he says, was about a search for truth. "What was truth? Yoga remained very appealing to me. I found Hindu philosophy and practices to be fascinating. This was an exotic universe of mysterious, supernatural phenomena, which attracted me with the allure of the unknown the taste for adventure, and promises of overwhelming magnitude."

Farasiotis had read *Autobiography of a Yogi* by Paramahansa Yogananda and was on the lookout for an advanced yogi named Babaji whom Yogananda referred to as an immortal god and the guru of gurus. Babaji, it was believed, could pass through walls, fly in the air, heal the sick, and raise the dead. When Babaji finally came into view after some searching, Farasiotis writes that he was taken aback because his features were not quite human. "It was clear that his soul was not human at all. I would have found it more credible and less shocking for someone to claim that he were a figment of my imagination or some extraterrestrial being. Everything about him was strangely alien, and his eyes were charged with a terrifying intensity and power."

While watching Babaji, Farasiotis writes that he lost consciousness for a time and he felt like he had been "seized and taken somewhere else." When he came to, he realized that he was "smiling from ear to ear." Farasiotis goes on to explain that the smile felt forced and he felt like he was being controlled by someone else, presumably by Babaji himself who by now was blessing people as they bowed or knelt to worship him. While watching the devotees, Farasiotis says he recalled the First Commandment, "I am the Lord thy God.... Thou shalt have no other gods before Me." Later, when the author had another meeting with Babaji, he made the Sign of the Cross before entering his ashram and asked God to help him. This action set the stage for what happened next. Babaji began to give the author dirty looks and then shrieked "Get out!" Babaji repeated the directive until Farasiotis left the ashram.

THE MAGNIFICENT AMMA: YOU NEVER KNOW
WHO HAS THE POWER

A number of Indian holy men and women have visited Philadelphia for extended stays while touring various U.S. cities. One noted avatar with a devoted following, Amma Sri Karunamayi, has been called the "embodiment of divinity" or the "incarnation of the divine" despite her insistence that she does not see herself as separate from the rest of humanity. Born in 1958 in South India, as a young girl, Amma loved to hear Sanskrit prayers. At twenty-one years of age in 1980, after reducing her intake of food, she traveled on foot to the Penusila Forest where Indians sages have gone to meditate for centuries. She spent years in the mountains, meditating, bathing in streams, and eating wild herbs.

When Amma left the mountains, she realized it was time to spring into action to help relieve suffering in the world. Contemplation and meditation without action is a useless endeavor, she teaches. Her message is generic and straightforward: One must be compassionate, merciful, and kind and be attentive to the plight of the poor.

Amma insists that she is not the head of a new religion and that anyone can come to her for blessings or guidance without giving up their spiritual traditions. The tenets of Hinduism teach that all religions are one and equal.

When Amma visited the First Unitarian Church of Philadelphia at 2125 Chestnut Street sometime in the late 1990s, her devotees were out in force. Only in a Unitarian Church, or perhaps a Friends Meeting House, could you expect to find the carpet rolled out for a Hindu avatar. Unitarian Universalists take great pride in describing themselves as unconventional Christians. Belief in the divinity of Christ for the average Unitarian is an option rather than a point of dogma. One can even be an atheist and be a Unitarian in good standing.

Noted for its extensive educational, cultural, and civic activities, the church at 21st and Chestnut has always been on the cutting edge of social justice programs. Founded in 1796 as the First Unitarian Society of Philadelphia, the present building was designed by Frank Furness for his father, Rev. Dr. William Furness. Martin Luther King, Jr., visited the church while a seminary student in Chester, Pennsylvania, and it is said that actor Kevin Bacon, a church member, had his acting debut there during a Christmas pageant. The church has served as a meeting space for the Americans for Democratic Action, the Islamic Relief Day of Dignity, and aerobics and meditation classes.

It is no wonder that Amma found her way to the church for a massive gathering of her Philadelphia devotees.

On the day that Amma visited 2125 Chestnut Street, I walked to the venue from my nearby Pine Street apartment, eager to discover for myself what the woman was all about. I had read that she could heal people from various ailments and that when she blessed you with sacred oil you came away changed in some way. I wanted to know if I would feel anything when Amma touched me, if there would be any tingling in my spine or any electrical impulses in my fingertips. I was also curious to see if Amma would say something to me when it was my turn to receive her blessing. Her followers called her a "divine mother," a rather ambiguous title that can be interrupted in a number of ways. Certainly as a Christian, I could not entertain the thought that she was a replacement for, or a cosmic antecedent of, the Virgin Mary. At most, I suspected that Amma had clairvoyant insight and "powers" comparable to the old Italian women psychics that used to populate Philadelphia's Italian Market area. When those old women psychics put your hand in theirs, it was not unusual to feel a minor electrical shock as if something was running through your body. These women taught me that clairvoyance and paranormal powers were real despite condemnations from professional skeptic-entertainers like James Randi.

As I entered the First Unitarian Church amid hundreds of Amma's followers, the scent of flowers was overwhelming. The atmosphere was much like that in a Catholic or Orthodox Church at the visitation of some miraculous icon or reliquary. The sense of devotion I saw among Amma's followers was startling.

Amma was seated in front of the Church in a throne-like chair surrounded by garlands of flowers and attendants. It was a scene out of a movie by Cecil B. DeMille: a living, exotic goddess being venerated by hundreds of people. I agonized over whether I should go up and receive her blessing. Would that be a terrible, sacrilegious act? After all, Hinduism, according to classic Christian theology, was paganism in the extreme.

I recalled a passage I had read in Farasiotis' book *The Gurus, the Young Man, and Elder Paisios*:

> Now, I neither liked nor disliked the Swami. I recall that the first time that I laid eyes on her, after waiting in the ashram just for this purpose, I saw through her mystique. I thought it was ridiculous the way the crowd of young people waited so impatiently for her to come out of her room. All of a sudden, she majestically came forth, like a queen emerging from her royal chambers in order to bestow gifts and favors upon her adoring subjects. A need for people to admire her seemed to be behind this second-rate theatrical performance, which I would see repeated on subsequent visits. She briefly glanced at me, but I refused to play the role of an admirer that both she and the others expected me to do. I looked at them for a moment, and then went back to minding my own business. I was disappointed, though I knew I had no reason to assume that all gurus shared the Swami's faults.

While deciding what I should do, I spotted someone I used to work with on Washington Square. "C" had been an avid professional and a very conscientious worker. She was also health conscious in the extreme and a fountain of information when it came to the best organic foods and drinkable spring water. A self-described germaphobe, I used to get a kick out of watching her scrubbing down her phone and headset in her work cubicle at the calling center where we worked.

One day, "C" informed me that her mother was a great devotee of Padre Pio, the Catholic Franciscan saint who received the stigmata of Christ as a young monk in 1918. Padre Pio, who died in 1968, was famous the world over for his paranormal abilities. He was an adept at bi-location, levitation, and seeing the future. People who went to Padre Pio for confession were told of their sins before they opened their mouths, others were healed of terminal cancer, hearing loss, severe bone injuries, and more.

After "C" told me that she grew up in a household devoted to Padre Pio, I began to associate her with the saint. In my mind, I began calling her "Padre Pio's blonde lady, the good worker." Yet here she was at the First Unitarian Church in full Amma mode, meaning that she was an official of sorts, one of the organizers perhaps. I watched her rush about talking to other organizers as everyone made ready for Amma's receiving line to start moving.

I approached "C," reminding myself that I should not mention Padre Pio. That would be an acknowledgement of her past and what she had possibly left behind. Instead I greeted her with, "I'm surprised to see you here, but I read about this Indian woman so much that I just had to come." "C" smiled briefly and uttered something officious, saying the name Amma with a special corrective emphasis, as I had called her "this Indian woman." At that moment, I had to wonder if "C" was keeping her new spiritual allegiance a secret given the devotional aspects of her Italian Christian family.

As I stood in line to receive Amma's blessing—an anointing of oil plus the gift of a scented card with a picture of Amma on it—I noticed that "C" was paying homage to Amma with the reverence of a cloistered nun. I barely knew anything about Amma except the most banal superficialities, and yet here I was about to face her and say a few words, but what those few words would be I had no idea. I did entertain the thought of asking Amma about Padre Pio but instead I asked her to bless the book I was working on. I was desperate for blessings in those days; I also entertained the thought that you never know who has the power.

The years passed. I kept Amma's card in an old book in my library. Often when I would open this old book, the card would fall out and then I would put it in another book, whereupon it would fall out of that book at a later date, and so on until the card had traveled the vast distance of my library. Sometimes I would look at the card when it reappeared and put it to my nose to see if it had retained the scent of flowers that it had when Amma first handed it to me, but it remained as unscented as an old bubblegum-scented baseball card from childhood. I thought many times of throwing Amma's card away, but I somehow always managed to keep it. Whenever the card crossed my path, I would sometimes think of "C" and wonder if she ever found her way back to Padre Pio.

Amma's card emerged shortly before I resolved to write about her for this book. When I spotted it, I went out of my way to put it in a special place so I would not lose it when it came time to do my research, but lose it I did, finally, after all these years.

I lost the Amma card, it seems, the minute I wanted to use it for a comparison of Amma to the Catholic saint named Padre Pio.

Years ago, when I journeyed to a Catholic Benedictine monastery for a week's retreat, I was introduced to a monk who had converted a section of the monastery into a Zen meditation garden. The garden, replete with quaint small fountains and an array of Bonsai trees and rocks, was a scene out of a Buddhist painting. The bearded monk explained that he prayed in the garden by squatting in the lotus position. Ironically, there was an absence of traditional Catholic iconography in the garden. I looked in vain for an icon or a small modernist crucifix, but the garden was Zen in the abstract. The Zen garden, of course, had come about as a result of Trappist monk Thomas Merton's book, *Zen and the Birds of Appetite*, as well as Merton's interest in Near Eastern Buddhism. So called Zen Catholicism was all the rage among certain Catholic intellectuals in the post Vatican II years, helped by a number of books on the subject, such as Dom Aelred Graham's 1963 tome, *Zen Catholicism.*

In an interview with Orthodox Christian monk, Fr. Gabriel Bunge, Nun Cornelia (Rees) asks about Zen practices among Catholic monks. Father Bunge comments follow:

The monks are the ones who practice yoga, Zen, reiki, and so on. When you tell this to Russian monks they are shocked, they can't imagine this is happening. I do not judge them; thank God, it is our Lord Who will judge the world and not me. But it means that people are not looking for a solution, an answer within their own tradition. They are looking outside of it, in non-Christian religions. To me, Catholic monks practicing Zen meditation is like Zen monks praying the Stations of the Cross. It is completely absurd. In Buddhism, suffering has a different origin; it is overcome in a different way from in Christianity. There is no crucified Savior. Why should they meditate on the Stations of the Cross? In those monasteries they have Zen gardens.... But could you imagine the Stations of the Cross in a Zen monastery? Buddhist monks kneeling before the Stations? It's unimaginable.

6

The Empire Cult of Scientology

I get fairly frantic when I contemplate the idiocy of these two goats [Jack Parsons and L. Ron Hubbard].

Aleister Crowley

My introduction to Scientology occurred when I was 19 and traveled to Colorado to visit the family of a former Philadelphia high school friend. After my arrival, my friend's father, Mr. West, offered to take me on a road trip where one of our "must-do" stops would be a visit to a famous Scientology Clear who would cure me of my stuttering and help me in my struggle to free myself from my Catholic upbringing.

Kay, the Scientologist Auditor-Clear, lived in a simple bungalow in a small sprawl of white houses not far from the Las Vegas casino district. *En route*, I kept asking Mr. West if Scientology E-meters hurt when the gizmo was attached to your wrist or if they stuck into the skin like a syringe. Mr. West said it was a meter with wires or straps connected to pulse points.

According to Scientology.org, an E-meter is a religious artifact called an electropsychometer, a calibrated device used for measuring extremely low voltages and psyche, the human soul, spirit, or mind. "The E-Meter measures the spiritual state or change of state a person and thus is of enormous benefit to the auditor in helping the preclear locate areas to be handled. The reactive mind's hidden nature requires the use of a device capable of registering its effects—a function the E-Meter does accurately."

Scientology.org defines Clear as "a state that has never before been attainable in Man's history. A Clear possesses attributes that are fundamental and inherent but not always available in an uncleared state, which have not been suspected of Man and are not included in past discussions of his abilities and behavior."

The Clear is freed from active or potential psychosomatic illness or aberration; self-determined; vigorous and persistent; unrepressed; able to perceive, recall, imagine, create, and compute at a level high above the norm; stable mentally; free with his emotion; able to enjoy life; freer from accidents; healthier; able to reason swiftly; and able to react quickly.

Mr. West had informed me that Kay, as an advanced Clear, was somebody who had washed away all of life's emotional garbage. Scientology, Mr. West reaffirmed, enabled Kay to reset her life on a new path. Her "dark" psychological history— "And indeed she had one," Mr. West confessed—was now a healthy blank slate.

My hope then was that I would not appear too screwed up to Kay, who was purported to be much more adept at dealing with life's vicissitudes than I was. Mr. West, in his desire to help—in retrospect, I can say that he was a well-meaning and true friend—thought that my upbringing as a Catholic had hampered my intellectual and emotional growth. Catholicism, he came very close to saying, had planted its repressive roots in me and was responsible for many hidden psychological damages as well.

Kay was a tall slender woman with brown hair that fell to her shoulders. She wore long delicate Native American earrings. Her welcoming smile suggested that it was possible to live a peaceful and moral life outside the orbit of organized religion. I was positive that she knew something that I did not know and I wanted to know what that something was. Her living room, awash in sunlight and southwest wall tapestries, had a light and airy feel. After Mr. West introduced us, Kay stared into my eyes. I knew that Mr. West had told Kay about me prior to our arrival, but now I wondered what she knew. Kay offered us tea and there was some small talk. I looked around for the E-meter, thinking it might be in a case or box somewhere, or even hanging on the wall like a religious icon or a sadomasochistic device.

"We are in endgame," Kay announced suddenly. "What a fantastic time to be nineteen years old. Everything is about to change. You need a clear slate. This is just wonderful!"

I marveled that sitting before me was a perfect woman who had gotten rid of all her personal baggage. How had she triumphed over the debilitating effects of growing up Mormon! Mr. West, when talking about himself, had always said that he had so much family crap tying him down that it was like a corpse riddled with bullets. Sometimes I wondered if he thought of me in the same way. In Kay's house, I could see that nothing bore any relation to the past I knew in Chester County, Pennsylvania. From the flat stretch of desert that appeared outside her window to the Native American artifacts that decorated her shelves, her past did not exist because she had turned it into an eternal present. I wanted her secret—the secret of Scientology.

I did not then know the dark side of this business-cult-religion, but in time Mr. West would come clean about former Scientology believers who were having trouble extricating themselves from the church. Years after my experience with Kay in the Las Vegas desert, Mr. West would write me and go on full-page rants about "scared and hiding Ex Scientologists who were running from the Church." These stories seemed incomprehensible to me. Catholics, certainly, do not go running after so-called drop outs or apostates. Members of my Irish German family were not sending committed Catholic uncles to abort my Las Vegas odyssey and then force me back to Philadelphia through intimidation tactics.

Sitting in Kay's Las Vegas living room, I wondered if I was up to the task. What did "flushing out" parents and family mean? Sitting there, I felt something close to hatred for my family and for their narrow world that would almost surely condemn me for sitting here with Kay. Flushing them out would not be easy.

"This is not a magical gadget," Kay insisted, finally revealing the cream-colored E-meter that for some reason reminded me of my great aunt's Chevrolet Impala. "The meter will show you where you need to do work." A long tube contained a Velcro-like wrist band, and there were wire ends that plugged on to your skin but held in place by suction cups and tape. It reminded me of a blood pressure pump. Other wires connected to the tips of the fingers. In this way, it connected to your pulse so that when you talked the reader could gage the responses of the needle.

Kay hooked me up, and then Mr. West and Kay began the questioning.

"Can you remember the first time you expressed your natural self and then received recrimination or punishment for it?"

I told Mr. West about wetting the bed as a child. Wetting the bed was about retention, holding things back and then letting them go inappropriately. My stuttering was another issue. Something or someone early on had blocked the flow of words from my mouth, causing me to lose my breath, turn red in the face, and speak as if I was slowly suffocating to death.

"Relive that memory for me now," Kay interjected, leaning forward. For some reason, my eyes drifted to a small Mayan artifact on a bookshelf where L. Ron Hubbard's book, *Dianetics: The Modern Science of Mental Health*, lay open like a bible.

"I was ten years old," I said, going back in time to that family Sunday dinner with Grandma Kelly, a truly saintly woman if there ever was one. "Grandma was seated at the head of the table. Mother had cooked a pot roast and had put out her best silver. Everyone was in good spirits when I blurted out that Grandma reminded me of a spider. We were playing a game where we were supposed to say what people at the table looked like. "

"What made you say a spider?"

"Grandma wore hats with netting in the front. They were popular hats at the time. Some of the netting covered her forehead. When I said that Grandma looked like a spider I was thinking of that netting because it looked like a spider's web."

"What happened after you said Grandma looked like a spider?"

"Father ordered me from the table and told me to go to my room. Then he came upstairs and beat me. He kept beating me until my brother came up and told him to stop. My brother threatened to punch him. Father must have been embarrassed. He stopped."

The E-needle was doing something strange. Both Mr. West and Kay were peering at it like scientists. They went on to ask some highly personal questions. I let everything out—stories about babysitters, and the death of my paternal grandmother and her sister in an automobile accident on my fifth birthday. Kay's ears perked up when I mentioned the accident.

"The needle is really going off," she said. I looked at the little Mayan god and recalled what I remembered of that day: a festive mood in the house with the dining room table set for the dinner and me watching mother ice the birthday cake. Then the phone rang. The heavy black rotary phone with white dials transmitted my aunt's frantic voice: "Tommy, get your mother! Get your Mother!"

The sad story of the double-casket funeral would be told and retold for years: how my aunt, the driver, had unwittingly driven across trolley tracks without paying attention to the stop, look, and listen sign. How a Philadelphia Red Arrow trolley had rammed her side of the car, fatally injuring my grandmother and her sister, my great aunt. Both were taken to the hospital where they died a couple hours apart from one another.

It was hard for me to talk about anything else after this, although Kay kept adjusting dials while Mr. West seemed to observe me with benign indifference.

"Calculations are not good," Kay told Mr. West. "He is going to take a lot of work. I wouldn't suggest his going home again. Prolonged exposure only leads to more layering. This may be his only session. He needs a working alternative."

What were they saying about me?

"We've got that figured out," Mr. West said:

He knows that by reliving past experiences he can get to the root of the problem. We've been talking about this for some time. It's in the writing down of these things that he will free himself. Unfiltered, unembellished, raw autobiography, that's the only way. When he does this he will be able to discover what's holding him back. He has the opportunity to erase the cause and effect and sometimes even the people who helped create the negative fields.

Kay undid the E-meter and replaced it in the box. Mr. West told me that my mission in life was to write about my life in an autobiography as if I had the E-meter strapped to my wrist at all times. Life overhauls are not done overnight, he said. I was glad that I finally had a mission. Although the E-meter was back in the box, I felt a pulsating in my arm and a vague tingling throughout my body. It was as if an energy form was rushing through my cells to every organ and limb in my body. I told Kay and Mr. West that I felt something "electrical."

"It's a process you know," Kay said, flinging back her long hair.

The next thing I knew, I was in Mr. West's car traveling through the desert. We had said a quick goodbye to Kay; Kay had hugged me and wished me luck on my journey. "Remember, you are your own god now," she said. In Mr. West's car, all I could think of was what lay ahead, the work it would take to undo the layers or engrams my family had imposed on me. Mr. West insinuated that if I could not undo the engrams, then I would not succeed in life.

It is Scientology or failure, he seemed to be saying.

The New York Times' 1986 obituary of Hubbard states:

> Clients paid Scientology up to $300 an hour for a one-on-one counseling process, known as auditing. To monitor a client's responses to questions, church staff members use an electrical instrument on the client's skin.
>
> The goal of "auditing," which can go on for years and cost clients hundreds of thousands of dollars, is to increase control over thought processes in a portion of the mind where, Scientologists assert, emotional problems and psychosomatic illnesses are born.

Lafayette Ronald Hubbard was born in 1911 in Nebraska and died in 1986 in California. He was a prolific science fiction and fantasy writer before writing the book that would change his life and earn him millions of dollars, *Dianetics: The Modern Science of Mental Health*. He once said, "You don't get rich writing science fiction. If you want to get rich, start a religion."

A Church of Scientology website describes Dianetics as remaining a bestseller for more than fifty years.

> And with over 20 million copies in print, generating a movement that spans over 100 nations, it's indisputably the most widely read and influential book ever written about the human mind.
>
> Here is the anatomy and full description of the reactive mind, the previously unknown source of nightmares, unreasonable fears, upsets and insecurities which enslave Man. This book shows you how to get rid of it, and so achieve something Man has previously only dreamed of: the State of Clear.
>
> Among the discoveries herein:
> * The Goal of Man
> * The Dynamic Principle of Existence—the one word that motivates all living things
> * The Four Dynamics—the drives upon which all of life is compartmented

- The Descriptive Graph of Survival—revealing one's true potential and how to achieve it
- The discovery of and complete anatomy of the reactive mind
- The painful experiences—engrams—contained in the reactive mind which command one to act irrationally against their own wishes and goals
- The impact of prenatal engrams—what took place before you were born and how it's influenced you ever since
- The complete Dianetics procedure to discover and eradicate these harmful experiences so they never affect you again, revealing the one person you've always wanted to know—you.

Scientology takes many of its metaphysical cues from the occultism of Aleister Crowley. Crowley's famous black magic line, "Do as thou wilt. That is the whole of the law," might be described as the backbone of Scientology. Crowley and Hubbard were friends.

In a diary entry, Crowley writes:

My memory is quite clear that I have been taking heroin continuously for many weeks: three or four does to help me get up, & others practically all day at short intervals. As to Cocaine, I must have had at least two or three prolonged bouts of it every week, plus a few "hairs of the dog" on most of the "off-days." Most of my mental & moral powers were seriously affected in various ways, while I was almost wholly dependent on them for physical energy, in particular for sexual force, which only appeared after unusual excesses, complicated by abnormal indulgence in alcohol. My creative life had become spasmodic & factitious.... I avoided washing, dressing, shaving, as much as possible. I was unable to count money properly, to inspect bills, & so on, everything bored me. I could not even feel alarm at obviously serious symptoms.

L. Ron Hubbard's son, L. Ron Hubbard, Jr., wrote about his father in 1985. In a piece entitled "Philadelphia," he recalls:

We were in Philadelphia. It was November 1952. Dianetics was all but forgotten; Scientology, a new science, had become the focus of attention. Every night, in the hotel, in preparation for the next day's lecture, he'd pace the floor, exhilarated by this or that passage from Aleister Crowley's writings. Just a month before, he had been in London, where he had finally been able to quench his thirst; to fill his cup with the true, raw, naked power of magic. The lust of centuries at his very fingertips.

To stroke and taste the environs of the Great Beast, to fondle Crowley's books, papers, and memorabilia had filled him with pure ecstasy! In London he had acquired, at last, the final keys; enabling him to take his place upon the Throne of the Beast, to which he firmly believed himself to be the rightful heir. The tech gushed forth and resulted in the Philadelphia Doctorate Course lectures.

Scientology was founded in 1950 with the publication of Hubbard's book, *Dianetics*. The book was written in Bay Head, New Jersey, not far from Philadelphia, in a house that has been restored by the Church of Scientology. In 2014, actor John Travolta and his wife, Kelly Preston, attended the dedication ceremonies at 666 East Avenue.

In 2015, *Philadelphia Voice* contributor Kevin C. Shelly wrote about Scientology's connections to Camden, New Jersey:

Created in Camden: the USS *Indianapolis*, the Navy ship sunk soon after delivering the uranium for Little Boy, the first deployed atomic bomb; Campbell's condensed soup; the Victrola phonograph; and later, RCA.

Oh, and one more: Scientology.

Yup, the faith associated with flashy Hollywood—Tom Cruise, John Travolta, Elizabeth Moss, Jenna Elfman, Laura Prepon and recruitment at "Celebrity Centres"—has its roots in blue-collar Camden.

On Dec. 18, 1953, the church's founder, science fiction writer L. Ron Hubbard Sr., and four others, met on the second floor of the Smith-Austermuhl Building at 5th and Market streets in Camden's downtown with lawyer William C. Gotshalk. The two-story brick and marble building, which still exists, housed insurance companies, financial institutions, and several law offices, including Gotshalk's.

Built in 1920, the building sits catty-corner from City Hall and just down the street from the Federal Court House, amid the once-bustling hub of commercial Camden.

In the legal papers signed that day, Hubbard is identified as a resident of Medford Lakes, a secluded borough about 20 miles east of Camden. Hubbard lived in a rented home there for about four months, an odd location for a man whose homes tended toward grandiose. All of the homes in Medford Lakes look as if they are part of a summer camp, with small log cabins ringing shallow lakes. Records show the community had just 434 homes and 1,704 resident in 1953.

Hubbard's son of the same name, and the son's wife, Henrietta, are both listed on the legal documents as Camden residents.

After travels to places that included Los Angeles, Spain and London, Runyon says Hubbard returned to New Jersey, "to one of those log cabins" in Medford Lakes, "where he apparently knew someone" who rented a home to him.

The homeowners group, Medford Lakes Colony, has no record of where Hubbard might have lived, but that's not surprising since he was a short-term renter, says Judy Smith, a resident for the past two decades.

From his Medford Lakes base, Hubbard gave lectures in Philadelphia in September, notes Runyon. The Camden talks began in October 1953.

"I think the area was a central point for printing and some of the groups," interested in Dianetics and Scientology, says Runyon. "And he found buildings available for his lectures. It was a matter of convenience."

By Christmas, Hubbard and his family had left the Camden area, apparently to never return. Scientology's presence in downtown Camden lasted until sometime in 1955. The Founding Church of Scientology in Washington, D.C., opened in July and operations shifted there, says Pouw.

But the Philadelphia region has continuing strong ties to the religion through the church's current leader, David Miscavige, who was born in Bucks County, but grew up in South Jersey's Willingboro, and then Broomall, Delaware County.

In January 2018, *Philadelphia Magazine* reported that the Church of Scientology planned to build an ideal church in Center City Philadelphia:

> Thanks to actress Leah Remini's A&E documentary series on the Church of Scientology, the ridiculously controversial (read: allegations of kidnapping, financial coercion, and physical abuse) religious group that counts among its flock such bona fide celebrities as Tom Cruise and John Travolta, is once again part of the regular news cycle all across the country. And here in Philadelphia, we have our own bit of Scientology news to report: The organization tells *Philadelphia Magazine* that it is moving forward with long-stalled plans to build a huge new Scientology church in Philadelphia.

In Philadelphia, the Church of Scientology bought two properties: the early twentieth-century headquarters of Cunningham Piano Company and an adjacent building on the 1300 block of Chestnut Street in order to create a skyscraper church. There has been no progress on the building to date. The current Philadelphia headquarters of the church is 1515 Race Street, where in 2008, 200 protesters from the group Anonymous protested the Church's alleged abuse of members and ex-members. The mostly circus-like protest occurred on L. Ron Hubbard's birthday and included dancing, protesters dressed in Guy Fawkes masks, horn blowing, and the waving of signs that read: "Ron is Gone but the Con goes on." The church ignored the protests but labeled the Anonymous group "terrorists" and "desperados" in the press.

The number of Scientology adherents in Pennsylvania remains unclear but most estimates have the number between 100,000 and 200,000. Unlike the first Scientology church building in Los Angeles, which resembles a vast Universal Studios like amphitheater with a visitor's information center, reading rooms, classrooms, and a state of the art gym, the Philadelphia center is fairly simple and low key. In the past, L. Ron Hubbard's books were displayed in the front windows of the Philadelphia building, but the practice of putting his books out for all to see seems to have changed. Today, you are more likely to see closed blinds or curtains where the books used to be.

Philadelphia has been disparaged in the past as a city located smack in the middle of the so called Dumb Belt. Although do-it-yourself store front churches exist all over the city, Scientology, a.k.a. the lavish creation of a famous science fiction writer, has always languished on the margins in the City of Brotherly Love despite the bevy of national A-list celebrities like Tom Cruise, John Travolta, and Kristy Alley who crowd the Church in Los Angeles.

In 1991, a *TIME* magazine cover story by Richard Behar, summed up the Church of Scientology this way:

The Church of Scientology, started by science-fiction writer L. Ron Hubbard to "clear" people of unhappiness, portrays itself as a religion. In reality the church is a hugely profitable global racket that survives by intimidating members and critics in a Mafia-like manner. At times during the past decade, prosecutions against Scientology seemed to be curbing its menace. Eleven top Scientologists, including Hubbard's wife, were sent to prison in the early 1980s for infiltrating, burglarizing and wiretapping more than 100 private and government agencies in attempts to block their investigations. In recent years hundreds of longtime Scientology adherents—many charging that they were mentally of physically abused—have quit the church and criticized it at their own risk. Some have sued the church and won; others have settled for amounts in excess of $500,000. In various cases judges have labeled the church "schizophrenic and paranoid" and "corrupt, sinister and dangerous."

7

Hare Krishna to All and To All a Good Cult

What religion isn't a cult?

Howard Stern

God wills a diversity of religions.

Pope Francis

In the 1960s, the Hare Krishna movement was everywhere. One could encounter groups of the saffron-robed monks with shaved heads and thin ponytails in airports, city streets, and public parks. Hare Krishna contingents first appeared in public at anti-war demonstrations and counter-culture events in the late 1960s. This was the age when western, traditionalist religions were being given the boot by people who described themselves as revolutionaries or advocates of political change. The war in Vietnam had caused many young people to rethink their allegiance to God and country the way their parents had done during the period around World War II. "Question Everything" had been enshrined as the quintessential 1960s mantra, and this included religion. The heretofore impenetrable power of Protestant and Catholic Christianity suddenly found their walls crumbling.

Questioning Authority, at least in the Roman Catholic Church, had grown out of the idea of reformatting the role of the Catholic Church in the modern world. This reformatting came to be known as the Second Vatican Council, an attempt by Pope John XXIII to bring an "unchangeable" church into modern times. Release the horses from the stable and there is generally no turning back. Often the expected "change" or modernization went way beyond expectations causing shock and dismay to those who assumed that the end result would be sensibly incremental and not affect unshakeable core values.

New forms are better than old forms: such was the "go to" message of the 1960s prevailing winds. The cult of Near Eastern religions supplanted on western soil had an exoticism exceeded only by the brash smell of patchouli oil worn by countercultural fashionistas.

As Peter, Paul and Mary sang in 1964: "Come mothers and fathers throughout the land/And don't criticize what you can't understand/Your sons and your daughters are beyond your command/Your old road is rapidly agin'/ Please get out of the new one if you can't lend your hand/For the times they are a' changin'!"

Changing indeed, for the old ways of believing were no longer valid for many. Young people searching for answers to the riddle of life no longer felt comfortable seeking answers within the old spiritual forms handed down to them from parents. The more exotic the new form, the better; the more alien and non-western the new form, even better still. In this brave new world, you had seventeen-year-old boys, possibly Vietnam War draftees, reading Zen philosophers like Alan Watts, *The Tibetan Book of the Dead*, Aldous Huxley's *The Doors of Perception*, and works by Herman Hesse, especially *Steppenwolf* and *Siddhartha*. The young were intent on finding their own truth and their own way through the spiritual underbrush, yet many came to the realization that cultivating a spiritual path can be a lonely and confusing endeavor. Many came to realize that they needed structure and some kind of community with like-minded believers with whom to share their beliefs.

Hare Krishna provided that spiritual niche for many seekers. It was eastern and exotic; it meant shaving your head and wearing a small pony tail; donning orange saffron robes; painting a stripe or two on your face. It meant separating yourself from a material-based culture and giving up much of your individual identity for the sake of the collective. In many ways, it was the perfect spiritual home for the disaffected hippie.

The Krishna Temple was also a far more refined and transcendental space than those free love-based hippie communes whose only code of ethics seemed to be *The Whole Earth Catalog*. Ironically, the Krishna moral code—the rules and regulations governing how individual devotees should behave—were as orthodox as the rules in Christian monastic communities. Krishna devotees were expected to be celibate if not married, and sexual outlets like masturbation and homosexuality were forbidden. A Krishna marriage was expected to last a lifetime; the idea was to produce children rather than design a cozy birth control plan for the comfort of the parents.

Swami Prabhupāda's views on homosexuality ignited many different reactions. A Wikipedia entry on Hare Krishna and sexual orientation, for instance, states that the founder of the International Society for Krishna Consciousness, A. C. Bhaktivedanta Swami Prabhupāda, taught that illicit sexual inclinations were "abominable."

Writing in a May 16, 1975, letter to Lalitananda dasa, Prabhupāda said:

> I am very sorry that you have taken to homosex. It will not help you advance in your attempt for spiritual life. In fact, it will only hamper your advancement. I do not know why you have taken to such abominable activities.... Even though you are in a very degraded condition Krishna, being pleased with your service attitude, can pick you up from your fallen state. You should stop this homosex immediately. It is illicit sex, otherwise, your chances of advancing in spiritual life are nil.

But an article posted on the GALVA, Gay and Lesbian Vaishnava Association site, Śrīla Prabhupāda and the Gays, is much more charitable in its assessment:

> Over the past few years it has become commonplace for devotees to depict Śrīla Prabhupāda as very hateful and condemning of gays. What a great disservice this has been to His Divine Grace! I suspect this is more a reflection of the mentality of such devotees themselves, and not that of Śrīla Prabhupāda. As far as I have seen, Śrīla Prabhupāda's exchanges with homosexual friends and disciples were always exceptionally loving and kind. Indeed, he was quite caring toward them and displayed a great deal of concern that they feel welcome and included in his Krishna consciousness movement.
>
> It is very sad that this loving attitude has become mostly absent today among many of Śrīla Prabhupāda's disciples and followers. Devotees seem obsessed only with the sexual aspect of homosexuality, while failing to address the more important human and personal considerations emphasized by Śrīla Prabhupāda himself. A pure devotee always looks for the good qualities in others, while foolish neophytes take delight in pointing out faults and weaknesses. In regard to gays and lesbians, Śrīla Prabhupāda personally taught us how to receive and treat them, so why not simply listen and follow his example?

But Krishna Temple sexual ethics differed very little from standard Christian and Orthodox Jewish practice but its non-western exoticism made it an easier pill for some to swallow. To an outsider, a Krishna Temple might be described as a strange, dolled-up place where one saw sculptural deities with lavishly painted eyes buried in garlands of flowers or jewels and mounted on altars or floats. The Hare Krishna chant, that intoxicating "Hare Krishna, Hare Krishna, Krishna Krishna, Hare Hare/Hare Rama, Hare Rama, Rama Rama, Hare Hare" made popular by George Harrison of The Beatles, became for many a kind of transcendental drug, a bubble-building spiritual cocoon that helped fortify one against the travails of the world. But one cannot stay in a religion forever if the reason you are there in the first place is because of its exotic allure. Eventually, the newness will wear thin and you will be face-to-face with the religion's substantive core or lack of a substantive core. Smoke and mirrors always gives way to reality. The Krishna Temple vegetarian feasts, after all, attracted and continue to attract many Temple outsiders who did not identify as Krishna believers at all. For these people, a Krishna experience is mainly about "the food." That is why for many young men and women in the 1960s and '70s, Krishna Temples were rites of passage experiences: it made sense in those hippie counterculture days for a smart young man intent on bucking the *status quo* to do a stint in a Vermont hippie commune, work a month or two with the Socialist Workers Party, then take a month-long Ken Keasey-style road trip (complete with psychedelic experimentation), and then finally do five months in a Krishna Temple.

The regular appearance of Hare Krishna groups at rock concerts and antiwar events in Philadelphia during the height of the countercultural era was for me an indication that some people were beginning to see the limits of free love and the doing your own thing. In those days, I saw the emergence of Hare Krishna as a barometer of things to come. Often I would ask myself: in an era of total personal freedom, why were some young people, at the zenith of their youth and beauty, turning away from the human appetites and opting for a life of harsh self-discipline and denial?

Hare Krishna Temple communes—minus the inclusion of women—were very much like a Roman Catholic or Eastern Orthodox monasteries. Devotees rose early, spent hours chanting in prayer, ate a restricted vegetarian diet, and were expected to perform certain tasks for the benefit of the community. This lifestyle of complete surrender and dedication to a religious ideal was certainly the opposite of the poetic mantras offered up by poet Allen Ginsberg, who, while chanting Hare Krishna, was also writing poems like, "This Form of Life Needs Sex."

As someone brought up Roman Catholic, the idea of venerating a plethora of strange-looking Indian deities, some with multiple arms and legs, some depicted as little children, was tantamount to embracing the mythology of a faraway galaxy. Nevertheless, I visited the Germantown-Mt. Airy Krishna Temple (ISKCON of Philadelphia) several times in the 1970s. I went because of the food and because a particularly hip vegetarian friend (who drank too much) liked the chanting, incense, and cymbal clanging prior to the splendid vegetarian feast. For many of the Temple guests chanting "Hare Krishna" was not seen as a "real" prayer at all; it was certainly not on a par with the Rosary or the Orthodox prayer beads in which the Jesus Prayer is repeated many times: "Lord Jesus Christ, Son of God, have mercy on me, a sinner."

The Hare Krishna mantra seemed to me to be more like a "soft-shoe" rendition of prayer as well as an incentive to dancing. Hearing the mantra over a long stretch of time did seem to put people into a kind of trance. I noticed that I felt a compulsion to dance like the monks despite the fact that Krishna meant nothing to me. Krishna was a just a made-up doll on a pedestal; he could certainly not compete with the strong panoply of Catholic saints that I had grown up with.

During my time at Temple feasts, I noticed that many of the devotees seemed to be excessively skinny people; some in fact were sickly looking in that over the top vegan way, although I did spot the occasional hefty devotee who was probably consuming too many carbohydrates. The hefty monks certainly were not getting fat eating city pizza. Or were they?

The International Society for Krishna Consciousness (ISKCON) Mt. Airy Temple was founded in 1969 when Indian Swami Śrīla Prabhupāda sent a disciple to Philadelphia to establish a temple. That disciple was Subala Dasa Swami who wrote in 1973:

We are not Christians, Jews, Hindus or Moslems, for these are all bodily designations. Because I have taken my birth in a Christian family I think I am a Christian, but I do not know that in my next life I may be a Buddhist or something else. A Christian may convert to become a Jew, or a Hindu may become a Moslem. These are all temporary designations having to do with the body. Therefore, they are not the one true eternal religion of all.

Śrīla Prabhupāda was born in Calcutta in 1896 and died in 1977. As the founder of Krishna Consciousness or ISKCON, he believed his mission in life was to spread Gaudiya Vaishnavism, a school of Hinduism. He established his first temples in London, New York and San Francisco.

ISKCON Philadelphia first established itself in a rowhouse in West Philadelphia. In 1972, the temple relocated to a Germantown rental house, switching then to a bought property on Germantown's Woodland Street in 1974. In 1974, Śrīla Prabhupāda came to Philadelphia for the Rathayatra parade and festival. Rathayatra, or the Chariot Festival of India, is an annual event with floats, music, dancing, and vegetarian food. The event attracts hundreds, sometimes thousands of spectators. After Prabhupāda's visit, the congregation grew so that in 1977 the temple was able to purchase its present location in Mt. Airy, taking over the former Gresheim Arms Hotel.

The relatively benign Hare Krishna cult attracted the respect and admiration of some leading Protestant theologians, including Harvey Cox. Cox, born in 1929, was professor of theology at Harvard Divinity School. In the 1960s, he achieved international prominence after the publication of his book, *The Secular City*. In 2009, the ISKCON News service printed an announcement of Cox's retirement from Harvard University:

Dr. Cox, who was with Harvard for 44 years beginning in 1965, spoke in defense of ISKCON during the anti-cult propaganda days of the 1970s and '80s. He once visited a group of concerned parents before the New York Ratha-yatra festival in 1977 and also spoke at the event. "As far as I can see," he once said, "Deprogrammers are simply hired-guns. They will deprogram anybody you pay them to deprogram."

Dr. Cox also held tremendous respect for ISKCON's founder. "The life of Śrīla Prabhupāda is pointed proof that one can be a transmitter of truth and still be a vital and singular person," he wrote in his forward to *Śrīla Prabhupāda-līlāmṛta*. "Śrīla Prabhupāda is, of course, only one of thousands of teachers. But in another sense, he is one in a thousand, maybe one in a million."

In 2009, former Hare Krishna member Elliot Miller wrote about his experiences in the cult in a piece called "Inside Iskcon." Miller wrote:

Swami Bhaktivedanta came to America in 1965. I joined in 1971, and it was that same philosophy that was being preached. In '71 and '72, we were still going out, but the people were not coming. I mean, there were people joining the movement, it was growing; but only young people, and only those who wanted to cut themselves off from society—the hippies, the people who were into back-packing, "back to the farm," you know; not the mainstream types of people. Lawyers were not starting to chant Hare Krishna. Businessmen were not putting their attaché cases down and joining us in the street. So the guru had been here for nine years preaching this message, and it wasn't grabbing; it wasn't catching on the way he had envisioned it would.

Miller continues:

So he came to New York's lower east side (Greenwich Village) and sat down on a little rug in Tompkins Square Park and started chanting with little hand cymbals—very quaint, very ascetic, very attractive to the late 1960's hippies who were already possessed by LSD and all kinds of hallucinogenic influences, and they really took to it. And this was his message: All we've got to do is just sit out here in the park and chant and distribute these little sweet foods that are offered to Krishna to people as they go by. By eating this sanctified food and by hearing the vibration of the names of Krishna (God), everyone's heart will become cleansed of all the dust, all the material desires that have been piling up for hundreds of thousands of years in countless lifetimes. So all these people walking by in the park, all these executives going to work, they will hear you chanting, they will be "zapped" by the vibration, and their hearts will become cleansed and purified.

Like Miller, I often observed that the joiners of the Hare Krishna movement were misfits, loners, and back-to-nature types, sensitive men searching for meaning. Of course, the same thing could also be said about Christian men who enter monasteries. Secularists, of course, could say the same thing about anyone who feels a need to join a church or religious organization. Belief in a deity or dependence on religion to get through life is seen by many as a weakness, the proverbial crutch as they say.

I am reminded of my old friend James, who lived alone with his father after his mother's death, and who seemed lost from the moment I met him. I happened to be renting an apartment in the same Port Richmond house where James and his father lived on the first floor. James was outside on the porch when we were first introduced. He was reading Alan Watts and had just left the Mt. Airy Krishna temple, the reason, he later told me, for his unusually short burr haircut. In many ways, he looked to me like the typical Hare Krishna young male recruit of the time: pale skin, white blond hair, a cluster of acne on his face, and sea shallow green eyes. As shy as a feral cat that had been abused, when you talked to James you had to draw him out. When we got to know one another better, he opened up and became more forthcoming and, as a token of our friendship, handed me an envelope containing his white blond Hare Krishna pony tail that he had clipped off when he left the temple. Long after I lost track of James after his enlistment in the Army and deportment to Vietnam, I would open the envelope, take out the pony tail, and hope that he was still alive.

In 2016, a *Washington Post* article, entitled "After 50 years, Hare Krishnas are no longer white hippies who proselytize in airports," reported:

> Back then, members of the Hare Krishna faith—more formally known as ISKCON or the International Society of Krishna Consciousness—were mostly young, white hippies drawn to a new version of counterculture spirituality. They gave up their jobs and their homes and then gave up alcohol and drugs and extramarital sex. They went to live in remote communes and proselytized to strangers in airports.

The *Post* went on to say that on the fiftieth anniversary of this homegrown religion, something remarkable had happened. "After waves of migration to the United States from India over the past two decades, the vast majority of Hare Krishna's believers in America are no longer white Americans. They're Indian immigrants … who hold down regular jobs and drive to temples to worship, rather than live in communes."

One Krishna devotee at Philadelphia's Mt. Airy temple, Vishnugada dasa, says he "got into" ISKCON after reading J. D. Salinger's novel *Franny and Zooey* in 1970 while in college. A theme of the book asked the question if it was possible to pray constantly and the Jesus Prayer was offered as a solution. Vishnugada dasa says that he began to say the "Jesus Prayer" until he met some Hare Krishnas at an event a few days later and was told that chanting the Hare Krishna mantra was "the same thing."

Who is Krishna? Krishna, according to ISKCON, "is a beautiful youth with a glowing complexion the color of rain clouds. He plays a flute, attracting the hearts of all, and His smile is enchanting. He wears a peacock feather in His curly black hair and a flower garland around His neck."

Beautiful youths, you might say, are a dime a dozen, but who is Krishna really? Nick Gier, Professor Emeritus at the University of Idaho, writes in *Krishna and Christ, Hindu and Christian Saviors*, that Krishna was born 3,000 years ago:

> There are many striking and instructive similarities between Krishna and Christ. Both were miraculously conceived; both had royal genealogies; both were threatened with death by a wicked ruler. Krishna and Christ were human incarnations of a triune God; both were tempted by demons; both worked miracles; both transfigured themselves; and both predicted their own deaths.
>
> Krishna and Christ rose from death and ascended into heaven. Christ died a gruesome death on a cross, while Krishna died, Achilles-like, by an arrow to his heel (left). Both Christianity and the religion of Krishna are theologies of grace. Krishna's favor, however, appears to go further than Christ's. In his battle with demons, Krishna dispatches them to heaven after killing them. The hunter who accidentally kills Krishna is also forgiven all of his karmic debt.
>
> Krishna is the eighth incarnation of the Hindu God Vishnu, who, according to Hindu belief, has come in every cosmic age to save humankind from its sin and folly. Perhaps in an attempt to gain favor with India's Buddhists, Hindus decided that Vishnu's ninth incarnation was Lord Buddha, whom the Hindu Gandhi called the greatest ever teacher of non-violence.

For the Krishna community, Jesus Christ and Lord Krishna are one and the same being. ISKCON's *Back to Godhead* publication points out:

- Both are believed to be sons of God since they were divinely conceived
- The birth of both Jesus of Nazareth and Krishna of Dwarka and their God-designed missions were foretold
- Both were born in unusual places—Christ in a lowly manger and Krishna in a prison cell
- Both were divinely saved from death pronouncements
- Evil forces pursued both Christ and Krishna in vain
- Christ is often depicted as a shepherd; Krishna was a cowherd
- Both appeared at a critical time when their respective countries were in a torpid state
- Both died of wounds caused by sharp weapons—Christ by nails and Krishna by an arrow
- The teachings of both are very similar—both emphasize love and peace
- Krishna was often shown as having a dark blue complexion—a color close to that of Christ Consciousness.

Seraphim Rose, a Russian Orthodox monk and author *of Orthodoxy and the Religion of the Future,* writes of how Hinduism came to the United States and influenced Christianity:

> In 1893 an unknown Hindu monk arrived at the Parliament of Religions in Chicago. He was made a stunning impression on those who heard him, both by his appearance—beturbaned and robed in orange and crimson—and by what he said. He was immediately lionized by high society in Boston and New York. Philosophers at Harvard were mightily impressed. And it wasn't long until he had gathered a hard core of disciples who supported him and his grandiose dream: the evangelizing of the Western world by Hinduism, and more particularly, by Vedantic (or monistic) Hinduism. Vedanta Societies were established in the large cities of this country and in Europe. But these centers were only a part of his work. More important was introducing Vedantic ideas into the bloodstream of academic thinking. Dissemination was the goal. It mattered little to Vivekananda whether credit was given to Hinduism or not, so long as the message of Vedanta reached everyone. On many occasions he said: Knock on every door. Tell everyone he is Divine.
>
> Today parts of his message are carried in paperbacks that you can find in any bookstore—books by Aldous Huxley, Christopher Isherwood, Somerset Maugham, Teilhard de Chardin, and even Thomas Merton.
>
> Thomas Merton, of course, presents himself as a contemplative Christian monk, and his work has already affected the vitals of Roman Catholicism, its monasticism. Shortly before his death, Father Merton wrote an appreciative introduction to a new translation of the Bhagavad Gita, which is the spiritual manual or "Bible" of all Hindus, and one of the foundation blocks of monism or Advaita Vedanta. The Gita, it must be remembered, opposes almost every important teaching of Christianity. His book on the Zen Masters, published posthumously, is also noteworthy, because the entire work is based on a treacherous mistake: the assumption that all the so-called "mystical experiences" in every religion are true. He should have known better. The warnings against this are loud and clear, both in Holy Scripture and in the Holy Fathers.

Rose, of course, is coming from an Orthodox Christian point of view which may be problematic for the neutral spiritual seeker. Rose's perspective, however, cannot be dismissed as dogma-speak.

The message of Vedanta is essentially this: All religions are true, but Vedanta is the ultimate truth. Differences are only a matter of "levels of truth." In Vivekananda's words: "Man is not travelling from error to truth, but climbing up from truth to truth, from truth that is lower to truth that is higher. The matter of today is the spirit of the future. The worm of today—the God of tomorrow. The Vedanta rests on this: that man is God. So it is for man to work out his own salvation." Vivekananda put it this way: "Who can help the Infinite? Even the hand that comes to you through the darkness will have to be your own."

In 1969, Śrīla Prabhupāda came to Philadelphia to lecture at Temple University. This followed his 1965 visit to the University of Pennsylvania where he met with Professor Norman Brown. He explained to Brown the meaning of Vedanta: Veda, he said, means knowledge and Anta means end, so Vedanta means the end of knowledge. About skeptics, he was harsh: "Skepticism, they do not believe in anything—everything is false. They are so disappointed, they think everything is false. We are not going to deal with such men. What's the use?" He reiterated time and time again that "The living entity, the Spirit soul, is by nature happy." Philadelphia's first Rathayatra festival was in 1970 when the small Krishna deities rode in procession on a decorated cigar box.

Śrīla Prabhupāda returned to Philadelphia again on July 11, 1975. After flying in from a Denver celebration, he took to the streets of Center City with his devotees. *The Philadelphia Inquirer* and other city newspapers reported on the visit and Prabhupāda's talk in the park behind the Philadelphia Museum of Art. While the parade made its way through downtown, office workers came out in droves to see what was going on and bystanders, caught up in the Hare Krishna chants, danced *en masse* in the streets. *Back to Godhead* reported: "Hecklers, Christian fundamentalists with big banners reading 'Get smart, get saved!' and 'Repent or Burn' were ineffectual amid the large crowd and the uproarious kirtana."

The many spiritual questions addressed to Prabhupāda included what happens to human beings after death. "In the human form, the soul can choose to go back to the spiritual world or to suffer birth after birth in the material world. But why should we remain in this material body and undergo repetition, change of body? Let us have our original spiritual body. That is wanted. That is intelligent."

The following day, Prabhupāda spoke to two Philadelphia reporters. According to *Back to Godhead*, one reporter was a freelance writer, Ms. Sandy Nixon, and the other, a Ms. Jones, was from *The Philadelphia Inquirer*. When Prabhupāda noticed Jopa beads around Ms. Nixon's neck, he felt he had an ally. "Krishna consciousness is already there in everyone's core of heart," he said. Then Ms. Nixon asked: "How do you feel about Women's Lib?" Prabhupāda replied that he saw that "the criterion for intelligence wasn't material. One's sex, race or nationality—but it was one's desire for spiritual life." *The Inquirer* reporter kept hitting him with Women's Liberation questions but Prabhupāda continually frustrated her with his responses.

Upsetting feminists even more, Prabhupāda equated abortion with murder.

During a discussion with a professor of religion (Hinduism) from Temple University, Prabhupāda asked the professor, "What is that Hinduism?" referring to his job title, to which the professor replied, "I don't know. You tell me what Hinduism is." The question was asked again and went nowhere until the professor said, "You teach me!" At this point, Prabhupāda, visibly annoyed, said: "A spiritual master is not your servant. First you become shaven-headed like my students, then I will teach you. You have to offer your obeisances and surrender to the spiritual master. Then he will reveal the truth."

Back to Godhead reported that the reporters' questions had been "asked in the typical reporters' attitude of irreverence and interrogation."

During his 1975 U.S. tour, Prabhupāda was reported by *Back to Godhead* to have made the following comment on political leaders: "The common man has no sense whom to elect; he proves this by electing an unqualified leader and later trying to change him or pull him down. Meanwhile, thousands of bureaucrats live off the taxes of the people and spend their time planning how to keep themselves in power."

On the flight from Philadelphia to Berkeley in 1975, *Back to Godhead* reported that the Captain of the United Airlines jet that took Prabhupāda from Philadelphia to Berkeley, California, talked with His Divine Grace:

Later on, Prabhupāda recalled the conversation. The captain asked that if God is all good, then why is there evil in the world? "I explained that for God there is no evil, just good. Just as my chest is as important to me as my back; if there is pain in my back I take care of it. I do not ignore it thinking that the front is more important. Evil is compared to the back of God. It is not different from His front, or goodness."

Then the question came, "If everything is good from God's point of view, then how can there be evil?" I gave another example to explain. It is just like the sun. On the body of the sun there is no shadow. We create shadow by turning our back to the sun. Similarly, when we turn away from God there is evil.

8

Tea for Two:
The Cult of Theosophy

Everything in the Universe, throughout all its kingdoms, is conscious: i.e., endowed with a consciousness of its own kind and on its own plane of perception.

Madame Blavatsky

In the late 1970s, I lived for a time in a second-floor apartment in a building that also served as the headquarters for the West Chester, Pennsylvania, Theosophical Society. The unusually shaped apartment looked out over the center of town. It also had a unique design: French doors that separated the living room from the bedroom and the large, suburban-style kitchen. A long narrow hallway ran from the kitchen to the bathroom. The one remaining apartment in the building was occupied by a Vietnam vet who shaved his head bald despite visible scars from injuries suffered during the war. Occasionally, this neighbor would ask me to shave his head clean with a razor, so for a time I became an amateur barber.

In a deal with the landlord to lower the rent, I cleaned and swept the offices of the Theosophical Society rooms. These rooms were decorated with Victorian-era sofas, various-sized mahogany and walnut tables, and different-sized lecterns. The windows were outfitted in thick drapery. The oriental rugs were bright and colorful, the lamps oddly Victorian with their heavily tasseled lampshades. There were two antique desks that displayed small framed pictures of various personages, the most prominent being Madame Blavatsky. There was a small library and various figurines—a Buddha, an Indian deity with eight arms, and miniaturized Far Eastern building replicas.

The rooms were rarely dirty, but I vacuumed the floors anyway and dusted the framed images, especially the larger portraits of Madame Blavatsky and Henry S. Olcott, the founders of the Theosophical Society, which hung over the fireplace in the main room.

The landlord liked to say that I had the makings of a Theosophist and urged me to attend the weekly meetings of the society. While I never followed up on his suggestion—one reason was that most of the women members seemed to resemble Eleanor Roosevelt—while cleaning the rooms, I would often put my dust pan and brush aside and stare into the eyes of the Madame Blavatsky portrait. Sometimes I would look at the portrait as if waiting for a revelation. But Madame never reached out to me; she never spoke; she never made one of the doors slam shut or an artifact fly across the room. Nothing happened, ever—there was no ray of light that sprung forth from her eyes, unlike the crucifix that came to life in front of Saint Francis of Assisi as the monk prayed in his monastery's chapel.

Fairly well read and experienced in the world of spirit visitations, Theosophy's emphasis on the existence of another world within our own did not frighten me. Dangerously ill as a child with double pneumonia, one day I thought I discerned an image of Saint Thérèse of Lisieux emerging from the white wall in front of my sickbed. The shadowy figure never quite "came off" but it hovered in the paint as a suggestion, an idea that something might be emerging.

Stories of spirit manifestations in the Nickels family were not uncommon. For years, my great aunt spoke of waking up one morning and seeing her deceased brother, John, dressed in white, seated in the rocking chair near her bed. She said she could clearly see her brother for a couple of minutes before the vision disappeared. Years ago, while working as a reporter for a local newspaper, I had an assignment to interview the owner of an Atlantic City B&B, a project that required me to spend the night in the house before the interview.

That night in the B&B, I dreamt that a traditionally robed Catholic nun put her face up to mine and hugged me in the most beneficent way. The dream was powerful, so much so that I told my press companion the next morning that a "nun had visited me in my sleep and squeezed me into her wimple." Later, during a tour of the house, I noticed a small stained-glass window by a stairway landing. When I asked the proprietor the meaning of the window, he said that in the 1920s and 1930s the house used to be a convent.

The first Theosophical Society was founded in New York in by Blavatsky and Colonel Henry Steel Olcott. Olcott met Blavatsky in 1874. Blavatsky was already famous as a clairvoyant. The pair met in Vermont where Olcott, an attorney-turned-journalist, had gone to investigate the Eddy Brothers, both self-proclaimed clairvoyants and mediums. Olcott was at that point a diehard skeptic along the lines of today's James Randi. His search for hard facts (empirical evidence) no doubt had its roots in his position as the head of the commission, which investigated the assassination of Abraham Lincoln. With his mutton-chop whiskers and pince-nez spectacles, Olcott took to Blavatsky; Blavatsky in turn took Olcott under her wing and became his mentor. The result was astounding. Olcott became a firm believer, and, together with Blavatsky, the pair worked to gather and diffuse knowledge of the laws that govern the universe.

Blavatsky believed that "The whole universe is filled with spirits," and that there was "a latent spirit in all matter."

Edward Hower, in an article on Olcott for the *Smithsonian*, wrote about the composition of one of Blavatsky's most famous book, *Isis Unveiled*:

> The author claimed that most of her book had been dictated to her by various "Masters," extraordinary men, some of them long dead, who for centuries had been guarding secret knowledge in Egypt, India and Tibet. They communicated with her telepathically, she said, using astral currents. They also wrote letters, some of which dropped from the ether into Colonel Olcott's lap as he sat working across from her at their desk. Needless to say, non-Theosophical historians cast considerable doubt upon the telepathic origin of these letters. But the Colonel duly reported their contents with great excitement.

"Spirits do not communicate through healthy persons," Blavatsky maintained. "Spirits are forever seeking a body to inhabit, seize on those which are defective, being unable to control those which are not. In the East, insane persons are regarded with peculiar veneration, as being possessed by spirits."

A reporter once asked Blavatsky if being possessed by spirits meant being possessed by the devil. She answered, "No ... Daimon is the word in Scripture and it doesn't necessarily mean a devil. It may mean a god. Socrates had a Daimon, and he certainly was not possessed by a devil."

Madame Blavatsky would eventually retreat to India with Olcott (Olcott would later separate from Blavatsky and branch out on his own) to establish the headquarters for the first Theosophical Society. Prior to India, Madame Blavatsky moved to Philadelphia in November 1874.

"The more respectable members of her society spent much of their time apologizing for her behavior," wrote Joy Dixon in *Divine Feminine, Theosophy and Feminism in England*:

> Her outspokenness, her vulgarity, and her refusal to abide by the niceties of drawing-room etiquette. Some wondered audibly why the new revelation had not been conveyed through someone rather more genteel, to which Blavatsky responded, "I do not care about public opinion. I despise thoroughly and with all my heart Mrs. Grundy."

For a time, Blavatsky lived in a brownstone at 3420 Sansom Street in West Philadelphia that later became a noted Philadelphia restaurant, the White Dog Café, founded by in 1983 by Philadelphia social activist Judy Wicks. The restaurant adopted the name White Dog because Blavatsky refused to cure a serious infection of the leg by following doctors' orders to have it amputated but instead had a white dog lie across her leg while she slept. Within a short time, the leg was cured and the amputation question became mute.

The Philadelphia headquarters of the United Lodge of Theosophists, at 1917 Walnut Street, has been in operation since 1945. The United Lodge of Theosophists was founded in 1909 by Robert Crosbie (1849–1919) as an offshoot of the Theosophical Society mainly to preserve the writings of William Q. Judge, an Irishman born in Dublin. Judge's most famous book, *The Ocean of Theosophy*, was published in 1893. Theosophy gave birth to a number of schisms and different brands of the movement. Judge, for instance, believed that Olcott and Annie Besant (who rose to prominence after Blavatsky's death in 1891) deviated from the original teachings of Blavatsky's Mahatmas (or teachers). Olcott and Besant's organization—Theosophical Society-Udyar—is based in India while Judge's organization, the Theosophical Society, is based in Pasadena, California.

Another schism occurred when Ernest Temple Hargrave formed the Theosophical Society in America. Other schisms arose, namely the Temple of the People, which broke from Hargrave's branch, and the United Lodge of Theosophists (ULT) formed in 1909.

Critics of Theosophy often cited the dangers of theosophists joining the "ranks of faddists and cranks." Others criticized the unconventional dress of Theosophists.

In 1911, Montague R. St. John wrote to *The Vahan*, a publication devoted to the exchange of Theosophical news and opinion that theosophists had to know when to pull back. He wrote that a vegetarian or fruitarian diet "was harmful to European bodies," adding that "There's no reason why members of the Theosophical Society should attract attention and excite ridicule by dressing in a markedly unconventional and occasionally totally inartistic manner."

Writer/novelist George Orwell wrote about how to dispel "the smell of crankishness" he observed within Theosophical circles with a socialist bent. "If only the sandals and the pistachio-coloured shirts could be put in a pile and burnt, and every vegetarian, teetotaler, and creeping 'Jesus' sent home to Welwyn Garden City to do his yoga exercises quietly!" Orwell believed that Socialists attracted cranks of every sort to their meetings, "every fruit-juice drinker, nudist, sandal-wearer, sex maniac, Quaker, 'Nature Cure' quack, pacifist, and feminist in England."

Judge recorded his impressions when meeting Madame Blavtsky for the first time in January 1875:

> It was her eye that attracted me, the eye of one whom I must have known in lives long passed away. She looked at me in recognition for that first hour, and never since has that look changed. Not as a questioner of philosophies did I come before

her, not as one groping in the dark for lights that schools and fanciful theories had obscured, but as one who, wandering through the corridors of life, was seeking the friends who could show where the designs for the work had been hidden. And, true to the call, she responded, revealing plans once again, and speaking no words to explain, simply pointed them out and went on with the task. It was as if but the evening before we had parted, leaving yet to be done some detail of a task taken up with one common end; it was teacher and pupil, elder brother and younger, both bent on the one single end, but she with the power and knowledge that belong but to lions and sages.

Madame Blavatsky, glad to be in Philadelphia in 1894, wrote: "America is the best and the worst, the kindest and most abusive country in the world." But she was a difficult woman who often in her later years referred to herself as "an old hippopotamus." Her general method of dress was loose flowing garments with a definite Indian cut. She called the spirits she communicated with "brothers." In her daily life, friends pointed out that she exhibited no traces of asceticism. At her citizenship naturalization ceremony on July 8, 1878, she described herself as a Buddhist. Olcott also described himself as a Buddhist. When she lived in New York City at 46 Irving Place, she was known as "the famous heathen of Eighth Avenue." On leaving New York City for India in December 1878, she remarked: "I shall go to Bombay, and be with my dear heathen who are free from the yoke of Christianity at least."

Many people wanted to know what her thoughts on Jesus Christ were. When one woman inquired about the "nature" of Christ, Madame Blavatsky answered: "Madame, I have not the honor of the gentleman's acquaintance."

Born into an aristocratic Russian family (she was a baroness), when Madame Blavatsky went into a trance sometimes she was known to have held a small Russian three-bar cross. Many described her as "a great Russian bear," and "a smart woman but ignorant of all the graces and amenities of life." She was described as "generous appearing" (when observers wanted to use the word "fat") and brusque in her general manner. She was a chronic chain smoker, with cigarette papers in one pocket and tobacco stuffed in another. One observer wrote: "The cigarettes were countless and the flowerpots were full of stubs." She is said to have smoked 200 cigarettes a day. Others marveled at her intensity. "Never have I seen such an intense creature, intense in purpose, intense in her endeavor."

When she was writing her first book, *Isis Unveiled*, she wrote twenty-five pages per day. *Isis Unveiled* can be summed up as an investigation of the origins of Christianity, including a study of the teachings of the gnostic sects of the first centuries, and an explanation of the mystery of Jesus, despite the fact that Madame Blavatsky had never "met the gentleman." The book was written in Ithaca, New York. Often she would write in bed from 9 a.m. until 2 a.m. the following morning. Another observer commented that she could improvise with great skill when she sat at the piano and that the raps people heard on her walls were produced by her own willpower, and not spirits.

Her willpower was noteworthy. A visitor to her New York home noted that "she caused a great table to rise up in the air without touching it." There are hundreds of other incidences of how she made things appear and disappear, and even of how Olcott learned how to cure people of serious diseases but was told to stop these cures in order to safeguard his "storeroom" of personal energy.

Blavatsky's aim was to study spiritualism more than it was to get in touch with peoples' dead family members.

Philadelphia attracted many mediums in 1874. According to John Vidumsky, author of a Hidden City retrospective of Blavatsky's life in Philadelphia, *A Castle of The Occult on Rittenhouse Square*, there were about 300 mediums in the city at that time:

> Two mediums, Nelson and Jennie Holmes, had unleashed a scandal that threatened the whole profession. Six months earlier, they had begun holding commercial séances at 50 N. 9th St, where "spirits" would appear in a large cabinet, showing just their faces or hands. These particular spirits called themselves John King and Katie King. John King claimed to have been the pirate Henry Morgan in life, and Katie King was his daughter. Katie would sometimes emerge from the cabinet, and male visitors remarked upon her graceful figure. You could buy photos of the sultry spirit afterwards. Clearly, this was fraud. But it convinced a lot of people, and the contested reality of "Katie King" consumed a lot of newspaper ink. It was then that Blavatsky came to Philadelphia to investigate.

Blavatsky, Vidumsky writes, discovered that the Holmeses were con artists, but felt obligated to defend them anyway. Blavatsky overruled her own misgivings about popular Spiritualism because she was far more worried about the spread of skepticism.

Philadelphia did one thing for Blavatsky: it provided her with a husband. Not that she needed a husband, of course. The steely Russian bear could handle most things on her own but at some point she attracted the attention of a certain Michael C. Betanelly, often referred to as a mentally unstable gentleman from Georgia who pursued her relentlessly until she consented to be his wife. The two were married by William H. Furness at the First Unitarian Church by the Rev. William H. Furness on April 3, 1875. The couple moved into what would later become the White Dog Café at 3420 Sansom Street.

The unhappy marriage lasted just several months. A divorce was granted in 1878.

If Philadelphia had taught Madame Helena Petrovna Blavatsky anything at all it was the fact that she needed a husband about as much as a fish needs a bicycle.

THE MR. SPOCK MACHINE COMES TO PHILADELPHIA

When I became a man, I put away childish things, but then one day a woman who lives on Rittenhouse Square talked to me about a Wishing Machine—or, as I like to call it, a Mr. Spock machine.

The Mr. Spock machine, I was told, is a device that makes personal dreams come true. The machine is a white box with nine black knobs. The wooden box is a perfect square, 10 inches by 10 inches with a copper and a plastic plate on the upper right- and left-hand corners. The plastic plate is also called a stick pad.

The master handcrafter of the Wishing Machine is a man named Dr. Mulder in South Carolina. Dr. Mulder insists that the Wishing Machine works.

You might call the Wishing Machine a fast-paced prayer box with dials only the machine works to make your wish come true long after you have put it away on a shelf. Some call the machine advanced magic or techno-shamanism. "Its all about intention and keeping that intended wish constantly conscious to the universe by sending out the intended signal every second of every day for your desired wish," Dr. Mulder states. "We have been told all our lives if we think about something long enough it will come true. Since us humans have a hard time focusing on one thought for long periods of time, this device will do that thinking and intending for us 24/7. We can sit back and wait for our wishes to occur."

If this sounds contrary to the world of logic, that is because it is but it is also what makes it so interesting.

Benign superstition tells us that when tourists go to Rome and visit the Trevi Fountain, they should throw coins over their shoulders into the foaming fountain pools—and make a wish. A similar "logic" applies if you find a "heads up" penny on the ground: if you pocket the "heads up" penny it is automatic good luck unlike a "tails up" penny which one is supposed to avoid. Of course, there are a million superstitions in the naked city, such as the prohibition against "cutting a tree" (or walking around a tree on the sidewalk in order to pass a slow walker in front of you).

The Wishing Machine is supposed to be something else entirely. It is about focusing on something you want—a car, a new house, money, a job promotion, or even a new boyfriend or girlfriend—and then getting it. The machine has no limits and no prohibitions unless of course your wish is preposterous like wanting to live forever. The machine, according to Dr. Mulder, has even been known to influence political elections. Imagine two hundred protestors on the street with Wishing Machines! If competing political parties had Wishing Machines, I imagine there would be an Armageddon of sorts.

When my Rittenhouse Square friend Connie offered to send me a Wishing Machine from Dr. Mulder for free, how could I refuse? The upshot here of course was Connie's hope that as a journalist I would write about the machine and give the Dr. Spock cult a big boost. I told her I would do that if the machine produced results. How could I not sing the praises of a lantern with a genii in the form of a box?

Connie described the Wishing Machine as a radionics device. "Radionics has been around since the late 1800s," she said, "when American physician Dr. Albert Abraham first brought it to light. Abraham's invention was a machine that could diagnose and cure almost any disease. The machine could also work across great distances, or reach a patient in the next room."

The Wishing Machine transmits the power of intention (your wish) to the intended source through scalar waves, Connie said. What are scalar waves? "They are a form of radio wave," Connie explained, mentioning a guy named Ed Kelly, head of Kelly Research Technologies in Lakemont, GA, which also manufactures radionics devices, especially to farmers who claim that Kelly's devices yield bigger crop yields.

If this is true, why is it not all over CNN and Fox News? Why does Walmart or Target not sell Wishing Machines? Why must people scout out a remote Dr. Mulder in South Carolina? "Well, I'm not a farmer," I told Connie, "but like most people I have a few wishes I'd love to see fulfilled, so please send the machine as soon as possible." I waited with baited breath.

When the UPS box arrived, I opened it with a great deal of anticipation, impressed at the quality of the machine's woodwork and yes, even the smell of the wood itself. I placed the Mr. Spock gadget on my kitchen table and read the instructions carefully.

I prepared a cup of tea in anticipation of making my first wish.

I wrote my wish on paper along with my name and then taped it to the copper plate on the box. The next step was to make sure that all the black dials were on zero (they go from 0 to 100). After this you are ready to turn one dial slowly at a time while meditating on your wish while simultaneously rubbing a finger over the plastic patch. As you rub, you slowly turn the dial up from 0 but the moment your finger gets sticky on the plastic patch you stop turning the dial and leave it where it is. You remove your finger from the plastic patch and start over with dial no. 2 and repeat the same process until you feel the sticky sensation. All the while you are supposed to be focusing on your wish.

You do this for all nine dials, then put the machine by a window or on a book shelf and forget about it. All you have to do now is bide your time until your wish manifests itself.

Connie, who happens to be a longtime paranormal investigator, told me that the timeline for the fulfillment of your wish can be anywhere from seconds to one or ten days and sometimes weeks.

She informed me that wishers from across the U.S., China, Germany, and Switzerland claimed that their migraine headaches went away, divorces finalized, job offers came out of the blue, and they were able to buy the house they always wanted. If this was true, then I had a powerful little box indeed, especially since it was claimed that some wishes came true within seconds of setting the dials.

Connie noted that some machines have amplifiers, hand held wands, even helmets designed to maximize the strength of your wish. The cost of these machines can get pretty ridiculous; they go from $800 to $100,000 and more. The Mr. Spock machine that was sent to me ordinarily sells for under $200.

My first wish on the Mr. Spock concerned a friend who had gone home to Allentown and then seemed to disappear off the face of the earth. My wish was that he get in touch with me. A week after I made the wish, the unexpected happened. I received a friend request on Facebook. It was this very friend informing me that he was headed to Philadelphia for a visit.

I chalked it up to coincidence, not wanting to try another wish right away. It never pays to get greedy. Remember that Brothers Grimm tale, "The Fisherman and His Wife," about the husband's catching a golden flounder that was really an enchanted prince? The husband releases the fish and then the wife demands that he go back and ask the fish for a reward of a new house for saving its life. The fish grants the wish but the wife is never satisfied. She keeps making bigger wishes until finally she demands of the fish that it grant her the ultimate prize: she wants to become the equal of God. The fish then takes away all of the wishes and returns the couple to their poverty. Greed never pays, so I held off but not for long.

My second wish concerned another long lost acquaintance. Again I asked the Mr. Spock machine to bring this person back into my personal orbit, and once again, amazingly, the lost person reappeared, causing me to inquire of my lost friend what made them contact me after such a long time. "Well, I just got this nagging feeling that we should reconnect," he said.

Did he really say a nagging feeling that we should reconnect?

When I wrote my Wishing Machine/Dr. Spock story for a Philadelphia newspaper and the *Huffington Post*, I received many inquiries and requests to view the machine. In one instance, somebody wanted to borrow it to make their own wish. But Wishing Machines are not to be shared, that is one of the rules of the game. I braced myself for more inquiries, but they did not come. My fears of city residents and neighbors storming my house to get their hands on the little box did not materialize.

My Mr. Spock machine is about two years old now and occasionally I have to dust the dials and the copper and plastic plates. I keep it high up on the top of a bookshelf so friends do not ask me what it is. I have used the machine more than twice, of course, and over time got used to strange things happening because of it. I have ignored it for months now because sometimes you just want life to take its normal course without "interferences" from Mr. Spock. But it is nice to know that in a pinch—an emotional rescue situation—I can suspend the logical part of my brain, tap into the "what if" factor, and take down Mr. Spock and make a wish and then watch it come true.

What more can an adult man ask for?

THE CULT OF DR. GOSNELL

For a number of years in my early twenties, I worked as an operating room orderly and technician. One of my tasks was to do pathology runs for the scrub nurses, which meant taking tumors, nodules extracted by surgeons, tonsils, and dermatological biopsies to the pathology department. At this particular hospital, there were also a lot of therapeutic abortions, so my tray of specimens was sometimes filled with jars of fetuses.

They called them fetuses, although I realize that many people would vehemently disagree. They would call the specimens "babies." I got ample opportunity then to inspect the specimen jars, to view the aborted fetuses up close, and I must say that it disturbed me. A lot of the women being wheeled into the O.R. for therapeutic abortions then were young single women who seemed to be using abortion as a form of birth control. Probably not in all the cases, but my sense at the time was that many of them were.

As a male, I felt I had to keep quiet about these procedures. What did I know about women's bodies? This was the apex of the age of feminism (the 1970s), after all, when books like *Our Bodies, Ourselves* made it to the bestseller lists, and when all good political radicals like myself were taught that men had no say when it comes to women's bodies.

But was it a woman's body issue or was it a "human life in a woman's body" issue? That was the philosophical question. I rationalized that if a big hospital such as the one where I worked approved of these T.A.'s, then who was I to cast aspersions, or to judge? After all, these surgical abortions were better than coat hanger abortions in back alleys. That is what everybody was saying then: Abortion must be legal to prevent coat hanger back alley abortions. Case closed. No discussion needed. In a way, it made perfect sense.

But the sight of so many fetuses—or babies—in jars floating around like astronauts in space disturbed me. I felt a bad vibe. In the operating room, when a scrub nurse would deliver a fetus/baby in jar to the hospital workroom, generally the nurses' aides would hide the jars on a tall shelf somewhere until it was time for me to take the basket to pathology. One O.R. nurse, I remember, refused to assist at a T.A. She was Russian Orthodox woman and she wore a silver three bar cross. "I made it clear to them that I would not assist in abortions," she told me then. "I told them they would have to find another nurse."

The high number of abortions in the O.R. seemed to upset quite a number of the scrub nurses but they could not bring themselves to do what the Russian Orthodox nurse had done. Once I saw a nurse crying after a particularly long abortion. She entered the workroom in tears. "It's about the abortion she just assisted," another nurse whispered. Something happened in that operating room, but what?

When Philadelphia (Powelton Village) doctor-abortionist Kermit Gosnell was arrested in 2011 for operating an out-of-control, illegal abortion clinic, I thought of all the little fetus jars in my specimen basket in that hospital in New England. Some of those specimens in the jars were as old as four months. In 2013, Dr. Gosnell was convicted on three counts of first-degree murder. Records indicate that his staff stuck scissors into the necks of three babies after failed abortions.

Now there is a film about the Powelton Village abortionist. Entitled *Gosnell: The Trial of America's biggest serial killer*, the film is making the rounds across the country and is getting pretty good reviews. But getting the film made was an effort because no Hollywood producer would touch the topic.

Hollywood distributors rejected the film, and this forced the film's producers to rely on crowdfunding. And Planned Parenthood, that paragon of free choice, leveled its guns in an attempt to prevent private screenings of the film. Even Facebook, that multicultural, diverse online matrix community center where "every point of view" counts, rejected scores of ads for the film. According to some reports, 200 theaters across the nation dropped the film like a hot potato. So much for freedom of speech.

Because the film is pro-life it is seen as Public Enemy Number 1. NPR, for instance, refused to advertise the film because the script calls Dr. Gosnell an "abortionist." That word is forbidden on NPR because it seems to suggest that there is something rotten with abortion—all abortion, even to save the life of the mother. Censorship like this should be everybody's concern. Dr. Gosnell was an abortionist. He was not a benign family practitioner trying to save the life of a pregnant woman.

Orthodox feminists view the death of fetuses or babies in the womb as unpleasant collateral when dealing with the far more important issue of women's healthcare. A well-meaning feminist reporter writing for the *Philadelphia Weekly* (PW) some years ago, had this to say about the Gosnell case:

> Gosnell is the result of politicizing women's health care, and his case, in turn, has been used to further politicize women's health care. Real information about the effect of shutting down abortion clinics—preventable injury, illness, and death, not to mention forced births, all of which happened at Gosnell's clinic—has been squeezed out of the conversation.

In a recent review of the film, a PW reviewer admitted that the acting was stellar but faulted the film for being filmed in Oklahoma and not Philadelphia. The reviewer said it was not a real Philly film at all and that the producers did not even have a Philadelphia premier. Did he say a Philadelphia premier? This comment borders on the hilarious. The film, now that it has been released, has not even been shown in city theaters, certainly not in any downtown theater. My guess is that it will never be shown in downtown theaters because it advocates the use of the word "abortionist."

If Philadelphians want to see the Gosnell film, they will have to head into New Jersey or to Plymouth Meeting, Pennsylvania. That is called censorship, I think.

An article in the *National Review* blamed the censorship around the film on the philosophy of radical leftists. "Radical leftists zealously believe that abortion must be defended at all costs, even if it means whitewashing its bloody, half-century legacy of mass genocide in our nation's inner cities."

As for Gosnell's former abortionist factory in West Philadelphia, the very conservative and often reactionary Life Site News reported that the 2,700-square-foot space "was an unsanitary, blood-stained site where Gosnell cut the spinal cords of hundreds of newborns; where witnesses described infants who survived initial abortion attempts as 'swimming' in toilets 'to get out'; where the feet of aborted babies were stored in a freezer."

As for the building itself, which has been boarded up for years, one real estate agent said it might be a while before it is rehabbed and turned into condos.

> When you have a horrific event that's inside a single-family residence, such as Jeffrey Dahmer's apartment, the effects on real estate are typically more profound because people live there and sleep there, and there are memories that you don't want to go home to. With commercial properties, while there can be an effect, it's usually different and typically less.

But that remains to be seen.

THE NATION OF ISLAM

It was not that long ago when the streets of Philadelphia were filled with groups of Catholic nuns in traditional religious habits. In 1960, Catholicism offered a rich array of women's communities with diverse religious habits that covered the waterfront in terms of style. Different religious orders had their own manner of dress so the streets were alive with colorful communities as nuns rode buses or subways and made their presence known in a forceful fashion. That changed after the Second Vatican Council of 1965. Women began leaving their religious communities as some convents began to eliminate the religious habit, allowing nuns to dress in secular clothing and live outside their communities in apartments. Gradually, the streets of Philadelphia showed a marked decrease in the number of identifiable nuns. Little by little their numbers dwindled as another type of religious garbed woman seemed to take their place.

Muslim women, the majority of them African American and converts to Islam, began to populate the streets and the subways. Their numbers trickled out slowly at first but soon that trickle became a deluge, relegating memories of the Catholic nun to the dustbin. Of course, for a short period of time Catholic nuns in modified religious habits could occasionally be seen on the streets, but soon even the modified habits disappeared so that the Catholic nun was no more. The "new nun" for the new age became the Muslim woman in a headscarf or turban, often referred to as a minimal hijab, generally most popular in Turkey, Egypt, Lebanon, and Iran. Or you might see another style of Islamic dress, women in loose scarves called rusari. Occasionally but not often a more orthodox manner of dress would be evident: a black chador, preferred by conservative Shiite Iranian women. You might also spot the jilbab or the tudong as worn by Muslim women in Southeast Asia. In the minority for many years was the very radical Arab Gulf niqab, a veil covering a woman's face, ears, hair, leaving only the eyes visible. The combination of the niqab with the Abayas on a woman in downtown Philadelphia always turned heads, but that is no longer true. This combination has become quite common, although still rare on the streets of the city is the full Burka of the Taliban, a full body and face covering with a screen over the eyes. But even the Burka is becoming commonplace.

What you almost never saw on the streets of Philadelphia in 1965 were prepubescent Muslim girls wearing the hijab. Generally the hijab is reserved for Muslim girls after puberty, but in Philadelphia it was not uncommon to see small girls dressed like their mothers. More stylish Muslim women might be spotted wearing a three-layer niqab, or a trendy maroon and fully lined, crew neck evening dress called a Refka. There are also workout hijab suits and a very fashionable hijab trench coat.

The Washington Post reported in 2018:

In Philadelphia, there is a plethora of Muslim-owned businesses, an Islamic history museum, and numerous Muslim community organizations and charitable initiatives. There is a Muslim city council member and a Muslim state senator; the chairman of the city Board of Commissioners is Muslim, and there has been a Muslim police chief. The Muslim holidays of Eid al-Fitr and Eid al-Kabir are observed holidays within the Philadelphia school system, and 2017 was the fifth year in a row that City Hall hosted an annual Iftar dinner in celebration of the holy month of Ramadan.

In 2017, *The Washington Post* also reported: "Philadelphia was once a Nation of Islam stronghold, home to 12 affiliated temples. After the group's leader, Elijah Muhammad, died in 1975, his son Warith Deen (W.D.) Mohammed broke with his father's theology of black racial superiority and led most of the Nation's members to embrace orthodox Islam."

Some "Nation of Islam" theories involved a cosmology that identified blacks as the original race and white people as "devils" created later by a mad scientist named Yakub. The nation also promoted other teachings, such as self-reliance, clean living and the promise of a future in which blacks would no longer be oppressed.

In 2016, Philadelphia's Billy Penn reported that "[Muslim] Community leaders estimate the amount [of Muslims in Philadelphia] at 150,000 to 200,000—about 10–15 percent of the total population. Few other big cities, perhaps only Chicago and Detroit, can compare. In 2011, Greater Philadelphia's mosque count of 63 was fourth in the country, behind Southern California, New York City and Chicago."

Billy Penn also reported that a minority of Muslims in the city are of Arab or Middle Eastern descent:

> They are scattered throughout the city but heavily concentrated in the lower Northeast, Feltonville and around Front and Girard by Al-Aqsa. Most of Philly's Muslim population is black. They're also spread throughout Philadelphia, but black Muslim communities are particularly strong in West, North and Northwest Philly.

This fact has led critics to describe the burgeoning rise in Islam in Philadelphia to racial issues, as a way to show black pride rather than a deference to "true theology." If your reasons for becoming Muslim, or any religion for that matter, are socio-economic-political, what has this to do with questions relating to the true nature of God?

"They say that I am a preacher of racial hatred," Elijah Muhammad once said, "but the fact is that the white people don't like the truth, especially if it speaks against them. It is a terrible thing for such people to charge me with teaching race hatred when their feet are on my people's neck and they tell us to our face that they hate black people." He later toned down his rhetoric, noting shortly before his death that "The slave master is no longer hindering us, we're hindering ourselves."

When Muhammad died of congestive heart failure on February 25, 1975, he left behind a thriving religious movement with a membership as high as 250,000. Its social and political influence was matched by the success of its financial enterprises: real estate holdings, a national newspaper called *Muhammad Speaks*, and numerous independent businesses.

Muhammad was succeeded by his son, Warith Deen Mohammed, whose attempts to reform the doctrines championed by his father drew a mixed response. As a result, another prominent leader, Louis Farrakhan, branched out to form his own version of the Nation of Islam in 1978.

The largely African American *Philadelphia Tribune* in 2016 reported that the Southern Poverty Law Center listed forty hate groups that exist in Pennsylvania and six hate groups in Philadelphia. On the Center's list was the Nation of Islam.

Others listed groups included As-Sabiqun, Keystone State Skinheads, Israelite Church of God and Jesus Christ, Israelite School of Universal and Practical Knowledge, and the Traditional Rebel Knights of the Ku Klux Klan.

According to the Southern Poverty Law Project —which states it is dedicated to fighting hate and bigotry and seeks justice for the most vulnerable—the Nation of Islam, led by Minister Louis Farrakhan, landed on the list based on its ideologies, including the belief of superiority over whites.

THE SILENT JIHAD IN PHILADELPHIA?

In August 2010, I reported for *The Philadelphia Bulletin* that Tom Trento, director of the Florida Security Council, was in Philadelphia to showcase the film *The Third Jihad*, and then shared his thoughts on what he calls "the silent jihad in Philadelphia."

Over 200 people packed the main auditorium of the central branch of the Free Library to watch the controversial film that one-time presidential candidate Rudy Giuliani calls "a wake-up call for America." *The Third Jihad* exposes the destructive aims of radical Islam, including the subtle dangers of "peaceful" cultural jihad and its influences on western society.

Among the many people interviewed in the film were Ayaan Hirsi Ali, the former member of the Dutch Parliament who made the film *Submission* with Theo Van Gogh. Van Gogh was later killed by a Muslim radical for his portrayal (in *Submission*) of the treatment of women in Islamic societies. Ali, a former Muslim, escaped to the Netherlands to free herself from an arranged marriage in Somalia in 1992.

After the feature-length film—a large part of which focuses on Western Europe's growing radical Islamist populations that call for the institution of Sharia Law in these countries—Mr. Trento took the podium. A power de-surge prevented the lights in the auditorium from switching on, so Mr. Trento was framed in shadows, as was the audience, symbolic, perhaps, of the dark nature of the subject at hand.

"Islam is a political system, primarily," Mr. Trento said:

Serious analysts and Islamists say this also. There's no separation of God and state in Islam. There's no separation of mosque and state. If this is true, then the essence of its quality, Sharia, also called the pathway or Sharia law, begs the question: Can this coexist with a Constitutional Democratic Republic? Is there a way to bring these two together?

Mr. Trento's answer is an unqualified no.

"We are talking about a clash of civilizations here," he said, going on to quote C.I.A. operative Claire Lopez, who also makes an appearance in the film: "We are in the battle for the essence of the United States of America."

Mr. Trento, in fact, calls it "the epic battle of our lifetime" but insists that most Americans are asleep when it comes to the silent jihad happening all around them.

"You have a battle right here in Philadelphia," he said. "In fact, on October 28, we are going to hold a 3- or 4-hour workshop on Jihad in Philadelphia and detail all of this in an evidentiary way. For instance, you have an individual in Philadelphia who made a lot of money in the Philadelphia Soul Sound. His name is Kenny Gamble, or Luqman Abdul-Haqq."

Mr. Trento reminded the audience that Mr. Gamble became a Muslim in the 1970s after a personal crisis and then "used his money to build a lot of companies that are working to rebuild the inner city."

"We are seeing this sort of thing all over the United States," Mr. Trento said, "This is what is part of the stealth jihad."

While quick to remind the audience that his desire was not to bash Muslims, Mr. Trento said that it was his intent to confront the ideology of Islam that desires to implement Sharia Law in place of the Constitution of the United States.

"If anyone wants to mess with the Constitution, they become an enemy of the United States. But the issue isn't Muslims; it's where you stand on Sharia Law. If you're for Sharia Law, you're an enemy of the United States."

Sharia Law governs every aspect of private and public life of an individual, from how one eats, dresses, grooms, and worships.

"Kenny Gamble has an operation going on," Mr. Trento said:

Now, when U.S. Intelligence starts to look at these guys—and they've been looking at them for a long time—they will see that a kind of organizational flow chart is being utilized by the Islamic world through an organization called the Muslim Brotherhood. The Muslim Brotherhood is the Costra Nostra of the Muslim world. So, when you look into this in Philadelphia, and you see the guys with black berets, the new Black Panthers, the Nation of Islam, all these various Islamic organizations tie into Kenny Gamble, and they all sit on boards together.

The next question Mr. Trento asks is: What is Kenny Gamble doing?

"If Kenny Gamble desires to save the inner city, we are with him 100 percent. If he desires to use Sharia Law and establish an enclave which is separate and distinct from the American Republic Democratic Constitutional system of government as is occurring in London, then he becomes someone that needs to be stopped."

"This is why Kenny Gamble is currently under a pretty intensive microscope," Mr. Trento said. An additional concern, Mr. Trento feels, are Kenny Gamble's "young shock troops ... boys anywhere from the age of five to 12. Called Jawala scouts, these young troopers are the exact duplication of the Hamas model," Mr. Trento explains. "The psychological impetus being that if you influence a kid when they are 7 years old, you have them for life."

"Part of the plan, whenever poison is introduced anywhere, is to introduce it in a nice container of some sort," Mr. Trento said.

> The container right now is trying to rebuild the inner city. We're going to give Mr. Gamble a chance to denounce Sharia for U.S. principles. Right now, the effort is to clean up the neighborhood and grow young men and women in the Islamic faith. I do believe there are sincere Muslims who want to do that, but there are higher officials and they are working out a grand plan, and they are using non Sharia Muslims as useful idiots, as Karl Marx did, to help usher in hundreds of billions of state and federal dollars to protect the progress of low income housing and job finding programs.

One audience member asked Mr. Trento's opinion of the proposed Islamic Center two blocks from New York's Ground Zero.

"There's a doctrine in the annals of the theology of Islam that allows it in wartime to deceive, to have a deceptive position," Mr. Trento said:

> It's affirmed by the four schools of Islamist theology. It's for real, folks. When we hear various Inman's saying, "We're building a building of love and compassion, so that Jews and Christians and everybody can get together, you can believe that if you want to." But it's important in Islamic theology that once you conquer something or have a conquest of some sort, you claim the land, then you own it eternally. That's why there will never, never, never be peace in Israel because the 1.3 billion Muslims believe that they own that land because they conquered it at one point.

"Tell your friends and family about this film, tell everyone," Mr. Trento said. "We are fighting a theocratic political system that's an irresistible force!"

PHILADELPHIA'S ISLAMIC POET PEACEMAKER

When the French poet Arthur Rimbaud wrote "You must change your life," he set the tone for future poets, including Philadelphia's Daniel Abdal-Hayy

Moore. Born in 1940 in Oakland, California, Moore's first book of poems, *Dawn Visions*, was published in 1964 by Lawrence Ferlinghetti of City Lights Books. This was the Beat Generation era, when Allen Ginsberg's "Howl," also published by City Lights, was changing the poetic landscape. In 1972, Moore followed up with another City Lights volume, *Burnt Heart/Ode to the War Dead*, about the human carnage in Vietnam.

In the late 1960s, Moore founded and directed The Floating Lotus Magic Opera Company in Berkeley, California, and later presented two major productions, *The Walls Are Running Blood* and *Bliss Apocalypse*. The world was changing, and for some meant a reinvention of the self. Moore, who was then a self-described Zen Buddhist whose normal routine was to get up early every morning, "sit zazen, smoke a joint, do half an hour of yoga, then read the Mathnawi of Rumi, the long mystical poem of that great Persian Sufi of the thirteenth century," life was about to change.

He met the man who was to be his spiritual guide, Shaykh Muhammad ibn al-Habib. "The man looked like an eccentric Englishman," Moore writes:

> He too had only recently come out of the English version of the Hippie Wave. He was older, refined in his manners spectacularly witty and intellectual, but of that kind prevalent then who had hobnobbed with the Beatles and knew the Tantric Art collection of Brian Jones firsthand. He had been on all the classic drug quests-peyote in the Yucatan, mescaline with Luara Huxley-but with the kif quest in Morocco he had stumbled on Islam, and then the Sufis, and the game was up. A profound change had taken place in his life that went far beyond the psychedelic experience.

Moore converted to Sufi Islam in 1970, riding a wave of spiritual self-transformation that affected other writers and poets in the Bay area, most notably Eugene Rose, an atheist and Marxist whose devotion to Nietzsche nearly drove him mad before his discovery of the wisdom of the early Desert Fathers. Rose, who would go on to become an Orthodox priest and co-founder of Holy Trinity monastery near Redding, California, is now considered by many to be a future saint of the Russian Orthodox Church. As for Moore, his spiritual transformation inspired him to travel to Morocco, Spain, Algeria, and Nigeria, but finally back to California where he would publish his book *The Desert is the Only Way Out*.

In many ways, Philadelphia would prove to be Moore's desert, although he did not become a Philadelphian until 1990. Before that date he lived for a while in Boston's North End, where he remembers meeting the poet John Weiners, the shy gay Irish Catholic poet whom Allen Ginsberg once referred to as "a pure poet" and who was really the Walt Whitman of New England.

While living in Philadelphia, Moore published *The Ramadan Sonnets* (Jusoor/City Lights), and, in 2002, *The Blind Beekeeper* (Jusoor/Syracuse University

Press). San Francisco poet, playwright, and novelist Michael McClure has written that Moore's poems are like Frank O'Hara's, where "there are no boundaries or limits to possible subject matter," and where "imagination runs rampant and it glides."

As a believer in something beyond himself, you might say that Moore is not a poet of empty things and ideas like some modern poets. Instead, aspects of the spiritual and the divine seem to invade every word he writes. He also finds a way to say the unsayable. Moore, it is said, was viewed as a legend in the California of the 1960s, in part because he was able to be "spiritual" without losing his sense of humor. One could almost say that he is the spiritual poet with the comedic wink. Others call him a surrealist of the sacred.

In this age of ongoing dialogue among Muslims, Christians, and Jews, the sacred personage known as the Virgin Mary, mentioned some thirty-four times in the Koran, stands out as important on the historical and the dogmatic plane. The sacred person concept is not lost on Moore, who writes in his poem, "Five Short Meditations on the Virgin Mary":

> I saw Mary board a bus at Broad and State
> her head covered and her face radiant
> small and held within herself
> careful and preoccupied
> a heaven seeming to be wrapped around her
> her cheeks red her lips dry her eyes lowered
> interior moisture her preferred cloister
> the bus passengers sudden ghosts before her
> her shoes small and tattered
> her hands carrying a book
> If any had spoken to her she might have become lost
> If she had spoken to anyone
> they might have become saved.

9

Processing Satan

Anton Szandor LaVey founded the Church of Satan in 1966 in San Francisco. LaVey's real name, however, was Howard Stanton Levey. The purported author of the *Satanic Bible* (many insist that LaVey plagiarized large parts of the *Satanic Bible* for AVON Books) died in 1997. On his deathbed in a Catholic hospital, it is said by some that he had a vision of something that terrified him. His own daughter reported that he saw something and said, "Oh my, oh my, what have I done? There's something very wrong." His daughter said that her father then begged God not to send him to hell. LaVey's followers dispute this claim, insisting that this was a rumor started almost a decade after his death by a Christian on YouTube.

Howard Levey was an atheist and did not believe in a literal Satan. As he told one reporter before his death, "Look, I'm an atheist. Satan is symbolically representative for us, and when you see the kind of liberating freedom that people are feeling when they say something like 'Hail, Satan,' well, it seems like it's needed. Hating yourself for being human seems pointless."

Generally, a lot of adolescent bravado surfaces when it comes to Satanism. I am thinking of kids in black clothing listening to heavy metal as they suck on five-pointed pentagrams. The superficial rebellion of lighting bonfires in cornfields or putting on dark Goth eyeshadow before going out to the local cemetery and toppling tombstones with crosses on them.

A 2018 article in *Philly Voice* asked, "Who Are the Philly Satanists? What Do They Do?" As was pointed out, they do not eat babies and they do not want churches to be burned down. "We are Satanists. Full stop. Most of us are also atheists," as one member told the reporter. A look at the group's Facebook page, Satanic Philadelphia, reveals posts like, "Pride is the most fabulous sin," and "We don't apologize for our nature." Satanic Philadelphia sponsored a so-called Black Mass on October 12, 2018, traditional Columbus Day, and the birthday of Aleister Crowley, "the Great Beast," a poet and founder of his own school of mysticism, Magick.

Philadelphia Magazine, always on the lookout for topical issues, reported on the Black Mass:

> New Jersey resident Joan Bell has been camped out in front of 12th and Spring Garden arts venue, the Philadelphia Mausoleum of Contemporary Art (PhilaMOCA) since 6 p.m. on Thursday. She has a three-foot-tall statue of the Virgin Mary. And she has her rosaries. She's there to prayerfully protest the appearance of the Satanic Temple at PhilaMOCA on Friday night.

The magazine went on to report that "the blasphemy-based Salem, Massachusetts religious organization" was actually performing the Black Mass ritual two times. That is because when the 8 p.m. Satanic Temple Black Mass sold out in a heartbeat, PhilaMOCA owner Eric Bresler added another Black Mass at 10:30 p.m. The 10:30 p.m. Black Mass sold out as well.

Who are these devoted satanic followers anyway? That *Philly Voice* reporter described his visit to the organization:

> It's a sweltering afternoon in late May. A group of mostly 30-somethings are relaxing in the air conditioning at a South Philly bar discussing movies and politics. To the untrained eye, this might look like a normal meet-up, but these 11 strangers aren't getting together to bond over foreign films or to try speed dating. They're Satanists.

The reporter goes on to describe the Satanists in a bar in Germantown:

> A chocolate cake covered in black icing topped with a blood red pentagram sits on the table before them. It's the group's first anniversary. They open the meeting with an invocation calling to Satan for power and wisdom. It ends with members intoning, "FIAT, IN NOMINE SATANAS."

The Philadelphia group is part of a Salem-based organization known as the Satanic Temple. Satanic Temple "franchises" are popping up all over the country. If a 2014 Pew Research Center survey is to be believed, then 1.5 percent of Americans now identify with Paganism, Wicca, and Satanism.

The Satanic Temple was founded by Lucien Greaves and Malcolm Jarry in 2012. The temple became famous when they initiated a Missouri Supreme Court lawsuit to reduce undue burdens in abortion procedures. The group also went to great lengths to place a satanic monument on the Arkansas capitol grounds to offset a 10 Commandments monument.

In the 1970s, a common figure in Philadelphia's Suburban Station was a tall, long cloaked figure mingling among regional rail passengers while passing out leaflets and magazines. The magazine, called *The Process*, was published by The Process Church of the Final Judgment, then headquartered in New Orleans with branches in Los Angeles. The Process Church, some say, had influenced Charles Manson and the Manson "Family." Process Church co-founder, Robert De Grimston Moore, was once referred to by Manson as his body double. "Moore and I are one and the same," Manson is on record as saying.

The Process Church was founded by two British ex-Scientologists, Mary Ann MacLean and Moore after their expulsion from the Church of Scientology as "suppressive persons" in 1962. The organization grew rapidly and *Process* magazine became popular with Hollywood celebrities, with its stories on death, sex, fear, and love. MacLean called herself The Oracle and Moore was known as the teacher although the one in control was MacLean. Process Church members had photo I.D.'s and in some cities there were Process coffee houses.

Process magazine featured stories on Marianne Faithful, Timothy Leary, and William Burroughs. A Process band was formed in Toronto and recorded a number of songs. The Process philosophy was that Jesus and Satan were one. Members were encouraged to participate in sex couplings, orgies, and go outside their comfort zones. Group sex was a rite of passage. After the Manson murders in Los Angeles, the Church of the Process, in a flush of embarrassment, changed its sinister black cloak and robes to a gray modern leisure suit. That was later changed to a blue modern leisure suit. The Process cross, which once had the look of a Nazi swastika was changed to resemble a soft version of the German Iron Cross. The standard Process cross was a cross with a curled-up serpent inside.

In 1974, there was a schism when Moore, who was seeing another woman, was kicked out of the church by the jilted MacLean. The name of the church was changed to the Foundation Church of the Millennium. In 1979, the name was changed again to the Foundation Church and all references to Satan were dropped. MacLean wanted a purely Christian Church. MacLean changed the name again, but this time all religious pretensions were dropped. The new name, Best Friends Animal Society, accompanied a move to a new place, Kanab, Utah. On November 14, 2005, in a satanic twist worthy of director Roman Polanski, a rumor circulated that MacLean's death was caused when a group of feral dogs tore her apart.

In Philadelphia's Suburban Station, the man in the cloak handing out copies of *Process* magazine went about his task with calm determination, chatting up mothers, families, students, and anyone who might offer a contribution. The Process man in the cape could also be seen throughout the city conducting lively debates with evangelical Christian groups.

Suburban Station in the late 1970s was a teeming metropolis. Within its walls you could find every facet of city life: proselytizing Jews for Jesus, processing Hare Krishna devotees, Nation of Islam evangelizers, as well as expressionless but always formally dressed Jehovah's Witnesses standing next to portable magazine racks. An iconic sight for years was an elderly Anglo-Catholic nun in full traditional habit who sat in a folding chair inside the station. At her side was a basket for donations. Day in and day out, year after year, the nun would sit in silence and accept whatever money was offered her. By the early 1990s, she had disappeared, a victim of passage of time. I was always sorry that I never approached her and asked me to tell me her story.

Suburban Station was also an early hangout for male prostitutes from the Fishtown and South Philadelphia neighborhoods. In 1975, it was where the murderers of thirty-year-old newspaper heir John S. Knight, who lived in the Dorchester in Rittenhouse Square, hung out and made their drug deals. *TIME* magazine reported on the John Knight murder:

> John Shivery Knight III was a young man with a future. At 30, he was special-projects editor of an afternoon tabloid, the *Philadelphia Daily News*. He had a $1,050-a-month apartment in a large building on Philadelphia's fashionable Rittenhouse Square and an art collection worth about $100,000. As a respected reporter for *The Detroit Free Press*, he had won an American Bar Association award. Most important, he was the millionaire grandson and a presumed heir of John S. Knight, 81, founder of the Knight-Rider Newspapers Inc., the chain that includes some 35 daily.

Knight's murder exposed his closeted homosexual life among what was then termed "the lowly." Police eventually arrested three male prostitutes, Isais "Felix" Melendez, Steven Maleno, and Salvatore Soli for the crime.

Sometime in the late 1970s, a Process missionary approached a young man named Makin, new to Philadelphia from the Midwest. Makin, a runaway, came to Philadelphia without any resources. When I spoke to Makin at that time as a reporter for Philadelphia's *The Drummer* newspaper, he could list no address. The phrase I used in my *Drummer* article was that Makin lived "hand to mouth," meaning that he was homeless.

At times Makin could be spotted carrying a free copy of Anton Szandor LaVey's Bible, given to him (so he told me) by the Process man himself. I would see Makin reading LaVey's book in Suburban Station. Makin explained his choice of reading material by calling himself a "spiritual investigator." There were times when he carried both LaVey's book and the Gideon Bible. It was as if he was deciding which path to follow.

It soon became obvious to me that Makin was one of the station's notorious rent boys. The rent boys hung round the indoor ice skating rink and the Alexander Calder sculpture in the Penn Center courtyard. These ragamuffin-roughnecks—H. L. Mencken might have called them "lintheads"—used the Calder sculpture as a leaning post and in the warmer months as a changing post where they would hang their "perspired" T-shirts up to dry.

Suburban Station in 1976 had a commercial sunken ice skating rink surrounded by floor to ceiling windows through which regional rail passengers waiting for departing trains could watch the skaters. Suburban Station provided Makin with new life, albeit under the radar but sometimes in the direct path of the police. He dressed well considering his "hand-to-mouth" life situation. He was often seen in pinstriped sneakers and Swedish boathouse trousers with big pockets and wide belt loops.

The city Morals Squad was alive and well in the late 1970s. There were long-haired undercover agents in London Fog coats who canvassed the station with watchful eyes, while other undercover agents wore faded blue jeans while pretending to "look available."

Homelessness takes its toll, however, and soon Makin was taking more drugs than he could handle. He began standing in the middle of Suburban Station wobbling and zoning out as hundreds of commuters would whirl past him on the way to their trains.

He eventually became so careless, he did not mind falling asleep outside the skating rink in the warm weather. At 8 a.m. on my way to work, I would sometimes find him flat on his belly on one of the station's outdoor concrete benches, pigeons fluttering about him in a wild fashion. And there beside him on the bench would be the nearly shredded and coverless Anton Szandor LaVey Bible.

THE CATHOLIC CHARISMATIC CULT: SHAKE, RATTLE, AND ROLL

In 2018, the online Catholic Philly.com published a piece on the Catholic Charismatic movement. "Some traditional Catholics might be turned off by the highly emotional exuberance of a Charismatic meeting, which can demonstrate such gifts of the Holy Spirit as prophecy, faith healing and speaking in tongues. Advocates believe this is simply the workings of the Holy Spirit," the article began.

Catholic Philly also carried advertisements for the 2019 Philadelphia Catholic Charismatic Renewal Conference. Those ads had the look of an old time southern revival. A traditionalist Catholic may have had to look twice to see if what he/she was seeing was really real. The ad was printed in big bold letters in the style of Big Tent evangelism. The following passages from Scripture were arranged around information surrounding the event.

"Then Jesus said, 'Did I not tell you that if you believe, you will see the Glory of God'" John 11:40. Other bold letters followed. The event would take place at the Clarion Hotel Conference, Essington, Delaware County, Pennsylvania. There would be a guest, Bishop Sam Jacobs, chairman of the National Service Committee for the Charismatic Renewal. A beautiful woman showing off her bright shiny dental veneers was the guest speaker. She was not just anybody but she was someone who was "baptized in the Holy Spirit in 1957." The woman's million-dollar suntan gave this event an even bigger biblical punch. The woman, the ad stated, "is committed to making Jesus known to the Nations by the preaching of the Gospel in the Power of the Holy Spirit."

Not only is all this not the way that Catholics have traditionally talked, I could not get over the fact that the event was not criticized by the normally staid Catholic Philly.

Karl Keating, in a 2017 piece for Catholic Answers on the Catholic Charismatic Movement, wrote:

> The Catholic variant of charismaticism dates from 1967. It began at Duquesne University, spread to Notre Dame, and then went viral, as the current saying has it. A Belgian cardinal, Leo Suenens, was an early patron. Pope Paul VI, while a charismatic event was in progress in Rome, said some positive things about the movement's emphasis on "communion of souls" and its promotion of prayer. Later, John Paul II encouraged Catholic charismatics to defend the Christian notion of social life against inroads by secularism.

"The popes," Keating continues, "never endorsed the notion of a 'Baptism in the Spirit,' nor did they speak in favor of glossolalia, or speaking in tongues." After all, so-called speaking in tongues was a one event at Pentecost. It had everything to do with "gifting" the early apostles and disciples with a knowledge of foreign languages so they could go out into the world, and nothing to do with rolling around on the floor in a fever. In fact, the modern concept of "speaking in tongues" (or shaking your booty with upraised hands) was virtually unknown throughout most of Christianity until 1830 when a certain excitable Scottish Presbyterian minister, Edward Irving, manufactured its appearance "through his enthusiastic preaching." Keating concludes: "After that, speaking in tongues died down until the turn of the twentieth century with the rise of the modern Pentecostal movement. There were no Catholic examples of it until two-thirds of a century later."

Keating's views were challenged in a Catholic forum by a pro-charismatic apologist:

> At the heart of the Charismatic Renewal is a call to a personal encounter with Jesus and ongoing discipleship through the power of the Holy Spirit. I think that we can all agree that those are worthy pursuits. Although our faith is rational, it must also transcend mere intellectual assent.

I grew up on the outskirts of Philadelphia's Main Line in Frazer, Pennsylvania, where an infamous landmark on Lancaster Pike attracted the attention of passing drivers. The landmark was a huge billboard with the words Jesus Saves in gargantuan block letters. The billboard was twice the size of any other billboard in the area, and missing it while driving on Lancaster Pike was impossible. The billboard's design included a rising sun with rays of light extending outward in massive bold strokes. There was a short Bible quote in smaller print underneath the main message. A longer quote, perhaps, might have been distracting and caused an accident. The "Jesus Saves" billboard was the subject of family conversations for years. A trip to the supermarket, to the Devon horse show, to my Boy Scout cabin in the forest, even while riding the school bus every day, it was always this billboard that caught my eye and got me thinking about the holy roller evangelicals in the area: the praise dancers, the polite Frazer Mennonites in their white bonnets and all the innumerable summer vacation Bible Schools, all decidedly un-Catholic.

We Catholics, secure in our knowledge that our Church was the original apostolic Church founded by Christ himself, didn't have to stoop to making cartoon billboards in order to win followers. Jesus was not a commercial product like Ipanna toothpaste or A&P coffee. He was far too serious to trivialize on a billboard along a highway.

In the years following the Second Vatican Council the Jesus Saves billboard became less of a freak display for Catholics. Suddenly area priests were referring to it during sermons.

In Philadelphia, a Redemptorist brother, Brother Pancratius (Panky) Boudreau (Joseph Andrew Boudreau), is credited for starting the Catholic Charismatic Movement. This was in the 1970s when Brother Panky was transferred to Philadelphia from Washington, D.C., where he had already kick-started the movement in the late 1960s. Brother Panky was stationed at Saint Boniface Church at the time where he started a prayer group that later grew to more than 160 prayer groups around the Delaware Valley.

Suddenly Archdiocese of Philadelphia Catholics were hooting and hollering. The era of staid, quiet rosary saying was seen as retrograde and Protestant-unfriendly. Although creeping Pentecostalism existed in mostly isolated parishes with special Masses and events, elements of the Charismatic movement began to seep into heretofore dignified parishes. Suddenly one saw people at Mass praying the Lord's Prayer in the Orans fashion while others took to holding hands with their neighbors in the pews, a few degrees away from swaying like those Big Tent hysterics. Other lay people, convinced that they had special spiritual gifts, would lay their hands on the heads of fellow parishioners. The only thing missing was outright dancing although that would come later when middle aged women, filled with something they called "The Spirit," would don chiffon capes and sashay around the altar in what would come to be known as liturgical dancing.

The Roman Catholic Church had clearly lost its mind.

On the heels of the charismatic movement came the Cursillo movement, founded in Spain in 1944 as a way to bring Spanish men back to the church. The Cursillo retreat was really the Catholic version of an EST or Lifespring retreat. The Cursillo three-day retreat emphasized non-stop group activity with little or no solitude. Criticisms of the Cursillo movement by traditionalists pointed to "in group secrets" and instructions. Some former Cursillo devotees have even compared it to a cult.

The two founders of Cursillo in Spain, Eduardo Bonnin and Bishop Juan Hervas, saw their movement transported to the United States in 1957, although Cursillo hit its stride in the states in the 1970s in conjunction with the Catholic Charismatic Renewal movement. The two movements might be said to have produced a "new" type of Catholicism: the "Jesus Saves" hand clapping "let it be emotional" school and the so-called Masonic "secret society" of Cursillo, which started out as a movement exclusively for men but which, falling victim to secular culture, went co-ed.

The confusing state of American Catholicism at this time can be seen in the 1969 Elvis Presley movie *Change of Habit*, which also stars Mary Tyler Moore who plays a nun.

This Presley Mass is what many considered to be "relevant" during the late 1960s. As Dr. Taylor Marshall commented: "I find it interesting how the presumably secular director prophetically captured the problem by showing the vocational angst of Mary Tyler Moore while interchanging scenes from traditional images of Catholicism (saint statue, crucifix, statue of Mary) with the novelties of the era (Elvis, guitars, dancing Gospel choir)." This is a wild mix Liturgy, so much so that one gets the feeling that all the traditionally robed nuns will soon strip off their traditional habits in exchange for a dark blue stretch pants suit. Hooting and hollering, indeed.

THE PERCEIVED CULT OF CATHOLIC TRADITIONALISM

Some years ago, a U.S. Catholic bishops meeting in Baltimore made a claim that there were far too few active Catholic priests familiar with the rite of exorcism.

Father Malachi Martin, who died in 1996, says that at the height of the Second Vatican Council in Rome, there was a ceremony to enthrone Lucifer in the Vatican (and the Chair of Peter). The church in question, Saint Paul's chapel within the Vatican walls, hosted a very different rite of Mass on January 29, 1963, just one week after the election of Pope Paul VI. (Years later, according to Fr. Martin, Pope Paul VI would write a note to his successor, John Paul II, and tell him of this ceremony.) Paul VI is also famous for his statement, "The smoke of Satan has entered the sanctuary."

For decades, this statement has been the source of much confusion and controversy.

The ceremony, Fr. Martin is on record as saying, was a Black Mass, or the Traditional Latin Mass said in reverse, complete with an animal sacrifice and a drugged young girl who may or may not be the victim of ceremonial sexual rituals. The ceremony was not the Novus Ordo Mass because, in Fr. Martin's words, "even the Satanists know that this Mass is not valid." Martin writes that the Black Mass was attended by high-ranking prelates in the church, important layman, business leaders, and politicians. At least one cardinal was also in attendance. A concurrent "Enthronement of Satan" Black Mass was also held in South Carolina on that date.

In his novel *Windswept House*, which Fr. Martin always maintained was 90 percent fact and 10 percent fiction, the opening chapter describes this Mass:

> In an atmosphere of darkness and fire, the Chief Celebrant in each Chapel intoned a series of Invocations to the Prince. The Participants in both Chapels chanted a response. Then, and only in America's Targeting Chapel, each Response was followed by a Convenient Action—a ritually determined acting-out of the spirit and the meaning of the words.

The presiding bishop then considered the victim. "Even in her near unconscious state, still she struggled. Still she protested." Finally, the Bishop began the Great Invocation: "I believe that the Prince of the World will be enthroned this night in the Ancient Citadel, and from there He will create a New Community: the Universal Church of Man."

Fr. Martin's bestselling book, *Hostage to the Devil*, described his many years as an exorcist. Some Vatican insiders insisted that Fr. Martin had an axe to grind, while others attempted to destroy his credibility with stories of illicit love affairs with the wives of friends. Towards the end of his life, despite a liberal sojourn when he worked for Cardinal Bea during the time of the Council, Fr. Martin maintained that the Catholic Church was in apostasy. He pointed to "liberal, heretical" theologians like Charles Curran and Hans Kung, as being given slaps on the wrist for ascribing to heretical doctrines but still allowed to practice as Catholic priests, while those whose only goal was to preserve tradition, such as Archbishop Lefebvre, were excommunicated by then Pope John Paul II (that excommunication was summarily lifted by Pope Benedict VI).

Father Gabriele Amorth, the onetime chief exorcist in Rome, wrote in his book *Memoirs of an Exorcist: My Life fighting against Satan* that there are active Satanic sects within the Vatican "where participants reach all the way to the College of Cardinals." This infiltration of Satanists and Masons forms what Martin calls the Vatican "superforce," or an organization of powerful prelates who work to destroy the Catholic Church from within.

The slow and insidious impregnation began as early as the 1930s and '40s when former United States Communist Party member Bella Dodd testified before the House on Un-American Activities in 1952 that the Communist Party in the 1930s "put eleven hundred men into the priesthood in order to destroy the Church from within."

Dodd told the Committee, "Right now they are in the highest places, and they are working to bring about change in order that the Catholic Church will no longer be effective against Communism."

The change, Dodd asserted, "Would be so drastic that you will not recognize the Catholic Church."

Confirming Dodd's testimony, another former American Communist Party official, Manning Johnson, told the HUAC that "the Communists discovered that destruction of religion could proceed much faster through infiltration of the Church by Communists operating within the Church itself."

While the Council itself did not call for the radical changes and abuses that occurred over the last forty years, "the spirit of Vatican II" led bishops to implement changes not authorized by the Council or the Pope. One such change was that regional conferences of bishops were given new powers that would later work to distort and change the original intention of the Council. One example is the Council's insistence that Latin be retained as an essential part of the Catholic Mass but conferences of regional bishops kicked this mandate to the curb.

Catholic life in the 1970s had become a choreographed dance macabre, according to Dr. John C. Rao, an associate professor of history at New York's St. John's University. Writing in *Love in the Ruins, Modern Catholics* in search of the ancient faith, Dr. Rao posits that entering into a dialog with the "Neo Catholics" was nearly impossible. "I simply found no means of engaging a discussion with Whirling Dervishes in the grip of renewal fever." Dr. Rao writes:

> All of their man-centered activities were defended by them with reference to the obvious guidance of a Holy Spirit whom I was said to despise, a Holy Spirit who had suddenly and inexplicably exchanged His friendship for Catholic Tradition for a Shiva-like passion for its annihilation. Mockery and distortion of Traditionalist arguments were the unchanging weapons in the progressive arsenal in those days...

Mary Ann Kreitzer, founder and president of Les Femmes, a Catholic group, writing in the same anthology, recalls home liturgies with "liberation theology" angles preached by Franciscan priests who then went on to celebrate a "noisy guitar and tambourine hootenanny home Mass with one of the priests presiding."

And what, if anything, did Malachi Martin know about Archbishop Annibale Bugnini, the designer of the Novus Ordo Mass? Was Bugnini, who was eventually dismissed from his post, part of the secret cabal behind Vatican Walls?

After all, it was Bugnini who said "We must strip from our Catholic prayers and from the Catholic liturgy everything which can be the shadow of a stumbling block for our separated brethren, that is, for the Protestants."

Vatican II's imprint on the liturgical life of the church was for many, including this writer, devastating. Gregorian chant and Mozart were kicked to the curb and replaced with hymns like "On Eagles Wings" and folk music. "The Great Dumbing Down" also affected Catholic Church architecture: Beautiful churches were stripped of their high altars, statues, and mosaics in the name of "ecumenicalism." In the American Church especially, experimentation and excess imploded with clown and jazz masses, Gucci nuns in lipstick and puffed up (or puffed down) feminist hairdos, some of whom were now calling God "Mother Goddess" and intoning the virtues of WICCA.

In the whacky 1970s, a priest might jump out from the sanctuary and do dance numbers in front of the congregation, tassel with a hula hoop, or shuffle about as if reliving his youth in New York's Peppermint Lounge. It was the age of the "cool" priest with the lascivious wink, a time when pretty much anything was acceptable if the parish priest said it was okay, even if that meant calling for a board of directors to replace the Papal Office in Rome.

The church in the 1970s seemed to be on a fast lane to the heart of the twenty-first century. In the end, however, instead of unity with Protestants the fruits of the Council were factionalism and schism. Traditionalist Catholics dubbed the Novus Ordo Church as misguided, while others formed organizations like the Society of Saint Pius X. When traditionalist seminaries and convents began springing up, the church realized it had a problem.

"The Catholic Church is really two Churches now," as one priest said to me recently.

The Traditional Latin Mass Community of Philadelphia was established to celebrate the Extraordinary Form of the Roman Rite in the Archdiocese of Philadelphia. The Archdiocesan churches that celebrate the Traditional Latin rite include Saint Mary Catholic Church in Conshohocken; Our Lady of Mt. Carmel Church in Doylestown; Our Lady of Lourdes Church in Overbrook; the National Shrine of Our Lady of Czestochowa, Doylestown; Our Lady of Consolation, Tacony; Our Lady of Mt. Carmel Chapel, Plymouth Meeting; and the Cathedral-Basilica of Saints Peter and Paul, Philadelphia.

CATHOLIC WORKER LEFT PROGRESSIVISM

I headed on out to Villanova University to hear writer and author Jim Forest talk about his new book, *At Play in the Lions' Den: A Biography and Memoir of Daniel Berrigan*.

When I was a conscientious objector during the Vietnam War, the brothers Berrigan, Dan, and Phil, both Jesuit priests, were heroes of mine. Never mind that in those days every Catholic I knew, including family members, were all "just war" types. Hardly any Catholic in my personal world then questioned authority. The concept of reading the gospels in an antiwar context was really foreign to the average Catholic. Good Catholic Irish boys did as they were told. If your country wanted you to serve in Vietnam, you went to Vietnam, you did not ask questions. When your draft notice arrived in the mail, you did not question the process but did as you were told, signed on the dotted line, and then willingly let yourself be shipped off to war.

Jim Forest, born in Salt Lake City, Utah, in 1941, is the author of numerous books. At age twelve, he became an Episcopalian. When he was in the U.S. Navy, he became a Roman Catholic and began working for the Catholic Worker Movement in New York City. He applied (and got) conscientious objector status while in the U.S. Navy. He was arrested for burning draft cards at a Vietnam War protest. His Catholic Worker connections enabled him to get to meet and know Dan Berrigan, Dorothy Day, and the famous Trappist monk Thomas Merton.

The Catholic Worker Movement was the central nerve of the Catholic peace and justice movement. As managing editor of the newspaper *The Catholic Worker*, Forest had amazing access to all kinds of people.

In his book about Dan Berrigan, there are his photographs of Thomas Merton in his hermitage at Gethsemane, Kentucky.

In the 1980s, Forest spent a lot of time in the Soviet Union and became acquainted with the Orthodox Church. He became an Orthodox Christian in 1988, something that he says slightly confused Dan Berrigan but which Berrigan supported nevertheless. Berrigan's Catholicism had Irish (family) cultural roots and could not be reconfigured.

In my talk with Forest after the lecture, he told me that his peace and justice work continues as secretary of the Orthodox Peace Fellowship.

At Villanova, Forest appeared with noted novelist and author James Carroll, author of the award-winning book *An American Requiem: God, My Father, and the War That Came Between Us*. Carroll, a Bostonian, was once a Paulist priest in Boston and part of the Boston Paulist Center, a place where I sometimes attended Catholic Mass when revisiting my old adopted city when staying with a friend there. My friend, a Catholic radical and a truly prophetic spiritual voice, saw the cutting-edge Paulist liturgy with its slide shows, rock music, and heavily non-traditional features as a thoroughly fitting worship venue in the modern era. During our friendly debates, he would often call me a liturgical reactionary, a label that at first struck me as having "intellectually challenged" roots but which I later came to embrace. Our differences never affected our deep friendship.

Forest began his talk with a warning to the audience that they might hear a tug or two of Parkinson's disease. In 2007, Forest had a kidney transplant donated by his wife. He lives in Amsterdam and is the father of six children. As I watched him speak and later sign books in the great hall of Villanova's nursing school, I could see that his face and general demeanor still retained much of its decades-earlier twenty-something vigor.

On the day of the event, James Carroll was in the throes of controversy thanks to a piece he wrote for *The Atlantic* in which he calls for the abolition of the Catholic priesthood. The former Paulist priest now lives with his writer wife in Boston.

"For the first time in my life," Carroll writes, "and without making a conscious decision, I simply stopped going to Mass."

> I embarked on an unwilled version of the Catholic tradition of "fast and abstinence"— in this case, fasting from the Eucharist and abstaining from the overt practice of my faith. I am not deluding myself that this response of mine has significance for anyone else—Who cares? It's about time!—but for me the moment is a life marker. I have not been to Mass in months. I carry an ocean of grief in my heart.

"Every sentence of James Carroll's recent article in *The Atlantic*, 'Abolish the Priesthood,' is theologically inept, historically anachronistic, self-referential, or all three. None of it is a surprise," *The National Catholic Reporter* stated in response.

Carroll is an elegant speaker with a captivating patrician air, especially when he looks at the audience over the rim of his reading glasses. His Catholic critics are many. Carroll is really Swiss theologian Hans Kung on steroids.

Forest recounted many things about the life of Dan Berrigan, especially how Berrigan wanted to shape his life around the Beatitudes, advising Catholics "to get out of the tomb and make some gestures…a little act of civil disobedience." Berrigan, Forest, said, "had powerful convictions but he was not self-righteous."

Forest recounted how Berrigan once handed him a check for $10,000 when the house that Forest was living in was in dire need of insulation.

He talked about Berrigan's view of the "micro-gods" that people have in society: obsessions related to gyms, work, sports, or politics. According to Berrigan, "If you're going to have a god, it might as well be God."

He recounted how at one lecture somebody asked Berrigan how he deals with priestly celibacy. "I am so sorry I forgot to bring my celibacy slide show with me," Berrgian responded.

Forest did not say much about Dorothy Day, although in one of his columns about her, he remembered her "Mass encounter" with a radical priest.

> Pleased as she was when home Masses were allowed and the liturgy translated into English, she didn't take kindly to smudging the border between the sacred and mundane. When a radical priest used a coffee cup for a chalice at a Mass celebrated in the soup kitchen on First Street, she afterward took the cup, kissed it, and buried

it in the backyard. It was no longer suited for coffee-it had held the Blood of Christ. I learned more about the Eucharist that day than I had from any book or sermon.

Note the emphasis on "a radical priest." Many of the radical priests in the 1970s and '80s went on to leave the priesthood. Certainly at Philadelphia's Saint Peter Claver Catholic Worker House (now defunct) where I used to often visit, there were many radical Masses, some celebrated by lay people, some celebrated by women, some celebrated by real priests, although the liturgy was often a patchwork of put together contemporary songs, verses, though occasionally a traditional text was thrown in for tradition's sake.

Yes, the Catholic Church is really two churches now.

MEET ME AT THE SWEDENBORG

"*All religion has to do with life, and the life of religion is to do good,*" Johnny Appleseed

The essence of the Swedenborg church is twofold: there is one God in one person Jesus Christ but a Trinity does not exist. Swedenborgians believe that the idea of the Trinity was a false misconception invented in the fourth century (called tritheism). In the Swedenborg church, there is no faith that is not a living faith of activity and good works.

Emanuel Swedenborg (1699–1772) believed that "All people who live good lives, no matter what their religion, have a place in Heaven."

In *Philadelphia Reflections: The musings of a physician who has served the community for over six decades*, the author notes that there are at least four divisions of the Swedenborgian religion in the Philadelphia region but that the Bryn Athyn branch is the most notable.

A very wealthy adherent of Swedenborg named John Pitcairn bought a large tract at Bryn Athyn and gathered the local church to live around a perfectly magnificent cathedral and church school. It is hard to think of any church in the Philadelphia region which approaches the magnificence of the Bryn Athyn cathedral. It has a special character that it was conceived and built during the crafts movement of the early twentieth century, with imported European workmen deliberately organized like medieval craft guilds. The central features of this workmanship reflect and then project the belief in personal individuality within the whole religion. No two windows, or doorknobs, or carvings are the same in the cathedral, reflecting the wish for each workman to devise his own unique creation and show the way of personal responsibility to the faithful. This cathedral is one of the things in the Philadelphia region most worth visiting, but to appreciate its quality you have to know what you are looking at.

Emanuel Swedenborg, the Swedish mystic who claims that he was guided by God to visit the realms of the afterlife in spirit form, wrote volumes on what lies beyond this life. Among his many books, *The Lives of Angels* posits the premise that there is a cosmic sex in the afterlife among married couples.

This is what Swedenborg reports that an angel told him during one of his heavenly tours:

> All men who are newcomers are examined, as they come up towards heaven, to see what kind of chastity they have. They are brought into the company of young women, heavenly beauties, who sense from their tone of voice, their speech, their eyes, their body language, and the aura they emit, what kind of people they are in regard to their love for the opposite sex. If they are unchaste, the young women flee and tell their companions that they have seen satyrs or priapuses. The newcomers themselves change as well, and to angels look all hairy, with feet like calves' or leopards. Before long, they are expelled so that their lust will not pollute the region's aura.

Swedenborg says that married partners experience the same love in heaven as they did in life, only it is stronger with greater feeling and sensitivity. What comes from sexual intercourse in heaven, however, is not the birth of children, but spiritual offspring: "The marriage of goodness and truth is a marriage of love and wisdom, and love and wisdom are the offspring of this marriage. Since in this situation the husband is wisdom and the wife is its love, and since both are spiritual, the only offspring that can be conceived and born are spiritual."

That is not all: rather than the letdown that usually follows human (earthly) intercourse, in heaven there is only a cheerful "constant flow of new vitality" that refreshes and illuminates the couple. Swedenborg also reports that there are various levels of Heaven, and that there are cities, towns, magnificent houses, and palaces.

Swedenborg continues:

> In heaven they [men] do not even know what infidelity is. They do not know that it exists or that it is possible. Unchaste love, extramarital love, chills an angel's whole body, just as chaste love, marriage love, warms an angel's whole body. For men, their nerves sag at the approach of a prostitute and become excited at the sight of their wives.

Swedenborg's message arrived in Philadelphia in 1784, when John Glen, sailing from England, introduced Philadelphians to the mystic's most popular work, *Heaven and Hell*. The book, states the church's website, Swedenborg.org, is a compendium of "Glen's lectures on Swedenborg's descriptions of the ever-present reality of a spiritual world. Many prominent Pennsylvanians attend Glen's talks and turn to Swedenborg's volumes. Some of these followers establish churches, whereas others simply become devoted readers of Swedenborg."

10

Philadelphia's Radical Faeries

Mark Thompson's anthology, *The Fire in Moonlight* (White Crane), is a collection of first person accounts of the Harry Hay-inspired Radical Faerie movement. Hay, a co-founder of the Mattachine Society, joined forces with Don Kilhefner and Mitch Walker to start the Faerie movement in order to add a spiritual dimension to the (often-dry) nuts and bolts world of emerging gay politics.

Inspired in part by the writings of Edward Carpenter and the Calamus poems of Camden's Walt Whitman, Hay saw the homosexual as much more than a creature fighting for rights in a hostile society. The homosexual, according to Hay, was a multidimensional being with roots in the mythic, a sort of alien spirit with special healing gifts for the world.

As Stuart Timmons notes in his introductory essay, "The Making of a Tribe," Hay once told a circle of 200 Faeries: "We Faeries need to stop saying, 'My consciousness is better than your consciousness.' That's heterosexist. No one person, no one group, no one ideology has the answer. You need a spirit."

Theologians may quibble with that relativist statement, insisting that if one truth is as good as another truth, then there is no truth anywhere. One thing's certain, however: You have to have spirit in order to "build." For Hay, this meant constructing a homosexual spiritual dimension outside the world of conventional religion.

In a 1975 edition of RFD, Hay wrote: "To be a true homosexual, is to be put at odds with home, school and society.... We are so other that we have to learn early how to protect our very survival."

While this perspective may seem dated, Hay was nonetheless insistent that a pronounced queerness was buried inside the homosexual's "stubbornly perverse genes." Hay's vision of a monastic-like collective of queer men of all ages coming together in friendship circles for a process of "shedding the ugly green frog skin of hetero-imitation" started with the first Faerie Circle in Colorado in 1979.

Called "A Spiritual Conference for Radical Faeries," at that Labor Day event, hundreds of men (the gatherings would later include women) participated in mud baths and neo-pagan, quasi-Native American rituals like circle hand holding, chanting, and taking turns speaking to the circle while holding a "Talking Stick." Many of these *ad hoc* talks were spiked with references to Aliester Crowley as well as Hay's own take on what it means to be "queer" and "other."

In these free-love pre-AIDS gatherings, there was ritualized group sex as well as individual couplings. As Timmons observes, "In selecting fairies as a role model for gays, [Hay] combined logic with inspiration to surpass the medieval Mattachines—to a pre-Christian time and beyond human limits."

With its emphasis on aspects of Native American culture and worship of the earth, the early Faeries attracted gay men who had had enough of the dead end clone life in the urban gay ghetto.

At the second Spiritual Gathering for the Radical Faeries in 1980, in Estes National Forest above Boulder, Colorado, faerie names were adopted and the emphasis on paganism was enhanced. As contributor Carol Kleinmaier notes, besides a denial of spirit-body and male-female duality, Faerie spirituality "was sourced in … the celebration of sacred sexuality, Wicca, paganism and shamanic traditions."

As one would expect, highly eclectic and a diverse range of spiritual references as well as divergent opinions about the Faerie experience mark these essays.

Allen Page, for instance, writes that during the first gathering he "asked the Goddess (which Goddess he doesn't say) to show him why he needed to be there." Meanwhile, "a young man shook a rattle and stands up in a speckled dress." The philosophy was to embody masculine and feminine energies, although one finds in many of these stories a distinct prejudice against patriarchy as well as an emphasis "to take the gifts of the Father back to the Mother."

Philadelphian Faerie Chris Bartlett notes:

> I like cultures that use rituals to embody choice: the Amish Rumspringa when Amish teens, following a year of exposure to the outside world, choose to join the Amish community (be baptized) or are shunned. Another example is the bar/bat mitzvah when young Jews choose to take on the responsibilities of adulthood. The investiture of a priest in various religions is another moment of powerful choice. When participants in a culture choose to embrace that culture, they become full actors, as opposed to full recipients.

In Faerie circles, identification with the feminine is assumed. It would not be unusual, for instance, for the males in a circle to cry while listening to reports of the rape of a female friend of a member. Since Radical Faeries spanned all age categories, older men were respectfully called elders and were regarded as purveyors of wisdom, even if that "respect" ended at the bedroom door. Wisdom cannot compete with beauty when it comes to a good lay.

Artwit, for instance, writes that at one gathering he got lucky three times so that his "usual depression at being alone while the slender twinks slept in pairs was less severe." Highly critical of many in the Faerie community, Artwit states that "self-righteous beliefs about food seem to be a hallmark of the Faeries. We used to joke in the kitchen about making 'Cream of Vegan' soup for our next meal."

Artwit also writes about the Faerie Drag Wars:

The first two Gatherings had that old rustic-northwest-jeans-and-flannel flavor and here come these queens from California doing wigs and make-up. So a small culture war was started at the Gathering, with the hosts deciding not to send the Call to California next year. [But] over the years, wigs and makeup won and overtook whatever Heart Circles there were.

For Artwit, the Faeries main problem was making social problems into personal ones. "I have no desire to be a Faerie Mormon and make breakfast while the pretty ones sleep in," he writes.

As Berbiar (Jerry the Faerie) puts it: "We need queers who have radical askance alternative viewpoints to dominant cultural mores. May the Radical Faerie movement continue to play its role in providing a cauldron of change so needed in this ignorant and repressive world."

At the end of the day, when the big parties are over and when youth has long since vacated our material bodies, we sometimes look for life's deeper meaning: Why are we here? Is the journey of life just a climb for success, status, wealth, and getting laid?

In 2012, *The Philadelphia Inquirer* reported on a Radical Faerie parade on Broad Street. The active Philadelphia Faerie community is friendly and tight knit, celebrating seasonal festivities like the Imbolc Gatherette and hosting Faerie arts and crafts shows at the city's William Way Community Center.

One thinks of the celebratory themes in Walt Whitman's poetry while reading this missive from the Philadelphia Faeries to its members:

The 2016 Philly Faerie Imbolc Gatherette is upon us * * *
Thursday January 28th–Sunday January 31st

Come for all or some part of it, and let's celebrate Imbolc, the center-point of the dark half of the year. It heralds the coming of spring (although, for many of us, it hasn't really left, and we have mixed feelings about that; [this could be a centerpiece conversation, and how we are responding, or not, to this]). It also celebrates the light returning, & we long for the sweet milk of Life flowing from our dark, creative wombs.

The last FIVE Winter Gatherettes have been amazing, magickal, confluences of sweet, faerie love. Let's add more beauty to this legacy that we've created together, and make this sixth Gatherette even more wondrous. Blessed be.

So come smell what's being stewed in our kitchens made by and for us!; taste the sweetness of enjoying hand-prepared soup with someone that you just shared a belly laugh with; feel the warmth of your couchmates leg just gently resting next to yours; take a gander and see what people look like when immersed in a space of acceptance and joy … can you hear our calls of "Welcome Home, we're so glad you could join us!"

THE RELIGIOUS-LIKE CULT OF THE PIT BULL

Here come the pit bulls, twenty in a row and howling like wolves in Germany's Black Forest. Where to escape? Many people slip inside their houses. Moms who had been sitting on stoops reach out and take their babies out of strollers and tell their other toddlers on tricycles to stop everything and get inside.

"The pits are coming! The pits are coming!" somebody shouts.

I witness the Stephen King scenario from my second-story window. "Does this explain the odd disappearance of feral cats from the neighborhood?" a friend of mine who dropped by asks.

"How's that?" I say.

"Feral cats slip in and out of backyard tiny spaces, the same private backyard spaces where the city's new breed of choice, the pit, lingers and waits. It's much like the fly going into the spider's web. The pit eliminates the feral!"

My friend may be right. The neighborhoods used to be filled with feral cats. On my own block, we used to see two or three a day. Suddenly there is an absence.

Of course, I never did see twenty pits in a row racing down my street, but given the popularity of pits, it could happen in the future.

It is not the breed, it is the people who raise the dogs, the pro-pit campaign posters state. We are supposed to commit this feel-good advertising to memory. We are supposed to remember this the next time we read an awful story in the press about a pit attacking a toddler on the way home from school. We are supposed to get it straight that pits are just like any other dog—the regal Greyhound, the cute-as-pie Chihuahua, the hot dog or Dachshund, or the supremely benevolent Collie. Blame the awful person who taught the pit how to be an indiscriminate fighter or growler, the pro-pit campaign says. The pit, by itself—as a blank slate—is as angelic as the lower order of angels.

Philadelphia is pit bull heaven, although it used to be that only the grungiest people owned them, like drug dealers, the corner tough guy, or people who just did not know any better. Pit bulls were associated with crime and filth and people with little or no class. Then there was a transformation. The pit bull's inherent ugliness (all jaw) was suddenly perceived as something beautiful. This reversal game reminds me very much of George Orwell's the Ministry of Truth in the novel *1984* standing for its opposite, the Ministry of Lies.

I have a neighbor who has three ferocious pit bulls. These dogs are not gentle. They growl in his backyard. They chew and eat everything. One time they ate through a wire fence. When this neighbor of mine walks his pits, three at a time, they storm the street ahead of him, growling, snarling, and racing as if possessed by demons.

I do not know how my neighbor deals with these animals. The pits are so uncontrollable he has to walk them very late at night. If he walked them too early in the day, they would lunge at people passing by on the sidewalk. These pits will attack anyone and everyone. At night sometimes I hear them growling and chewing through rubber and wire. When I am on my patio, I hear them in my neighbor's house growling and clamoring to get out so they can attack me.

These pits sometimes appear in my nightmares: Twenty charging pit bulls in a pack howling like wolves in Germany's Black Forest. There is nowhere to escape. In these dreams, I see people running into their houses.

The pits are coming. The pits are coming.

As an animal lover, I have a hard time with pit bulls. I like my dogs to be graceful and sleek, not barrel shaped with bulbous round heads and eyes that are always defensively on edge. I like a dog's face not to be all jaw. The all-jaw look is a giveaway: this animal is about violence and death.

A friend of mine insists that the odd disappearance of feral cats in the neighborhood has something to do with the popularity of pit bulls.

City feral cats slip in and out of my backyard patio and then they walk into my neighbor's patio. Before he was forced to keep his pit bulls indoors because of all the damage they were causing, they roamed the patio and attacked and devoured feral cats. It was much like the fly going into the spider's web.

"It's not the breed it's the people who raise the dogs," pit bull enthusiasts say. "Remember this the next time you read an awful story about a pit attacking a toddler on the way home from school. It's the fault of the owners, the people who trained the pit, not the pit." In other words, it is comparable to a teen boy who bullies people. Blame the parents. The kid was not trained properly. He is innocent.

Pit bull lovers are like people who belong to religious cults. They have lost the ability to reason and think rationally. The pit bull to them is a golden calf, an idol that must be protected at all costs.

On the Pennsylvania SPCA website, most of the dogs up for adoption are pit bulls with names like Machiatto and Brown Sugar. The underlying philosophy of the SPCA is that pit bulls are beautiful and loyal pets and they are just like any other dog. The SPCA has become part of the pit bull propaganda machine when they spout mantras like: "Don't blame the pit bull if it turns violent, blame the awful person who taught the pit how to be an indiscriminate fighter or growler."

Yet we never read how five Collie's mauled a Philadelphia toddler to death, as was the case in August 2018 when Newsweek reported that five pit bulls killed a toddler.

In January 2019, Philadelphia police shot pit bulls attacking a woman in her Northeast neighborhood. These same pit bulls had attacked the woman on a previous occasion.

Like the Pennsylvania SPCA, ACCT Philly, the largest animal care and control service provider in the region, hosts countless pictures of dogs up for adoption, and 90 percent of the dogs are pit bulls with names like Bahama Mama, Dobby, Star, Chase, Marathon, Harper, and Chance. The name Chance is appropriate. You take a chance with a pit bull. Many pit bull attacks occur after the dogs have been relatively well behaved for long periods of time. Then something snaps. That something is called the breed; it is called genetics.

Pit bulls are not "mean" or "aggressive" when they maim and kill, any more than labs are mean or aggressive when they retrieve, pit bulls simply maul and kill because of genetics. Denying the truth will not reduce the killings by these intentionally bred blood sport animals.

There is only one solution: Spay and neuter pit bulls to extinction.

The breeding of pit bull traits into the larger classic dog population has essentially destroyed the dog world. Dogs with half pit bull traits are now as common as the Cocker Spaniel was only forty years ago.

Pit bulls were practically unheard of when I was growing up. There were only Collies, Dachshunds, (real) Boxers and Shepherds, although the term junkyard dog (breed unknown) made the rounds from time to time, referring to ill-mannered ugly dogs who were so nasty they would attack their own tail.

Perhaps the most infamous dog in my family was the black French Poodle, Monsieur Faux Pas.

Monsieur Faux Pas was an indiscriminate, shameless cad. He loved legs, all sorts of legs, young and old, even leggy furniture stumps. As a teenager, I would walk Monsieur Faux Pas all over the streets of West Chester, Pennsylvania. He was well behaved during these walks but he showed his Jekyll and Hyde side at family gatherings as the adults sipped cocktails in the living room.

That is when he would go on a leg romp. There is nothing in life that brings one down to earth faster than having a dog greet you with a leg hump. My venerable grandfather, dressed to the nines, would suddenly be jolted forward on the sofa as Monsieur wrapped his beastly paws around his argyle socks.

"No, no, no!" grandmother would interject. .

Monsieur, undeterred, would proceed to Aunt Dora—silk stockings always made the grade—then proceed to grandmother herself, and then after that to each of my siblings, going down the line.

"He needs to be locked in a room," Aunt Dora would say, and so Monsieur would be ushered upstairs until the terrible spell that had possessed him had passed. In an hour or so, he could be released into polite company.

But had Monsieur been a pit bull, he would have eaten his way out of that room and then punished us all with certain death.

11

The Cultic, "Scenic" Amish

In Philadelphia's Reading Terminal Market, one can see Amish and Mennonite farmers working their food stands of fresh produce, meats, and various bakery items. The women wear hair nets or bonnets while the men dress in dark trousers, white shirts, and suspenders. They work with precision and focus and are rarely distracted by the large crowds that filter through the market. Some farmer vendors will occasionally bring their children so the sight of boys in bowl cut haircuts and girls dressed like their mothers in bonnets holds a certain fascination for city shoppers.

The Amish at market presents a quaint picture, reminiscent of what used to be called a "Saturday Evening Post" or a National Geographic moment. Meanwhile, outside the market, you will sometimes see Mennonite families riding the Market-Frankford El or the Broad Street subway. What one notices right away about these groups is their politeness and air of quietude. On the surface, these Plain People seem to be worlds away from the "living dangerously" pitfalls of city life, although this does not mean that these Plain People are protected from big city fallout.

No longer can it be claimed that the Amish live within a bubble. A check of contemporary newspaper and online news headlines will reveal that Amish country life is changing. An example might be Lancaster, Pennsylvania, a mere 60 miles from Philadelphia. As one of the central areas of Amish life, Lancaster was the location of the 1985 Harrison Ford film *Witness* (Paramount Pictures) that told the story of a Philadelphia detective on the run who hides out with an Amish family then falls in love with an Amish widow. When it was announced that the film would be shot on location in 1984, many of the Lancaster Amish objected despite the huge promotional efforts put forth by the Pennsylvania Bureau of Motion Picture and T.V. Development.

Filming began in the summer of 1984 and the Amish were quick to initiate protests. Donald B. Kraybill, in summing up the situation in his book *The*

Riddle of Amish Culture, wrote that the Amish had always opposed television, films, and photography:

> They resented being portrayed in a medium that they had historically condemned. Second, they have typically shunned publicity, and a commercial film would publicize Amish images on screens around the world.... Hollywood, perhaps more than any other word symbolized worldliness in the Amish mind—a "den of iniquity" that imprints sex and violence on the minds of viewers around the world. Thus to have Hollywood, the symbol of moral vice, make a film of the Amish and catapult them into international publicity was a triple insult. Finally, the Amish knew that they were being exploited commercially by the tourist industry. Writing in protest to the film to Pennsylvania Governor Richard L. Thornburgh, an Amishwoman said: "We Amish feel we are serving as a tool to lure tourists to Lancaster County."

The situation grew in intensity when Amish bishops warned their congregations not to cooperate with Paramount production crews. The warning, however, did stop huge crowds of curious Amish from watching the filming of the movie. Kraybill writes that *Witness* director Peter Weir made a promise not to use Amish persons in the cast, but apparently that did not stop actress Kelly McGillis, who played Harrison Ford's love interest in the film, from going undercover and spending several days in an Amish home before the ruse was discovered and she was kicked out:

> Upon identification, she was asked to leave. This breach of trust added insult to injury. An irritated Amish grandmother said: "Now, that was an intrusion. I thought that was pretty bad. We wouldn't do that to them [the public] and they wouldn't want us to either. They'd hike us out the door faster than we ever came in." Although the Amish stayed aloof from the filming, they felt betrayed by government officials who eagerly assisted Paramount Pictures. And as the Amish suspected, the monetary rewards were lucrative. The filming alone pumped several million dollars into the local economy.

After heated negotiations, an agreement was reached between the Amish and the director of the Pennsylvania Bureau of Motion Picture and T.V. Development regarding any invasion of privacy regarding the Amish.

The agreement stipulated:

> Will not promote Pennsylvania Amish as subjects for feature films or television productions.
>
> Will not promote any script that uses the Amish and/or its culture as subject matter.

Will refuse to deal with film companies that attempt to film the Amish without their consent or to trespass on their property.

Will inform potential producers of the Amish community's strong opposition to having photographs taken and having its culture represented in any theatrical production.

Witness no doubt helped the city of Lancaster become a major tourist destination, although the city was already climbing the population charts before Hollywood showed up. Lancaster long ago shed its "cow town"/hick town label, popular in the 1960s and '70s. Downtown Lancaster today resonates with the sophistication of New Hope, Pennsylvania. There one can find art galleries, antique shops, high-end restaurants, and cafes. The town's popularity, however, has created a downside for many Amish. Many families now see the area as becoming too crowded and congested; some Amish have even chosen to leave Lancaster for Amish enclaves in Ohio or Indiana while others have chosen to settle deeper into the Pennsylvania countryside.

With a big boost in population, a small town can become subject to the plagues and plights of big cities like Philadelphia. Reading, Pennsylvania, once a relatively quiet and still an architecturally fascinating town (it was the birthplace and childhood home of Pulitzer Prize-winning poet Wallace Stevens), is now a shell of its former self, thanks to exponential growth in the wrong direction. Roving gangs now pretty much control and patrol Reading's streets while longtime residents head out for safer environs. Lancaster's touristy main thoroughfares may not be gang-populated, but the city has been beset with enough drug trafficking to put a dent in the Amish bubble, so that pipes of crack, crystal meth, and lines of cocaine make for a new kind of chem.-trail over Lancaster skies.

Recent newspaper headlines like "Drug Epidemic Tearing Through Amish Countryside," "73 Amish Arrested; Mob Boss banned from PA Casinos," and YouTube videos like "Heroin use growing Problem Among Amish Youth," and "The Mennonite Drug Connection—the fifth estate," are not uncommon.

Who are the Amish and what makes them that way?

The vast generic Amish community is divided up into multiple church districts, each under the supervision of a different bishop. Each church district has different rules for members. There is the Old Order Amish (almost 90 percent of the Amish in Lancaster County belong to this group), distinguished by their practice of house worship where members take turns hosting Sunday services. Progressive Amish communities deviate from Old Order Amish in their allowance of electricity and automobile ownership. One Amish community may ban cell phones while another permits their usage; another community may permit the use of tractors while 10 miles away there may be Amish who can only use their tractors as in-place generators, never to be removed from the barn for field work. Other groups of so-called Plain People (defined as strict Christian sects that emphasize a simple way of life), namely the Church of the Brethren and various factions of Mennonites have (as Kraybill notes) a "colorful array of religious practices [that] perplexes outsiders and insiders alike."

> Although many of the groups have similar theological and cultural origins, they have split into factions with spirited fervor over such issues as cars, tractors, Sunday schools, television, and shunning. Some permit central heating in their homes and others oppose it.... One faction of Mennonites paints its car bumpers black to avoid an ostentatious appearance.

The German word *Gelassenheit* means submission or obedience. It also means giving something of yourself to the community. "The early Anabaptists used the term *Gelassenheit* to convey the idea of yielding absolutely to God's will with a dedicated heart—forsaking all selfishness." (Kraybill). On the raising of children, the Amish seem to have unlocked considerable wisdom. Kraybill notes:

> Using a standardized personality test administered to Amish children in several settlements, John Hostetler found that Amish personality types differed significantly from non-Amish ones. Indeed, the Amish personality exemplified *Gelassenheit*: "Quiet, friendly, responsible, and conscientious. Works devotedly to meet his obligations and serve his friends and school ... patient with detail and routine. Loyal, considerate, concerned with how other people feel even when they are in the wrong."

The Amish spank their children and believe it is never good to let a child have their own way. "By the time that the child reaches the age of three the mold has started to form and it is the parents' duty to form it in the way that the child should go." The goal is to teach children how to lose their selves, "to yield to the larger purposes of family and community."

The Amish trace their roots to the post-reformation following the Martin Luther-led Protestant Reformation in 1517. The pace of the 1517 Reformation, however, proved to be too slow for a group of believers in Zurich, Switzerland. This group of mainly young people found fault with the traditional practice of baptizing infants. The group wanted a complete break with this practice from ancient Christianity and became advocates for adult baptism. Infant baptism was a normal custom in the early Church. Saint Augustine himself wrote: "The custom of Mother Church in baptizing infants is certainly not to be scorned, nor is it to be regarded in any way as superfluous, nor is it to be believed that its tradition is anything except apostolic" (The Literal Interpretation of Genesis 10:23:39 [A.D. 408]).

The new movement became known as the Radical Reformation and its adherents given the name Anabaptists (or "rebaptizers"). Merriam-Webster defines Anabaptist as "a Protestant sectarian of a radical movement arising in the 16th century and advocating the baptism and church membership of adult believers only, nonresistance, and the separation of church and state."

The Anabaptists were considered heretics by the newly formed Protestant establishment. For 200 years they were tortured, imprisoned, and condemned to death by both Protestants and Catholics in a purge imitating The Inquisition of the twelfth century. The stories of Anabaptist persecutions can be found in the Amish *The Martyrs Mirror*, a book of over 1,100 pages that can be found in many Amish homes. An often-cited case of martyrdom in the book is the story of Dirk Willems:

> Willems was originally captured in 1569 by 'papists' for the crime of following and promoting the idea of rebaptism, a precursor to today's Amish and Mennonite practice of adult baptism.
>
> Willems ended up imprisoned in a tower near his home in the Netherlands. He later escaped by tying cloth together and shimmying down the walls.
>
> As he fled, a guard saw him and took off in hot pursuit. Coming to a pond covered with thin ice, Willems chanced it and crossed, making it safely to the other side. His pursuer was not so fortunate. The "thiefcatcher" cracked through the ice to plunge into the freezing water below.
>
> Amazingly, instead of making an easy getaway, Willems turned back and rescued the guard from a likely death. He was subsequently recaptured and later burned at the stake.

The Anabaptists known as Mennonites and the Amish have their roots in Catholicism. In the sixteenth century, Menno Simons (1496–1561), a Catholic priest, came to accept the Anabaptist view of Scripture. An article in *Christianity Today*, "Menno Simons, Anabaptist Preacher," explained:

> Believing the Bible to be authoritative, Menno developed the reputation as an "evangelical" preacher. "Everyone sought and desired me," he recounted. "It was said that I preached the Word of God and was a good fellow." But to Menno, it was a lie; his life was still empty and full of "diversions" like gambling and drinking.
>
> Three years later, an otherwise unknown Leeuwarden Anabaptist was beheaded, sending Menno into another spiritual crisis. "It sounded very strange to me to hear of a second baptism," he wrote. "I examined the Scriptures diligently and pondered them earnestly but could find no report of infant baptism." Again, he wrote, "I realized that we were deceived." But his life changed little: "I spoke much concerning the Word of the Lord, without spirituality or love, as all hypocrites do."

Eventually, he was hit with a final crisis. Three hundred violent Anabaptists, dreaming of the imminent end of the world and attempting to escape persecution, captured a nearby town—and were savagely killed by the authorities. Among the dead was Menno's brother, Peter.

"I saw that these zealous children, although in error, willingly gave their lives and their estates for their doctrine and faith.... But I myself continued in my comfortable life and acknowledged abominations simply in order that I might enjoy comfort and escape the cross of Christ."

The realization led to an emotional, tearful cry to God for forgiveness. For nine months thereafter he essentially preached Anabaptist doctrine from his Catholic pulpit, until he finally left the church and (a year later) fully cast his lot with the radical Reformers.

Simons's influence was so great that many Anabaptists came to be called Mennonists, or Mennonites.

The Amish branch of the Anabaptist movement was founded by Jacob Ammann after he came into conflict with a Swiss bishop named Hans Reist. The main issue was differences of opinion regarding banning troublesome members and whether or not these members should also be shunned in the larger social community. Ammann, who had strict views on the subject and would not compromise, opted for shunning. The congregations that supported Ammann's view became known as the Amish Church in 1693. Ammann, a conservative in other matters as well, was against beard trimming, fashionable dress besides being a rigid disciplinarian. Kraybill writes: "Although the Amish and Mennonite churches are parallel streams nourished by a common Anabaptist spring, they have remained organizationally separate to the present day."

Mennonites arrived in Philadelphia's Germantown section in 1683, some ten years (as Kraybill notes) before the Amish-Mennonite division. Then, in 1710, a group of Mennonites purchased 10,000 acres of land several miles south of Lancaster. In the years between 1717 and 1732, the Lancaster area was flooded by large groups of Swiss Mennonite settlers.

"...Historians are uncertain when the first Amish arrived in the New World," According to Kraybill: "...Amish immigration in the eighteenth century peaked between 1727 and 1770. *The Charming Nancy*, the first ship carrying a large group of Amish, docked in Philadelphia in 1737 after an eighty-three-day voyage. Thus in 1737, some twenty-seven years after the establishment of the first Mennonite colony in the Lancaster area, the Amish established their first two settlements."

Growing up in the farmlands of Chester County, I often heard stories of Amish youth carousing in cars, hiding liquor in barn haylofts, and acting like their hoodlum English counterparts. It was hard to make sense of this riddle especially considering the strict and repressive lifestyle the Amish came to represent. My childhood home sat at on a tract of land once owned by a Mennonite farmer and his wife. The land was sold to a developer in the 1950s; six modest split level homes were then built on the property. The farmer still owned a vast cornfield behind our house that included a small creek that meandered through a wooded area and near his large red barn. We played in the barn as children, wandering through the rustic corridors or engaging in a dangerous game called Jumping the Hay, which meant climbing to the highest point in the hayloft and then jumping down onto the hay bales that formed a false floor—false because often the small spaces between the bales would open up after a jumper landed. This was fine as long as there was an underlying cushion of more hay bales, but occasionally the spaces revealed a hole that went straight through to the actual floorboards of the barn, a good 40- or 50-foot drop. One day, my brother, in the exuberance of youth, jumped into the hay from the highest point in the barn and flipped in the air so that he managed to dive head first into one of the dangerous spaces. It was only after much effort that I was able to pull him out by his feet. To this day, he credits me with saving his life.

Every spring and fall, the farmer's two sons worked the field behind our house with rigorous authority. As their father drove the hay bale tractor, the sons bundled and threw the bales of hay on to the loading platform in the rear. We sometimes lent a hand, thinking the exercise more fun than work, but we soon tired out and retreated to the sidelines where we watched in amazement as the sons kept lifting bales until sunset.

In the Mennonite farmer's red barn were a variety of pigs and chickens. Cows and sometimes horses grazed in the enclosed barnyard and were sometimes led to the cornfield to graze in off season. An occasional cow found its way through the fence that separated it from our property and would make its way to our kitchen window where it would spook my mother while she was cooking or washing dishes. The barn was never locked so walking through it became routine. One day while rummaging through a deserted alcove on the barn's second floor, we spotted a pile of girlie magazines buried under a hay bale. They were obviously hidden there by the farmer's sons.

Were these magazines examples of the Mennonite version of the Amish rumspringa? The farmer's sons were about sixteen, the age when Amish youth are encouraged to go out into the world to experiment and explore. During this new freedom cycle, the behavioral restrictions of the past fade, although the slice of freedom is short, two years, but when it is over, Amish youth are expected to make a choice: to be baptized into the fold (which is tantamount to taking a vow to remain in the Church forever) or go their own way. Over 80 percent of Amish youth choose to be baptized, but those who do not choose baptism are not shunned but accorded a life outside the community where their visiting privileges remain intact. Shunning enters the picture only if, after baptism, one breaks their baptismal vows and leaves the community.

Tom Shachtman, in his article "Rumspringa: To Be or Not to Be," writes:

Rumspringa is a Pennsylvania Dutch term, usually translated as "running around" and derived in part from the German word *Raum*, which means "space"" in the sense of outside or outdoors space, room to roam. "Running around outside the bounds" is a more complete translation. The rumspringa period begins when an Amish youth turns sixteen; at that age, since the youth has not yet been baptized, he or she is not subject to the church's rules about permitted and forbidden behaviors. During rumspringa, Amish youth—a large percentage of them for the first time in their lives—go on their own in the outside world. Nearly all continue to live with their families, however, and many, maybe even a majority, do not go to the parties or otherwise engage in behaviors that Amish parents and church officials consider wild. Rather, they attend Sunday singings, occasionally go bowling, take part in structured activities supervised by church elders—tame stuff—but they have license to do things they have never done before. An individual's rumspringa ends when he or she agrees to be baptized into the church and to take up the responsibilities attendant on being an adult member of the Amish community.

Some of the Amish who do not return to their families for baptism may wander into cities like Philadelphia, especially those who fall victim to the drug culture.

In my area of Philadelphia called the Riverwards, I have met more than a couple of renegade ex-Amish and Mennonite youth on The Road.

A couple of years ago, while helping a friend with an errand, I wound up near East Somerset Street in Philadelphia's Kensington section. It was a bright summer afternoon. During that time, I was approached by no less than five people offering to sell me heroin, crack cocaine, and an assortment of prescription drugs. The blatant, in-your-face salesmanship of the dealers was shocking. The whole thing had an end-times feel to it, like I had walked into a Philly redux version of *Mad Max*.

Although my immediate neighborhood is rather nice, since moving here more than a decade ago, I have found that the big kahuna in the immediate region is opiates, followed by a variety of prescription drugs hawked by a new class of "criminal": ordinary people trying to make extra money by selling prescription drugs to friends and strangers.

In other words, you do not have to go far here to meet Klonopin or Xanax-trading moms or their stroller-pushing "distribution" daughters. Walk the streets in some parts of the Riverwards and you might see impromptu sidewalk haggles over this pill or that. Although there are standardized prices—four Klonopins for $10, Xanax coming in at 50 cents more, and Percocet drawing a top $6 a pop—people engage in unorthodox trades: ten Percocets to fix that toilet, twenty to clean out a basement, a dime bag of dust in exchange for old-time Valium and a case of Coors Light.

Sometime ago there was a University of Pennsylvania-sponsored Kensington "safari," meaning that a busload of Penn professors and anthropologists toured Kensington streets in the style of those Center City tourism buses for out-of-towners. For one day, the academics were able to get a first-hand look at prostitution and open-air drug transactions under the El.

Images of an Ivory Tower bus filled with Margaret Mead and Jane Goodall types in wide-brimmed sun hats staring at the natives through binoculars would be amusing if it were not such an exercise in futility.

"It's not hidden from view. You can see it along many streets. People scattered as the bus passed," *The Inquirer* quoted one professor as saying then. The absent-minded professor was talking about the same things that I see every day when I take the 39 bus to the Huntingdon El station. I laughed at the phrase, "People scattered as the bus passed." To a professor stuck in an Ivory Tower, the sight must have been shocking. Hey, there is real gritty city life going on here! Of course the natives are going to run. Nobody likes to be on the statistical end of an anthropological study.

"Oh, look at that one will you!"

"Get a load of her—no teeth!"

"Check out the hunchback!"

"Look at that prostitute in the beehive hairdo!"

While it is the business of universities to do serious studies—often these studies wind up in glossy binders or as graphs in textbooks where the print is too small—they rarely, if ever, produce any kind of change in society.

So what kind of change do "the experts" want for Kensington?

Many say that the Northern Liberties neighborhood should be Kensington's role model. Kensington advocates, in fact, like to talk about "tipping points" and "a positive transformation of the area led by artists and entrepreneurs."

I have accompanied them during walks around the city and listened to their stories and complaints about store managers and the police. I heard a number of success stories: how Jesse, who used to walk in traffic with his "Anything Will Help" sign, got off drugs, returned to school, and then became an important counselor and speaker on the topic.

During my travels, I met Mark, who has been working the Wawa doors for five years (meaning holding the door for customers). Mark makes as much as $40 a day working the doors. Whenever he sees a homeless newcomer working in his place, he gets up in his face.

"My spot," he says. "I've been here for five years. Leave now or else!"

Inevitably, the newcomer slinks away to wait out Mark's shift. In the meantime, other homeless drift in and stand on the sidelines waiting for a chance to take Mark's place. Challenging Mark to share the door is an iffy proposition—Mark's penchant for street drama is legendary.

Karl, who hails from Lancaster and grew up next to an Amish farm, knows all about working the doors. He tells me how the women homeless generally station themselves along the front of the store but rarely work the doors themselves. The women's panhandling style is generally more conversational than the men's. The women will walk and talk with people and occasionally whisper, "Do you date?"

The homeless who get squeezed out of working the doors are forced to find other locations. Other homeless drift to a smaller WAWA nearby while others stand in the front of Dunkin Donuts. Dunkin Donuts is not a good money venue, but it works as a gathering spot. Other homeless make their way to the 7/11 at Front and Girard.

Karl says that the homeless who work the trains (walking through passenger cars begging for money or selling pilfered candy) rarely beg outside convenience stores. Working the trains takes personality and the ability to speak in public. It helps to have to have a story ("I was robbed at gunpoint and have to feed my five children who are waiting for me in a hotel room," etc.) If you embarrass easily, you will not do well asking for money on the trains: All those commuters staring at you and analyzing your clothes and thinking those thoughts. Many of the train homeless think they are better than the convenience store homeless in the same way that those addicted to Xanax think that they are not as bad as "those scrappy heroin users." Everybody thinks they are better than their neighbor.

As one train-begging homeless guy told me, "I would never, never stand outside a store and beg."

Theft among the homeless is rampant. Clothes and blankets are stolen, although the most sought-after objects are cell phones. Thefts often occur at night when the victim is asleep. I have heard stories about how the most secret of secret stashes—belongings and such—are discovered and raided by other homeless. When a homeless person tells you that they just got a new phone, you can almost hear the clock ticking to the hour of its theft.

Most of the homeless praise the generosity of Philadelphians and say that they expected the opposite to be true when they first started to panhandle. After all, Philadelphia can be a hard nuts-and-bolts town, and for the homeless, it is even harder, especially when police and others tell you to leave the premises. Hardboiled homeless have told me how touched they are by the "good people in this city" when it comes to gifts of money, pizzas, cheese steaks, salads, and bags filled with deodorant, laundry detergent, shampoo, toothpaste, and socks. One person even offered Karl a one-way ticket back to Lancaster.

After World War II, the homeless populations in American cities were mostly confined to skid-row areas. Philadelphia's skid row or tenderloin district (on Vine Street from 8 to 11th Street), as it turns out, was much smaller than the tenderloin districts in most other cities. In 2017, however, nearly every city neighborhood has its own skid row.

How to deal with the homeless population has always been a perplexing problem. In 2017, Philadelphia mayor Jim Kenney, fresh from a fun Icelandic holiday, made the suggestion that Philadelphians stop giving cash to (homeless) panhandlers—which he contends is helping to fuel the city's opioid epidemic—and instead donate $5 by texting the word "Share" to 80077. The donated money would then be directed into the Mayor's Fund to End Homelessness and matched by the city's Office of Homeless Services.

This sterile, hands-off method of helping the homeless has a (cold) Icelandic feel to it. It seems to absolve all personal responsibility: "Just say no," as Nancy Reagan once quipped, and walk away from that panhandler with the dirty hands. But if all Philadelphians followed the mayor's suggestion, it would just make panhandlers more desperate and almost certainly increase thefts from local convenience stores. Panhandlers, whether on or off drugs, sometimes just need something to eat.

But does that change when all the panhandlers seem to be junkies? I used to think that only a portion of the homeless were junkies until I stepped into the nether world of the streets, talking and getting to know as many people as I could. I soon discovered that almost all of the people there were, in fact, addicts who refused to go into shelters, rehabs, or (supervised) community living houses because to do so would have limited their access to drugs.

The mayor's suggestion made me wonder if perhaps he had learned something new about the homeless during his vacation in Iceland. In 2004, the number of homeless people in Iceland was put at forty-five to fifty people, with those low numbers increasing somewhat recently but still worlds away from Philadelphia's shocking homeless statistics. (According to Project HOME, as many as 1,000 people live completely unsheltered in the city, depending on the season, and thousands more are in and out of dedicated shelters.) Certainly the cold weather has something to do with Iceland's minuscule homeless population, but the small numbers have also been attributed to the fact that homeless shelters there are not meant to be permanent homes, but revolving-door spaces—there is always room for other homeless person to come in off the streets.

Philadelphia's homeless shelters, in contrast, usually order all occupants out by 4 a.m. or 5 a.m. every day, at which point the homeless hit the streets with nothing to do. Since they do not have jobs, they panhandle. They panhandle because they need money for drugs and because they need the "left over" money for food.

In 2016, the city felt it had the solution to the panhandling problem when it began issuing citations (fines) to public beggars. This was big news among the homeless who ask for money at my local WAWA. The police were issuing $35 tickets to men who could not even afford to buy a cup of coffee. I spoke with several men then who told me that they tore up the citations and put them in WAWA's recycling bin. "How can we pay this when we have no money?" they said. When the $35 citation blitz finally subsided, the cat-and-mouse game between police and homeless resumed, but it was never consistent—some officers ignored the panhandlers while others issued walking orders to every panhandler in sight. It was a random game of bad cop/good cop.

While the city's opioid crisis needs fixing, it needs fixing at a point long before addicts are forced to resort to panhandling. Panhandling, after all, is usually the end-stage behavior of serious addiction. Tweeting a donation to a city agency is a superficial fix: Whatever benefit it promises to those in need, much of it will most likely be lost in overhead and personnel costs—the endless bureaucracy of so-called charitable giving—not to mention the potential financial "losses" of all those tweet donations, given the city's legendary tendency to mismanage funds.

The homeless in nineteenth-century America were called many names: hobos, tramps, and vagrants. In 1909, a man named Edwin Booth pretended to be unemployed and toured America's homeless shelters. Many of these shelters at that time were called wayfarers' lodges. A writer named Kenneth L. Kusner notes in his book *Down and Out, on the Road: The Homeless in American History* that Brown in his research noted that these lodges had similar characteristics:

(1) There was no pretense of bedding
(2) The occupants covered themselves with their ragged overcoats
(3) The food was almost inedible
(4) In Kansas City, the breakfast was dry bread, stewed prunes and watered down coffee without milk or sugar.

While no one expects a homeless shelter to ape the environs of a Hilton Hotel, very often the characteristics described above came with a price. In Louisville, Kentucky, for instance, the homeless had to work for the (free) water, soap, coffee, and coarse bread by chopping wood. In most wayfarers' lodges, the (free) meals distributed on a Sunday had to be worked for during the week. The usual lights-out time was 10 p.m. when all talking in the lodges had to cease.

Occupants were forbidden to drink, smoke, and swear. In many ways, the homeless were forced to live as monastics, although modern-day monks are sometimes free to indulge in wine or beer at special times.

The nineteenth century was a very judgmental time. The poor were seen as being "worthy" or "unworthy" when it came to receiving charity. The Salvation Army, to its credit, refused to make any such distinctions and served all the poor, or homeless, equally.

A curious Philadelphia connection can be found in "The Vagrancy Dockets of 1875." The Dockets surveyed 614 men and 147 women convicted of vagrancy. The Dockets found that 63 percent of the homeless were not married, while seven out of ten were literate with the average age being 34.6 years. About 60 percent of the convicted were born in the United States while over half of the group was native to Philadelphia.

Why Philadelphia? Was there something in the water here that caused so many to become homeless? The Dockets do not say, but they do state that a man in 1875 with more than one conviction of vagrancy could expect to be sentenced to twenty-four months in jail.

In the 1870s, tramps would often band together in aggressive packs, attacking farmers while giving the police a run for their money. After World War II, the homeless populations in American cities were mostly confined to skid row areas. Philly's skid row or tenderloin district (on Vine Street from 8 to 11th Street), as it turns out, was much smaller than the tenderloin districts in most other cities.

The assumptions many people made about the homeless in the nineteenth century (tramps = chronic drunkards) or in our own time (homeless = drug addiction) do not account for those homeless who defy categorization. In many ways, homeless people are just like you and me. Some former homeless go on to become public figures. Consider the personal homeless stories of Sylvester Stallone, Steve Jobs, Halle Barry, and Drew Carey. If we look at homelessness through a wide historical lens, the field becomes even more diverse. Elijah, in the Hebrew Bible, often appeared in the guise of a homeless person during his wayfaring days of prophesy.

VOYAGERS TO NOWHERE

They come into Philadelphia's Riverwards in droves. Sometimes they come as couples and occasionally they have a dog in tow. They set up camp in the strangest places: in front of convenience stores, pizza shops, Dunkin Donuts, dollar stores. They canvass traffic at stoplights with large cardboard signs. They all have slightly different stories. Some come from good homes, like Francis, who grew up in Lancaster in a religious Mennonite family, went to college to study film production, and traveled to New York before his life crashed.

Heroin caused his life to crash. He left New York for Philadelphia where he met a girl who had a knack for making a quick buck under the Frankford El. She was twenty-four years old, slender, and her almond-shaped face and eyes attracted men far and wide. This was a world millions of miles away from his Mennonite upbringing.

Couples bonded by heroin addiction rarely celebrate fifth or tenth anniversaries. Francis and Tiffany soon planned a road trip to Texas where they dreamt of a bohemian existence with Houston's music community. The road trip began with a bang. They posted Facebook photos of themselves eating tacos on Greyhound, and then Texas photos showing them bathing in a creek. Tiffany then met a man with money and Francis was history. Devastated, the former film student disappeared into that overcrowded nightmare known as the state of California. He then returned to Lancaster to regroup with his parents, but in the end he found that too boring. He kept thinking of Philadelphia's Heroin Trail in the neighborhood known as Kensington.

The vast majority of the homeless in Philadelphia are addicts. A miniscule percentage of the homeless are down on their luck but rebound quickly when offered a job and a place to live. Then they rejoin normal society. Some addicts are road trippers who travel from city to city. Like the legendary American hobos of the 1940s, '50s, and '60s, they ride the rails and sleep in boxcars, following a rustic tradition that has its roots in American literature. The poet Carl Sandburg and the novelist James Michener, for instance, both lived as train hobos for a while. Generally, these road tripper types have no intention of settling in Philadelphia.

Francis once introduced me to two homeless guys from his hometown of Lancaster. My impression was that one or both of them were from Amish or Mennonite communities, but when I asked about their background, they spoke in vague generalities.

The two men, Chris and Ron, said they usually hang out in lower Kensington by the Somerset El stop where they panhandle for drug money. Chris, aged twenty-eight, had a beard reminiscent of Saint Francis of Assisi or a stereotypical Amish farmer. He looked quite at home perched on top of a metal recycle bin as he told me that he had just come from a hospital where he tried to get himself committed. As if to prove his story, he showed me the hospital Johnnie under his shirt. He tried to commit himself, he says, because he was tired of life on the streets. He talked about returning to Lancaster but he was not ready to "settle" with his parents.

Chris has been on the streets for three years, although he says he showers and keeps himself clean when he visits friends or finds a hospitable spot to wash up. Chris' friend, Ron, who has been on the streets for a year, grew up in Northeast Philadelphia.

Chris says he misses his family "something awful," though he is careful to add that his family problems have nothing to do with his drug addiction. Ron will not even talk about his family. His eyes tell me that it is just too painful to go there.

Both Ron and Chris love the idea of getting clean. This comes into play when a guy their own age walks by and hears them talking, then offers Chris a job as a dishwasher for $10 an hour at a local eatery, Chris asks how he can apply. "Online," the manager says, "It's easy." But it is not easy. How is Chris going to get access to a computer unless he goes to a city library? Gone are the days when you could just walk into a place and fill out a job application. He would also have to get clean before he starts work. One of the disadvantages of being homeless is that you are always losing or getting your state I.D. stolen. "Well, maybe I'll see you," the manager says, "Remember, ten dollars an hour!"

Chris and Ron continue to talk about making $10 an hour long after the manager leaves. Chris says that if he got the job he would save his money and find a "nice place to live," but Ron does not say much. Perhaps Ron sees that housing in today's world is just too expensive for people with low income jobs.

Suddenly we are joined by a homeless man with a black eye (he just had a fight with his girlfriend) who is pushing around a set of golf clubs. The scene is becoming as bizarre as an independent foreign movie.

The man trying to sell golf clubs obviously stole them. At least that is what Chris thinks. "Who plays golf in Port Richmond," he says. "Nobody here wants golf clubs!" He is right, of course. Port Richmond and Fishtown have nothing in common with Haverford or Bryn Mawr. Besides which, the clubs look like really cheap golf clubs.

The man with the clubs dusts off all the knobby tops like they are Lions Club trophies. He looks around the parking lot for potential buyers but there are only a few people headed to their cars. Most are drinking WAWA Big Gulps as ten Puerto Rican kids ride by on bicycles doing wheelies. The golf guy reluctantly shoulders the clubs and leaves, but no sooner does this happen than he is replaced by a pretty woman with braided hair in green camouflage pants and a corded vest that must have once been on the racks at Nordstrom's.

She has a striking profile and, together with Chris—after a hot shower and a pedicure—they could make a living as Calvin Klein models. The girl sits down in front of WAWA with her change cup as another homeless person comes up from the rear. I ask Chris if this is some kind of homeless convention and if he knows any of these people. He shakes his head no. The newcomer carries a triple-tiered knapsack straight out of the Apollo Moon Landing. It is a wonder he can move under its weight. There is not enough time to get his story, but I introduce myself anyway and tell him that I am gathering stories.

Life gets stranger when another homeless man approaches and asks if anybody has a cigarette. He is a tall guy with a scar on his right arm and, lighting up after finding a butt on the ground, tells Chris and Ron (the girl with the braids will not join us) his story. He says he is the only person to ever survive jumping off the Ben Franklin Bridge. Ambrose Bierce could not invent stories like this, but what I am telling you is true. From his lips to my pen.

He lifts his shirt up and shows everyone the scar on his stomach from the operations he has had since he jumped off the bridge. Everyone wants to know how he survived the long drop to the water. What was he thinking on the way down? Did it hurt when he landed in the water? He says he lost consciousness immediately after jumping and "woke up" underwater with his shoes planted in the mud on the bottom of the river. Somehow he managed to free himself and swim up to the surface where he saw a patrol boat. Lucky for him, the people on the patrol boat saw him jump and were ready. He says all the nurses and the doctors at the hospital still call him the Bionic Man whenever he goes for checkups.

There are many different types of homeless as there are birds in the sky. There are the ground sitters who have pretty much lost any sense of embarrassment about being homeless and who are either too drugged out to stand up when they panhandle or so anti-social to look people in the eye. Their bent over posture, eyes-to-the-ground stance with a cup or inverted baseball cap placed beside them is often an admission of total defeat. They are counting on sympathy, even pity, especially when they look as if they have been in a fight or the victim of a mugging.

Francis, for instance, told me how he was jumped by three guys who blackened his eyes and bruised his torso. The motive was not robbery but hatred of the homeless. Tiffany never experienced such abuse, although she says she sometimes miscalculated safety factors when she went with a man who wanted to date her. Tiffany's "fresh from the suburbs" look meant she did not have to work hard to find caretaker men. Many of these men were lawyers and some were Asian businessmen who set her up in their homes or in a separate apartment. The arrangements always ended when Tiffany had had enough and would leave in the middle of the night. She was always leaving in the middle of the night.

"It's all about using these men," Francis told me. "She'll pretend she's in love while sometimes they actually fall in love but the minute she gets a better offer, she's gone.... She's gone."

While arranging my notes and latest observations on a table in a Dunkin Donuts near the Girard El stop, I happened to bump into Peter whom I helped months ago when he asked me for a cup of coffee. Just twenty-five years old, Peter found himself on the streets through a series of misfortunes that had nothing to do with drugs or drug trafficking. He said that some "stupid things" he did were responsible for his plight, and that he "was paying for it now." He was very light on specifics and talked in generalities but did mention missed meetings with parole officers and a theft that he was somehow involved in, although his part in that escapade, he says, was "mostly accidental." Peter lived in a hand-built shelter near the railroad tracks and was out shopping for laundry detergent when we crossed paths for the first time.

An incessant talker, Peter told me more about his life as time went on. He said he was a New Jersey resident who came to Philadelphia to look for work, although he was quickly finding that the employment scene in Philadelphia was "impossible." The influx of millennials into the city from surrounding states was causing a job glut in the service industry. It was even next to impossible to find a job as a dishwasher, he said. Peter found the city inhospitable and looked forward to the day when he could move back to New Jersey to be with his young son, if not the son's mother, with whom he did not get along. He told me that he was baptized in the Russian Orthodox Church and remembers how his grandmother used to take him to Divine Liturgy as a young boy. "The icons, the candles," he mused, "I've been to every Orthodox church in the area."

I invited Peter to take a look at my notes on the homeless. He was especially interested in the graphs illustrating how the numbers of homeless moving into my neighborhood had quadrupled over an eight-year span. The exponential growth was nothing less than mind boggling and can be blamed on opiates. In many ways, the present opioid crisis is an updated replay of what happened in the 1960s when Timothy Leary announced in a 1966, "Like every great religion of the past we seek to find the divinity within and to express this revelation in a life of glorification and the worship of God. These ancient goals we define in the metaphor of the present—turn on, tune in, drop out."

Peter told me he did not want to go on living like this. "I miss my son," he said. "I want to live with my son but I can't do that now." He told me he felt an urge to call his ex-wife so that he could set up a time to visit his son.

Peter started to talk about Keith, his spiritual guru, a homeless pop-up messiah with a good heart, who lived near the Frankford El Huntingdon stop. Peter said that Keith counseled a lot of guys on the street.

When I heard the name, I remembered that I had heard other homeless men mention Keith. Until I met Peter, I assumed that Keith was just another addict with father figure attributes. There were a number of older, homeless men who acted as mentors to the younger ones. Keith, I had heard, became addicted to heroin relatively late in life after a career in sales and raising two children. After his wife died suddenly in an auto accident, he lost his job and the will to live. A friend introduced him to opiates to assuage the pain of his loss, and from there it was a downward spiral until at last he was holding doors at WAWA and sitting in front of dollar stores with homemade signs.

Keith was an example of someone who could survive multiple winters sleeping outdoors while maintaining his daily fix with only a few arrests over several years. The young were attracted to him because he never seemed to come apart at the seams.

Keith had street smarts and practical "how-to" wisdom, but one could see that he was very tired of life on the streets. His countenance remained fixed in an expression of worry, resignation, and regret, although one Christmas I saw him pocket a fistful of large bills, a once-a-year bonanza that had him walking fast to the drug dispensary at Huntingdon or Somerset. A slight smile managed to cross his face on Christmas Day, but on the 26th, he returned to his usual depression, facing a New Year that would find him dead by the end of summer, the victim of an overdose. God rest his soul.

As for Francis, his life also changed when he finally agreed to go back to his parent's farm in Lancaster and to begin the hard process of starting over. His long and convoluted Rumspringa-like odyssey had come to an end.

Bibliography

Bawer, B., *Islam, The Essays* (Swamp Fox Books, Oslo, Norway, 2019)

Boyette, M., *Let It Burn: Move, the Philadelphia Police Department, and the Confrontation that Changed a City* (Quadrant Books, San Diego, CA, 1989)

Brewster, R. H., *The 6,000 Beards of Athos* (D. Appleton-Century Company, New York, 1936)

Brookhouser, F., *Our Philadelphia* (Doubleday & Company, Garden City, New York, 1957)

Bunge, Gabriel, *Earthen Vessels* (Ignatius Press, San Francisco, CA, 2002)

Cayce, E., *Individual Reference File* (Association for Research and Enlightenment, Inc., Virginia Beach, Virginia, 1970, 1976)

Dass, R., *Grist for the Mill* (Unity Press, Santa Cruz, California, 1977)

Divine, M., *The Peace Mission Movement* (Imperial Press, Inc., Philadelphia, 1982)

Fallaci, Oriana, *The Rage and The Pride* (Rizzoli, New York, NY, 2001)

Forest, J., *At Play in the Lions' Den: A Biography and Memoir of Daniel Berrigan* (Orbis Books, Maryknoll, New York, 2017)

Chesterton, G.H., *What's Wrong With The World* (Ignatius, San Francisco, CA, 1994)

Genet, Jean, *The Criminal Child*, Selected Essays (New York Review Books, New York, 2020)

Guinn, J., *Mason: The Life and Times of Charles Mason* (Simon & Schuster Paperbacks, New York, New York, 2014)

Guinn, J., *The Road to Jonestwon: Jim Jones and Peoples Temple* (New York: Simon and Schuster, 2017)

Hope, J., *Father Divine: His Words of Spirit Life and Hope* (Imperial Press, Inc., Philadelphia, 1961)

Hubbard, R. L., *Dianetics: The Modern Science of Mental Health* (Bridge Publications, Inc., Los ANGELES, California, 2002)

Kraybill, D. B., *The Riddle of Amish Culture* (Baltimore and London: The Johns Hopkins University Press, 1989)

Lawson, R. F., *Patterns* (Chrysalis Reader. Swedenborg Foundation Press, West Chester, Pennsylvania, 2013)

Levy, S., *The Unicorn's Secret: Murder in the Age of Aquarius* (Prentice Hall Press, New York, 1988)

Maritain, Jacques, *The Primacy of the Spiritual* (Cluny, Providence, Rhode Island, 2020)

Martin, M., *Peter in Chains* (Triumph Communications, Wellesley, ON NOB 2TO Canada, 2010)

Martin, M., *Windswept House, a Vatican Novel* (Doubleday, New York, New York, 1996)

Merton, Thomas, *Turning Toward the World* (Harper San Francisco, CA, 1996)

Mitrophan, Monk, *How Our Departed Ones Live* (Holy Trinity Publications, Jordanville, New York, 2015)

Prabhupāda, S. B., A.C. *Bhagavad-Gita, As It Is* (Bhaktivcedanta Book Trust; International Society of Krishna Consciousness, Los Angeles, California, 1968, 1972)

Roberts, J., *The Unknown Reality, Volume One* (Amber-Allen Publishing, San Rafael, California, 1977, 1996)

Rose, Fr. S., *The Soul After Death* (Platina, Calfornia: St. Herman of Alaska Brotherhood, 1980)

Rose, M. S., *Ugly As Sin* (Sophia Institute Press, Manchester, NH, 2000)

Schall, James, S.J. *On Islam* (Ignatius Press, San Francisco, CA, 2008)

Moser, Benjamin, *Sontag* (Harper Collins Publishers, New York, NY, 2019)

Sutin, L., *Do What Thou Wilt, A Life of Aleister Crowley* (St. Martin's Press, New York, 2000)

Swedenborg, E., *True Christianity, Volume 2* (Swedenborg Foundation, West Chester, Pennsylvania, 2012); *Our Life after Death* (Swedenborg Foundation, West Chester, Pennsylvania, 2013)

Vogl, A. A., *Therese Neumann, Mystic and Stigmatist, 1898–1962* (Tan Books and Publishers, Inc., Rockford, Illinois, 1987)

Watts, A. W., *The Way of Zen* (Vintage Books, New York, New York, 1957)

Wiesinger, A., *Occult Phenomena in the Light of Theology* (London: Forgotten Books, 1957; 2015)

Yogananda, P., *Autobiography of a Yogi* (The Philosophical Library, New York, 1946)